DEATH WAS OUR COMPANION

DEATH WAS OUR COMPANION

THE FINAL DAYS OF THE THIRD REICH

TONY LE TISSIER

SUTTON PUBLISHING

This book was first published in 2003 by
Sutton Publishing Limited · Phoenix Mill · Thrupp
Stroud · Gloucestershire · GL5 2BU

This paperback edition first published in 2007

British Library Cataloguing in Publication Data
A catalogue record for this book is available from the British Library.

ISBN 978-0-7509-4588-2

Typeset in 10/12pt Berk Old Style.
Typesetting and origination by
Sutton Publishing Limited.
Printed and bound in England by
J.H. Haynes & Co. Ltd, Sparkford.

CONTENTS

Maps and Diagrams	vi
Introduction	vii
Retreat Across the Rhine	1
Schoolboy Diary	22
Counterattack	62
Fighting in the Oderbruch	71
Musketeer	80
Luftwaffe Infantryman	88
Diary of Defeat	93
Death Was Our Companion	106
Retreat via Halbe	131
The End of the 21st Panzer Division	139
The Siemensstadt *Volkssturm* Battalion	144
The Skorning Report	185
Searchlight in Spandau	198
Surrender Negotiations	233
Index	257

MAPS AND DIAGRAMS

No. 5 Troop near Wriezen 27
No. 5 Troop at Letschin 34
No. 5 Troop at Alt Tucheband 42
The New No. 2 Troop near Wriezen 45
Closing the Corridor – 22–23 March 45 65
The German Counteroffensive 27–28 March 45 75
The Approaches to Seelow – 16 April 45 81
Fahnenjunker-Grenadier-Regiment 1241 at the Front 107
The Lebus Battleground 110
Counterattack at Schönfliess 115
Withdrawal of the 9th Army to the Spreewald 116
The Battle of Halbe 119
Breakout of the 9th Army from Halbe 124
VS Bn 3/115 – Biesdorf-Kaulsdorf-Mahlsdorf – 21–22 April 45 156
VS Bn 3/115 – Friedrichsfelde-Ost – 22 April 45 166
VS Bn 3/115 – Central Cattle Market – 23–24 April 45 169
VS Bn 3/115 – Samariter Strasse – 24–25 April 45 172
VS Bn 3/115 – Richthofenstrasse & Löwen-Böhmisch Brewery – 25 April – 2 May 45 174
VS Bn 3/132 – Siemensstadt – 21–26 April 45 178
Successive Defence Lines – 2nd Bn, 60th Fortress Regiment 186
Combat Group Skorning's First Engagement 191
Combat Group Skorning's Final Engagements 193
Searchlight in Spandau 199

INTRODUCTION

Consequent upon the successful publication of twelve articles from my archives in *With Our Backs to Berlin*, I am venturing to follow up with a sequel portraying further incidents in the German Armed Forces during the final phases of the Second World War. Again, this is no apology for the German cause, just a collection of straightforward accounts as related by the individual authors.

Werner Mihan, a *Luftwaffe* officer cadet, recounts his experiences with a field flak unit in the retreat across the Rhine from the Palatinate, and a *Luftwaffe* auxiliary, Friedrich Grasdorf, recalls his time as a fifteen–sixteen-year-old gunner transferred from the Home Flak to a front-line role on the Oder.

Erich Koch describes his company's experiences in the German attempt to break through the Soviet bridgehead to relieve the vital fortress of Küstrin, and Colonel von Lösecke takes up the tale of the same battle as a regimental commander.

When Marshal Zhukov launched his breakthrough battle on 16 April 1945 with a terrifying barrage from over 14,000 guns and 1,500 rocket launchers, Günter Labes was right in the line of fire below Seelow. Zhukov's use of 143 searchlights, a 'secret weapon' that would blind the enemy, help guide the advancing infantry and give them extra hours of 'daylight' to enable them to achieve their goals, had a totally unexpected effect, as Labes describes, but the German infantryman's laminated ammunition was equally useless. Herbert Böker's ambition to become a fighter pilot led him to an infantryman's role nearby in the same battle, but he managed to survive and eventually reach the American lines across the Elbe.

Further north, Lieutenant Hans-Werber Klement's Army Flak battalion was involved in a fighting retreat right across Mecklenburg to reach the Americans minutes ahead of the Russians.

Rudi Lindner, who was to attain the rank of major-general in the East German Army, but then an officer cadet, describes his experiences in the struggle for the Reitwein Spur, and the eventual horrific breakout attempt of the German 9th Army from the Halbe encirclement.

Erwin Bartmann, an instructor at the *Waffen-SS* depot east of Berlin, found himself assigned to a makeshift regiment trying to block the Soviet 33rd Army's attempt to seize the Frankfurt/Oder–Berlin autobahn. Caught up in the German 9th Army's withdrawal into the Spreewald, he too became involved in the breakout from the Halbe 'pocket', eventually crossing the Elbe and passing through the American lines only to be captured later. Then a curious twist of fate in due course resulted in Bartmann becoming a British citizen. Also involved in the Halbe encirclement of the 9th Army, Major Brand tells of the fate of the 21st Panzer Division, where it reached a state of near mutiny before being captured by the Russians.

Dr Pourroy's report on one of the *Volkssturm* battalions formed from employees of the vast Siemens concern shows just how combat-effective such a makeshift unit could be when properly organised and led. The battalion fought in the eastern suburbs of Berlin to end up in a well-stocked brewery before finally surrendering to the Russians.

Colonel Skorning, an ammunition technical officer, found himself commanding a makeshift battalion in the defence of Berlin's southern suburbs, only to see it eliminated.

Werner Mihan returns with his account of the fighting and breakout from Spandau, when he voluntarily rejoins his old searchlight battery from convalescent leave.

Lastly Colonel von Dufving, then Chief of Staff to General Weidling, the Defence Commandant of Berlin, recounts how he accompanied General Krebs in the abortive attempt by Goebbels to secure a ceasefire to enable the formation of the government dictated in Hitler's will, and then had to conduct negotiations for the surrender of the Berlin garrison, roles that earned him imprisonment as a prisoner of the NKVD and not as a normal prisoner of war.

Several of these articles refer to the so-called Seydlitz Troops, the turncoat German prisoners of war used by the Soviets for psychological warfare and also in these final stages for spreading false information and orders as well as, when mixed with Soviet troops, actual combat with their former comrades.

A H Le T
Frome, Somerset
November 2002

RETREAT ACROSS THE RHINE

WERNER MIHAN

Born in Potsdam in 1927, Werner Mihan was drafted as a Luftwaffe *auxiliary three months before his sixteenth birthday to serve with his classmates on searchlights and radar equipment in a battery located at Falkensee, due west of Berlin, from February 1943 until September 1944. Seven weeks of Labour Service followed before he was conscripted into the Flak arm of the* Luftwaffe *in January 1945. He then attended a short course for officer cadets in Denmark before being posted to an active service unit in the Rhineland–Palatinate.*

14 FEBRUARY 1945

Our train left Hamburg at about half past midnight. There were nineteen of us for Stuttgart, nearly all former *Luftwaffe* auxiliaries who had seen action in the Berlin area. Of course there were several air alerts. The train was completely packed. I spent the night dozing in a car tyre. A civilian was taking his car tyres with him wherever he went. I sat comfortably next to him, despite the circumstances. One can get used to anything when tired. In the morning I discovered why my seat had been so soft – I had been sitting on the cheese I had bought in Denmark!

Meyer, the dope, found that he had lost his paybook and one of his boots. 'Bad luck!' I said to him, but that was little consolation.

During the course of the day I managed to get a window seat and so the rest of the journey went well.

We had another air alert in Thüringia, and we were well aware how the ground-attack aircraft loved to attack trains.

Beyond Kassel our train came to a stretch of open track and we were able to see another train some distance away being strafed by four fighters. Some squadrons of heavy bombers were flying over us on their way back from attacking Dresden. I sat at the window looking out at the mountainous countryside. It was beautiful, with woods, deep valleys and elevations – a peaceful scene had it not been for the streams of bombers overhead!

Suddenly I saw two fighters coming straight at us out of a valley cleft. 'Take cover!' I shouted. 'Aircraft!'

In the last instant I saw both machines swinging outwards and streams of fire coming from their wings. We fell flat on top of each other on the floor of the compartment as the aircraft thundered over only a few metres above the train. The four-barrelled anti-aircraft gun mounted on the rear wagon of our train fired after them without success.

The brakes screeched and our train stopped. 'Open the window!' and out we jumped quickly. In ten long strides I reached some good cover offering protection from all sides. I looked back at the train, where a mass of people was being disgorged from doors and windows to rush over the fields in panic.

I was lying in a small hollow about 1½ metres deep. 'Another attack!' cried out somebody above me and then jumped, landing with both jackboots right between my shoulder blades and knocking the breath out of me. I would have given him a good hiding, but I could not move a limb for at least another minute.

And the attack? The bloody fool had been dreaming. There wasn't a fighter in sight. Four-engined formations were flying high above us with their fighter escorts criss-crossing above them, but our four-barrelled anti-aircraft gun had earned their respect. They did not like having to deal with such a weapon.

Our crowd went up to the engine, with me limping along. It had received several hits but was still functioning. Pale-faced, the driver and engineer perched on top of it and showed us where it had been hit.

Then back to the flak-wagon, the second wagon behind our carriage. The armour plating had hardly been damaged, but the gun crew's accommodation had been riddled. Even their saucepan had been shot through and their lunch spattered over the ceiling. One of the soldiers showed us his trousers.

'I was the last to get to the gun,' he said, and pointed to his torn trouser bottoms. 'I was lucky!'

'Heck, Heimann, another two carriages along . . .'

'Look at the hits, all at the same height!'

The whole of my back was very painful.

The train set off again two hours later. 'Never mind,' said Frede, a former student at our school, but from one form lower than myself, 'It doesn't matter! It might have been us having to live in there!'

There was a six-hour long alert in Würzburg. It was night, but when a night-fighter fired some bursts, we got moving and sought cover.

Something was bound to happen next day, for it was 15 February, and it was on 15 February in 1943 that I had been called up, and on 15 February in 1944 that we had the attack on our Finkenkrug position. So what would happen on 15 February 1945?

We spent the whole day in Bietigheim[1] under constant air alert with the traffic standing still. The Americans and British had won complete air superiority over Germany, and gave us no peace any more, either by day or by night. The routes for the attacking streams of bombers had been shortened now that they had sufficient bases in virtually the whole of reconquered France. If it wasn't bomber squadrons flying over the cities, there were almost continuous fighter squadrons in the air, shooting at everything that moved: trains, individual vehicles, individual people. Faces were always looking upwards. Life had become unbearable, and still the war went on!

We waited for our train at Bietigheim station, from where it was due to leave at 5 p.m.

'We'll wait for the next one at 6 o'clock,' Sergeant Muth, our movement NCO, told us. 'The air is still "unclean".'

Later he ordered us on to the overcrowded carriage of the narrow-gauge railway train, while he remained on watch on the outside platform. We eventually reached Gross Sachsenheim.

'Air attack!' shouted someone, and we jumped straight out of the window and ran for cover. Three fighter bombers were diving down on the train, but didn't open fire! From some distance off we could see Sergeant Muth running for cover and laughed. The machines were wheeling round and diving down on the train again without firing in the type of attack we knew as 'carouselling'. There was a third attack, but still no gunfire.

'Wow!' said Heimann, 'How about that for a game! Obviously they are out of ammo and only want to see us run. I bet it gives them a good laugh!'

'Perhaps it is also a pilot's training exercise!'

'That's it! Without ammo, so that nothing can happen!'

We laughed out loud. I think the others must have thought us mad, but the idea was so amusing, and the pilots must have enjoyed it too.

That evening we reached Vaihingen.[2]

'Vaihingen is the front line station for the western front,' Heimann declared, 'and thank God not for the eastern front!'

We had something to eat and soon fell fast asleep. We were not alone. One hundred officer cadets from Grove[3] were already there.

In the morning I marched off to the field hospital, where a bruised back was confirmed: nothing serious.

The duty schedule existed only on paper; we just lazed about, ate and smoked. We could walk out in the evenings at 6 o'clock. The first night Heimann and I looked for a wine bar, but without success. The second night we sought female company, this time with success.

The following evening we were told to prepare to leave, but we still walked out.

We set off at 3.30 a.m. to avoid the fighter-bombers and drove in a truck 50 kilometres alongside the Enz river, via Pforzheim, through the beautiful Black Forest. The weather soon cleared up and the sun shone out of a cloudless sky.

We reached the Division at Bad Herrenalb at 9 a.m. and took advantage of the situation to have a look around the town and eat at a hotel.

That evening the senior office cadet told me: 'Take these nine men on to Neuburg and report to the regiment there.'

We went on by train to Karlsruhe, spending the night in an air-raid shelter. The city had been badly damaged, like everywhere else.

'Neuburg? There are several Neuburgs around here!' A fine mess!

Finally we settled for Neuburg-am-Rhein, the nearest one, and took the early train across the Rhine to Wörth, where there was several hours delay.

'Go and ask where the goods train over there is going. Perhaps they can take us with them!'

The engine driver was prepared to take us as far as Hagenbach, but from there we would have to continue on foot. Hagenbach, which, like

Wörth, lay within range of the American artillery, had been destroyed. We got off there and I thanked the driver for taking us.

'So, lads,' he grinned ironically. 'Carry on marching to victory!'

'Let's not go straight on,' I said. 'Let's eat first.'

As the door was locked, we got into the station waiting room through the window, and had our second breakfast that day. It was bitterly cold.

Then we shouldered our kitbags and slouched along at Flak Auxiliary speed alongside the railway line to Neuburg. We had to march through a thick wood until we eventually saw the place, which took a long time.

During the winter the village had been in no-man's-land. The West Wall ran through here and during the offensive at the beginning of January it had been abandoned by the Americans. There were bomb and shell craters everywhere, with fallen telephone lines and pieces of equipment lying around – a battlefield.

The front grumbled away in the distance.

We reported to the regimental staff. The major who received us nearly fell out of his boots when he found out that I had been a *Luftwaffe* auxiliary for over one and a half years without ever having been near a gun. My three-day course on the 20 mm gun hardly counted. It was the same with the others.

'And we want to win the war!' he groaned. But that was not our concern.

We were allocated accommodation in an abandoned house, and at midday we were issued wine, one and a half litres each, with the inevitable outcome. We did not need our waterbottles on the way to our accommodation!

Next morning we were put to polishing shells, but if others have not polished them since, those shells will still be unpolished! That afternoon we withdrew into a quiet corner to avoid being detailed for further work. We were already in bed when someone shouted: 'Pack up everything! We're going forward!'

It was 20 February. It was completely dark, all lights being forbidden, and we had to pack! Within a short space of time we were loaded into a truck for a 50 kilometre journey.

'Where're we heading for?'

'Kutzenhausen.'

'Where's that?'

'When the firing starts, you'll soon find out!' was the comforting reply.

It was becoming increasingly dangerous but, putting this aside, we settled down in the straw and hefty snoring soon accompanied our healthy sleep.

Next morning we were split up. Five, including Heimann, were allocated to the 4th Battery, a 37 mm gun battery, and the remainder to the 5th Battery of 20 mm guns, all of the 1st Battalion, 10th Flak Regiment.

The battery quartermaster sergeant described the route to the 5th Battery's command post to me. I gathered my sheep and we marched off, but beforehand we had a fine breakfast from a farmer and filled our waterbottles with red wine.

Martin Frede was also in the team. He came from Lehnin and had attended the Realgymnasium in Potsdam, like myself. He also had had some experience with 20 mm guns. Jürgen Meyer came from Apolda. He was a quiet chap, dreamed a lot and always went into shock when woken up. Then there was Gert Mally from Dresden. Unlike the rest of us, he had not been a *Luftwaffe* auxiliary. He had a low, piping voice, and was always friendly and comradely. These made up the four that reported for duty at Hölschloch.

We looked round our new location with critical eyes. The village of Hölschloch lay a little north of Hagenau, where there had been some fierce fighting during the winter.

The battery commander, Lieutenant Kontradewitz, summoned us to his command post. After I had made my report, he gave us the usual lecture on duty, the operational task, etc. When he discovered the extent of our training on the 20 mm gun, he almost had a heart attack. Our new commander made a good impression on us. He was tall, lean and athletic, wearing the Iron Cross First Class; he was about twenty-five years old.

When he learned that we were all seventeen, he asked me about my Sports Badge, which one usually got only at the age of eighteen, and also about my Flak Badge. We four were allocated to the 4th Platoon under Sergeant Just, and our training was given to Officer Cadet Sergeant Gensberger: both had a unique conception of training, but we will come to that later.

We got on very well with the other personnel, although Sergeant Just was dead against that kind of friendship. As he was an ardent 'Ja-soldier',

I suspected that he would try to train us in the same mould. But others had already failed to do so. He hoped no one would back us, but didn't take into account the Chief's sympathy for us. Even Sergeant Gensberger, who was about twenty, wanted to train us, but soon gave it up.

Sergeant Just was sharp, but only when not under fire!

We first dug a pit six by three square metres and one to one and a half metres deep, and as this was to be our sleeping quarters, we raised the sides about a metre. Then trees were felled and laid over the bunker in two layers, one lengthways and the other across, the gaps between being filled with twigs and earth. Although it was still cold, the work brought us slowly but surely into a sweat. The paths were soft and muddy, the weather mainly rainy. Within three days the bunkers were completed and we settled in comfortably.

We were then issued with camouflage jackets and could move about more freely. The camouflage was necessary because of ground-attack aircraft. Once they found something they would not leave it alone until it had been reduced to smithereens.

About 500 metres from us was an abandoned American gun position, from where we removed useful things such as wood, sticks of compressed gun-powder and boxes.

'Look, a detective novel! *Mr Fortune's Best Stories!* I must have that!'

'And I'll take some more gunpowder sticks.'

Suddenly there was a bang, a howling and an explosion. This was the second time that we had been surprised by artillery fire, the first being in Hölschloch. Another howling and explosion.

'That was Number Two!'

We ran back from this discomforting place, taking the book and gunpowder sticks. We had discovered that we could use the sticks to heat our little stove. If we set fire to one, it would burn for some time before the powder was consumed, and solved the tedious warming-up problem.

One day the Chief came into our bunker with a cigarette in his ... ding 'Anyone got a light?' At first he shrank back when he saw ... heartily powder stick being held out to his cigarette, but t... amused with our device.

'Training begins tomorrow!' said Se...geant Gensberger would be in charge.

Only seven kilometres behind the front line we were now expected to go through the same training routine we had seen in cartoons with 'Lie down!' 'Get up!' 'Take cover!' and so on, in an attempt to combat our idleness.

'That idiot should try running around "fresh and lively" with three kilos of mud on his boots!' complained Martin.

Mally also had grounds for complaint, and Meyer added: 'Just the senior soldier! When he comes into the bunker it's "Hey, more left shoelace!" "Hey, right shoelace tighter!"' and he mimicked Sergeant Just accurately.

'He already has a nickname,' I said. 'Do you know what he is called? Sergeant Kroelschnitt!'

'Why Kroelschnitt?' Meyer wanted to know.

'Kroelschnitt is the least popular tobacco on issue. So, as nobody likes Sergeant Just, he got the name. It suits him fine!' explained Frede, our non-smoker.

The Americans directed artillery fire on us from time to time, just so that we would not get the idea that it was peacetime.

Training on the 20 mm flak gun, Solo 38, also went on. We learned a lot in a short time.

Lieutenant Kontradewitz tried some indirect shooting, which was quite unusual for the 20 mm gun, firing over a hill into the open countryside. He took us up the hill and gave the order to fire by telephone. The burst of fire whistled over our heads as we lay on the reverse slope of the hill, not wanting to lie where the shots fell at a theoretical rate of 400 per minute!

Enemy air activity left nothing to be desired. The two Mustangs, 'Max and Moritz', appeared daily on reconnaissance, and should they find anything, a little later four to eight Thunderbolts would come and reduce everything found to smithereens. Squadrons of Marauders also laid bombing carpets here and there.

We were now issued with carbines.

Inspection by Sergeant Just: 'What, not ready for inspection? Another ... an hour!' Then usually followed another inspection, and yet ano...

We line... ...nt of the bunker.

'Your carb... ...not clean! Dirt and rust everywhere!'

One would ... a magnifying glass to have seen a speck

of dirt, despite the fact that the carbines had been issued to us in a rusty and dilapidated condition. Just stood in front of me: 'Do you see the dirt here?'

'No, sergeant!'

'Here on the screw!'

I demonstratively turned the carbine from side to side, up and back down again: 'I don't see anything, sergeant!'

The others were grinning.

'Right, you four! Inspection every two hours. Understood?'

No answer.

'Do you understand?'

We remained dumb.

Sergeant Just: 'One hundred metres to the edge of the wood, double! You cheeky lot! This is insolence! You wait, I'll show you!'

We trotted off at flak unit speed for 100 metres.

'Do you understand?' we heard faintly.

'Yes, sergeant!'

'What sort of an answer is that? A whisper!' and he shouted: 'About turn! Double!'

After a few metres he shouted: 'Halt!

'Keep going!' I whispered to the others. 'He'll have to shout again.'

And again he shouted: 'Halt!'

'Keep going!'

Then I stopped, held my hand to my ear and listened.

'Halt! Halt!'

I let the others stop.

'Didn't you understand me?'

In my usual voice, I replied: 'Yes, sergeant!'

'I can't hear anything!'

Then the Devil got into me, and I shouted at the top of my voice: 'Yes, sergeant!'

The others giggled, and Sergeant Just detected the ridicule. 'If you think you can make a fool out of me, you're mistaken!'

And again I bawled out at the top of my voice: 'Yes, sergeant!'

Just gave up the struggle, and from that point on in his opinion I became the stupidest, most obstinate, idle and uncouth officer cadet in the battery. Since we had not breached regulations, he was unable to report us to the Chief.

Once he held seven inspections in a row. There was a toothbrush inspection. Mine was pristine clean, which baffled him: 'That must be a spare one! I know that trick. I want to see the proper one!'

Hesitantly I produced a second toothbrush from the back of the shelf.

'So, also completely clean. You're lucky, Mihan!'

He failed to notice that I had a third one for everyday use! I also had three combs: another old *Luftwaffe* auxiliary trick!

Infantry drills were increased for everyone; something was in the air. American air attacks became conspicuously stronger, with 'Max and Moritz' appearing more frequently, and the villages being carpet-bombed. So it came as no surprise when one day the order was given: 'Prepare to change location!'

Soon everything was packed up and loaded, guns hitched on and everyone made ready for the move. We moved off at 3 a.m. on 11 March. Farewell Hölschloch!

Shivering, we stretched our limbs in the brand-new day. We had arrived at the foot of a hill with a destroyed railway station a bit farther on and a town beyond it.

'Dig in!'

Second Lieutenant Elbinger, our platoon commander, indicated the locations.

'A fine Sunday activity!' grumbled Sergeant Limburg as he shovelled the fresh clods out of the ground with gusto.

There was a smell of spring in the air.

'A change of air is fine, but having to work . . .'

We looked at the destroyed town with the mountains just visible behind through the mist. 'What town is that?'

'I think it's Weissenburg,' answered Sergeant Roop. 'Over there, where our quarters are, is Altenstadt.'[4]

On the edge of the position I found the deeply cut bed of a brook, with a lively stream flowing through it. A quickly constructed bridge led over it to the tent in which we slept when we had guard duty.

The sun shone most welcomely upon us, spreading its warmth all day long. Spring had driven the long winter away.

I liked best lying in the grass beside the brook writing letters or reading Mr Fortune's adventures. We only had guard duties to do, nothing else, and this idle life suited me fine.

Ground-attack aircraft came over, crossing overhead, and their bursts of machine gunfire became our daily concert. One day four Thunderbolts attacked a target near Altenstadt, diving down low and coming close by us as they climbed up again, playing 'Carousel'.

I took my carbine as our No. 1 Platoon shot a Thunderbolt on fire. As it climbed, it exposed the whole of its underside. I aimed several aircraft lengths ahead of the machine and fired. At the same moment our own platoon opened up in a hellish concert and the Thunderbolt crashed ten kilometres away.

Something new for us was the horizontal dropping of bombs by fighters. Six to eight Thunderbolts flying in formation would release their bombs simultaneously. We called this 'rug-bombing' instead of 'carpet-bombing', but they were not to be ignored!

On Sunday, 17 March, we had a film show. The show continued despite bombs falling close by and the frequent bursts of machine-gun fire. The surprise followed: 'Prepare to change location! All of Weissenburg is being evacuated!'

Feverishly we packed up again, loaded up, stowed things away and hooked up the guns, setting off at about 11 p.m.

The vehicle engines roared as the column moved off northwards through the night with dimmed headlights. We stopped at about 2 a.m. and slept.

We climbed aboard our fine captured American truck again in the morning and made our way up a gully that led up a fairly steep mountain, but the strong truck made it.

'Dig in!'

Once more we dragged the guns into position, dug them in and camouflaged everything, not knowing how long we would remain here. Even our captured extra-heavy 12.7 mm machine-gun was deployed. Once the position was ready, we looked around at the landscape.

As already mentioned, we found ourselves on a height, which appeared to be of considerable size. A wood covering both sides of the gully blocked our view to the north. The wooded peaks of the Rheinpfalz rose to the west, where a castle could be seen. We could see far across the countryside to the northeast and east, but the best view was to the west.

Sergeant Roop, Mally and myself were manning the gun.

'Marauder at 10!'

The Marauder formation, consisting of groups of seven machines, flew quite fast, their cockpits alight and flashing in the sun. There were seven or eight of these groups.

'Formations turning in 2! Flying back to 12!' and then '"Carpet!"'

Dark clouds billowed from the earth. Sergeant Roop looked at the map: 'That must be Landau that they are bombing. It is already destroyed, so what are they looking for?'

The Thunderbolts kept wheeling round.

'They've spotted us!' said Sergeant Roop.

One dived down and began attacking from 600 metres. We fired several bursts, and then it was gone. We could even see the pilot in his cockpit. Two bombs fell in No. 4 Battery's wagon park, but only caused some minor damage.

19 March 1945

Early in the afternoon several Thunderbolts wheeled down on the area in which No. 4 Battery was located.

'It'll be our turn soon!' declared Sergeant Limburg. He went on: 'You take over as No. 4 on the gun when it starts and make sure the magazine exchanges go right!'

He watched through his binoculars.

'Here comes one! He's attacking!'

Our 20 mm gun thundered away and flashes came from the Thunderbolt's wings as we fired together.

'Magazine's empty!'

'Ready!' The new magazine was in.

The Thunderbolt vanished and did not return to renew the attack.

About an hour later an officer cadet appeared whom I recognised. It was Heimann from No. 4 Battery, where one of their 37 mm gun positions had been hit, killing one and wounding four others. He left again after an hour.

Towards evening heavy artillery fire fell on the southern slopes of our mountain, using explosive and phosphorous shells. The effectiveness of the bombardment was soon visible from the dense smoke rising.

'Time for us to up sticks again soon!' Sergeant Roop remarked.

That evening we went back to our quarters, walking around the village, even though it was dark. We could hear aircraft engines, but did not know what they signified. We were soon to find out. Somewhere close machine-guns rattled their greetings and we dived for cover. Fortunately nothing happened.

We made for our beds, but as we crawled into the hay, the firing started: whistling followed by an explosion. Shells were landing on the village, but we were so tired we nevertheless fell asleep in our barn.

20 MARCH 1945

At 2.30 a.m. came the order: 'Change location!'

Swearing, we searched for our clothing in the hay. It was pitch dark.

This time it was a long drive via Landau-Neustadt. The morning dawned and it became light. The drive could not go on for long because of enemy aircraft.

'Air alert!'

Into the nearest hiding place, a village called Niederkirchen, not far from Bad Dürkheim.

In the woods before us our army was retreating from the Americans. The American reconnaissance had apparently worked well. The enemy aircraft attacked with bombs, machine-guns and cannon, so that there were continuous explosions, and there were always twenty to thirty ground-attack aircraft in the air at any one time.

Two or three of these machines attacked the wood simultaneously with hammering guns, bringing death and destruction. A whole army was bleeding to death in those woods, the carnage continuing from morning until evening, and we could only stand and watch helplessly all day long.

That afternoon I consumed a whole bottle of wine.

In the evening we drove on to Bad Dürkheim, where we rested overnight in the wine cellar of a castle within a park. I was roused at midnight to take over guard duty. Second Lieutenant Elbinger arrived shortly afterwards. When I tried to make my report, I vomited right in front of him. Athletic as he was, he was able to jump back just in time. Fortunately, he let me off, as he had been drinking too.

After my guard duty I obtained a stiff slug from the castle porter. It did me good.

Then at 4 a.m. came: 'Change location! We're going back across the Rhine!'

21 MARCH 1945

The first day of spring! A beautiful sunny day broke. There was still some light mist to be seen and the dew lay in fine drops on the young seedlings, but the sun appeared on the horizon, breaking through the veil of mist, and soon drove the last traces of the cold, foggy night away.

We hauled our guns into their allocated positions, the wheels of the special trailers sinking deep into the soft soil. Soon we were shovelling away in mad haste, and when ground-attack aircraft appeared at 7 a.m. the position was fully camouflaged.

The sun climbed higher and higher. It became warm and finally hot. There was a wonderful, cloudless sky.

We lay on the edge of Dannstadt with our truck parked in the yard of one of the houses. Wine was still available and, despite my bad experience the previous night, I had my fair share. The lunch was good, and afterwards I retired to our truck.

Enemy aircraft appeared, racing only a few metres above the roofs of Dannstadt, but our gun crews were ready. There was a burst of firing and the second aircraft flew right into it, bits blowing off as shells bored into the engine, and the plane pulled up before crashing, with its engine on fire.

There was jubilation among us. We had bagged an Airacobra.

An Auster artillery spotting plane appeared high in the sky, keeping out of range, and then things started getting serious, with guns firing phosphorous shells at us.

Sergeant Wurm and Corporal Niermann went into the village with panzerfausts as an anti-tank team. Sergeant Wurm was a jolly chap who dis-regarded his rank status in the pursuit of fun.

'I've a funny feeling,' said Sergeant Roop, 'that things are going to get serious! We don't have a particularly good field of fire. We have the gardens in front of us and the houses on our right. On the left is an 88 mm battery. It doesn't look rosy to me!'

'Before it starts, I would like to go across to the truck,' I said.

'You can take a couple of boxes of shells with you,' said Sergeant Limburg. 'Then we won't have so much to carry when we have to move in a hurry.'

'OK,' I said and grabbed the two boxes, each weighing half a hundredweight.

Sergeant Limburg called out: 'Wait a moment! I'll come . . .'

There was a howling and a hissing sound.

'Take cover!'

Bang! an explosion went off close by.

Soon rifle fire was whistling past, a strange feeling hearing bullets coming towards you for the first time. Some were pinging against the wall. This was what our baptism of fire was like.

Sergeant Roop cocked his sub-machine-gun ready for firing just as the order came: 'Change location!'

'Schmalz,' called out Sergeant Roop to our driver, 'drive the truck out on to the street and behind the barricade!'

We rushed back to the position, where the shells were flying.

'Dismantle the gun!'

Soon the shield, seat, gun and its mounting were dismantled. We lifted the gun carriage out of the position, packed it all together and pulled it across the field to the street.

'Let's hope the Americans won't be as fast,' murmured Sergeant Limburg as the first infantryman came back.

'Hey, where are you going?'

'Disengagement from the enemy has been ordered, to Schifferstadt.'

'What's happening up front?'

'You wouldn't believe it. There's firing!'

'Idiot!'

The next one came by. 'Who ordered a retreat?'

'What retreat? We're attacking in the opposite direction!'

They were off, and soon there were no more infantry to be seen.

The Americans began sweeping the street with machine-gun fire. We brought our gun into position behind the anti-tank barricade that extended right across the street, leaving a small gap between the building and the barricade, through which our gun was directed against the approaching Americans.

Corporal Niermann came back wounded in the upper thigh.

'Where's Sergeant Wurm?'

'The last I saw of him he was firing a machine-gun when a Sherman tank rolled over him. I don't know any more than that.'

Sergeant Roop went forward: 'Mihan, are you coming with me to get the rest of our stuff from the position? You can stay here if you like, and I'll take Sergeant Limburg.'

Was he suggesting that I was scared? Not yet!

'OK, I'll come!'

We turned off into a side street that led on through two gardens. Constant explosions could be heard from either artillery or tanks. Sergeant Roop selected the items he wanted, three panzerfaust 60s, two boxes of shells, explosives and a cap, handing me his sub-machine-gun and his pack.

My first trip back was with the panzerfausts, which I propped up in sight against a wall. I shouted to Mally: 'Take that stuff away! I have to go and get some more!' But Mally didn't move.

On my second trip I picked up Sergeant Roop's things and the explosives. Bullets were flying everywhere and I was sweating and sweating. I pushed my helmet back against my neck.

On the third trip I brought back the shell boxes, a whole hundredweight. It was too much for me. Like an idiot, I set them down in the middle of the street and sat on them to get my breath back. I could hardly breathe.

'You'll go to hell,' shouted Sergeant Limburg, 'if those damn things explode!'

I laughed: 'Weeds never die!'

'Where are you going?' called out Second Lieutenant Elbinger.

'Getting the rest of the stuff, sir. Sergeant Roop is still there.'

Back down the side street. Then an ammunition truck belonging to the 88 mm guns blew up, sending bits and pieces flying. I was hit in the hand, which hurt. The ammunition kept exploding. I wanted to get to the position and tried once or twice, but could not make it. Then Second Lieutenant Elbinger came to the street corner and took me back to the gun.

With his face contorted in pain, Sergeant Roop hurried past us and went off to the rear. He seemed to have been wounded in the hip.

At that moment our gun received a direct hit down the barrel from an explosive bullet, but we tried it out and it still worked.

American infantry appeared at the far end of the street with sub-machine-guns on their hips and started filing up both sides of the street.

Sergeant Limburg took aim: 'Fire!'

A long burst, using a whole magazine, ripped through the files. Then we had some peace. They had not got us yet!

Suddenly there was a burst of fire, and there were our old friends, the ground-attack aircraft, presumably ordered up in support when we cleared the street. They were firing straight at the street as they came in. I jumped for cover into the nearest house entrance and there saw with astonishment someone I had not seen for some time, Sergeant Just. I simply looked at him. Immediately after the air was clear and I came out again.

Sounds of combat were coming from our left.

A flak captain came running out of a side street. 'Pull out! Pull out! We've been outflanked!'

Schmalz, our driver, engaged the starter and got the engine running. Mally was already sitting inside the truck. Should I jump in, or not? The truck drove off. Two strides and I jumped up, one hand got a grip and my feet skidded along. I was hanging on like this as Schmalz accelerated. Finally Mally managed to pull me aboard with some difficulty.

We stopped a few streets further on and I went back to see if Second Lieutenant Elbinger, Sergeant Limburg and our corporal clerk were to be found. They were coming towards me.

'Is the gun blown?'

'Oh, that damned gun! No sooner had we left it than it got a direct hit!'

We raced at high speed through the streets of Dannstadt, where the Americans would soon be marching. The inhabitants stood beside the buildings and waved.

Sergeant Limburg examined my hand, which was bleeding profusely. 'It doesn't look too bad,' he said, 'but there is some dirt inside. Be careful not to get blood poisoning.'

'You go straight to hospital when we get to Schifferstadt!' ordered Second Lieutenant Elbinger.

'I would prefer to remain with the battery, sir.'

'Very well, if you don't want to go to hospital, you can stay with me as a runner, but it'll be on your own responsibility!' said Second Lieutenant Elbinger.

Orders had been given for Schifferstadt to be defended. In our 'attack to the rear' – the word 'retreat' no longer existed in the German vocabulary – everything, panzerfausts, ammunition boxes, carbines, was simply being thrown haphazardly into the back of the truck.

Our platoon paraded. Of the original twenty-two, only sixteen remained. The truck took the wounded away.

I was a runner now, and stood guard over our equipment. It was a bright night. A group of several men started clearing away the beams from an anti-tank barrier. That wasn't right!

A sergeant appeared with his men. 'You must be mad dismantling that barrier! What sort of outfit is this?'

'*Volkssturm*!'

'Surround them!' he ordered, 'Cock your weapons!'

Then he went across to the old men of the *Volkssturm*. 'So you are the kind that as soon as our last truck has passed through hoist the white flag!' he raged. 'None of you will leave until this barrier has been rebuilt!'

22 MARCH 1945

We spent the night in a factory. Then the order came from Regiment to move into the suburb of Speyer and prepare its defence.

The garden of a convent seemed to us a suitable site. We rolled up the fence and set up our gun. The nuns from the convent received us in a friendly manner, bringing us food and drink, and also giving us the opportunity to wash, etc. We ate, drank, sunned ourselves and were happily at ease.

Then the sirens sounded the tank alert!

'I don't understand you,' said the priest. 'Everyone is rushing around like mad chickens, not knowing what to do, and all worried about the future, but you just sit there peacefully and smoke at ease. Aren't you keyed up for action, excited?'

'No, your honour,' grunted Friedrich, offering him a cigar: 'Have a smoke and you'll be just like us!'

We chatted up the village beauties who were besieging us and were interested in our gun. Then came: 'Change location!'

It was hard to leave, but we only went a short distance, as far as the Speyer cemetery, entering it from the south and driving up to the northern side. A loophole was then smashed through the cemetery wall with a pick. Beyond the wall were some trenches and an RAD flak battery.[5] There were some freshly dug graves near us. We were not superstitious, but still were shy about looking at them.

'We won't have far to go!' quipped Sergeant Limburg drily.

'We can fall into them straight off the gun!' capped Martin Frede.

We had only just settled down when the order came: 'Change location!'

'Damn it! That's three times in one day!'

And once more we drove off through the night, through Speyer and past the venerable cathedral.

We stopped at Berghausen, where we found quarters and slept well.

23 March 1945

In the morning came the order: 'Dig in!'

'I've had enough of this!' ranted Frede. 'Always having to dig in! It's killing me!'

Meanwhile my hand had gone septic. 'There's dirt in it,' said the medic. 'Let's hope it doesn't get worse.'

I climbed up into an attic to keep a look-out for tanks, as they had been reported and we could hear their tracks faintly in the distance. I was getting hotter and hotter. I threw up a plate of pea soup that occupants of the building brought me. I felt dizzy and unwell.

At the end of my one and a half hours' tour of duty I reported to the medic, weak-kneed like a drunk. My temperature was 39.9°. I wrapped myself up on a feather-bed and slept.

That afternoon the call came again: 'Change location!'

I dressed as if in a dream and put my gear on the truck. Second Lieutenant Elbinger came along and announced: 'So, comrades, we are to cross the Rhine at Germersheim, and apparently we have to fight our way through. Cock your weapons! Helmets on!'

A shot of white wine eased the blow, but I was trembling and my skull was throbbing. I was only half conscious, seeing everything through a veil. My head ached like mad and at times I was completely unconscious.

We stopped short of Germersheim and I came to for a while. There was artillery fire and ground-attack aircraft activity. The road was blocked. We took cover on the roadside. Heavy artillery was firing on the bridge and the explosions were towering up.

At about 9 p.m. we were taken by ferry across the Rhine, but I was no longer conscious. The convoy stopped in Schwetzingen. Second Lieutenant Elbinger and the battery commander came and asked after me. I was unconscious with a temperature of 41°. I was taken to a field hospital, but it was over-full and they were not accepting any more patients, so I was taken on by motorcycle to a second one, where I was given a bed.

Next morning the doctor came to see me. 'How are you?'

'Better, better than yesterday, sir.'

'Still pain?'

'My head is clearer.'

'In that case we can release you back to your unit today. All you needed was some sleep.'

So I was thinking myself recovered, until the nurse showed me the thermometer reading 40.5°! I stayed.

On 24 March we were moved to Sinsheim, the Americans having come considerably nearer after crossing the Rhine farther north. At times I was high with fever, and at times it abated, but I was vomiting constantly. The diagnosis was food poisoning.

Then I began to feel better, could even taste the food, and started helping in the kitchen.

The Americans were already occupying the Heidelberg area, were thrusting towards Würzburg and threatening to encircle us. At about 10 p.m. on 30 March came: 'All those able to walk report to the quartermaster sergeant for leave passes!'

I was now fully recovered with convalescent leave from 31 March to 13 April. So, home to Potsdam!

I packed my things – there were not many as my pack had gone with the battery – and got away from the field hospital. We took a truck and climbed aboard, the quartermaster sergeant too, roaring drunk. When it stopped unexpectedly he fell out and rolled down the embankment without hurting himself. A sober person would have broken his neck, but he just scrambled back up, swearing.

We arrived at Heilbronn at about 7 a.m. and at about 10 a.m. transferred to Wehrmacht jeeps heading for Stuttgart.

Air activity increased, so we kept a sharp look-out. We had hardly left Heilbrunn when twelve machines flew over and we had to dive for cover in the ditches. This happened every ten minutes.

We eventually reached Stuttgart, where we split up at the railway station, each making his own way home.

Mihan reached home on 2 April, Easter Monday, to the surprise and delight of his parents. While still on leave he experienced the heavy bombing raid of the night of 14 April in which Potsdam was severely damaged.

He had been lucky not to have experienced the fate of his battery. Two years later he received a letter from Martin Frede relating how only a few of them had survived the retreat. *His story continues on page 198.*

NOTES

1. 20 kilometre north of Stuttgart.
2. 24 kilometre northeast of Stuttgart.
3. An air base in northern Denmark.
4. Weissenburg is the German name for Wissembourg, which lies on the Alsace side of the French/German border, but Alsace and Lorraine had been incorporated into the Third Reich in 1940.
5. Flak was primarily a *Luftwaffe* responsibility, although the Army had its own integral flak units. The so-called 'Home Flak' eventually included many units manned by schoolboy *Luftwaffe* auxiliaries under *Luftwaffe* supervision, but there were also some *Reichsarbeitsdienst* (RAD) flak units of Labour Service personnel.

SCHOOLBOY DIARY

FRIEDRICH GRASDORF

When his classmates, a year or two older than himself, were conscripted into the Home Flak as Luftwaffe *auxiliaries in January 1944, fifteen-year-old Friedrich Grasdorf volunteered to accompany them, and thus became a member of the 9th Battery of the 36th Motorised Flak Regiment involved in the aerial defence of Hanover, his troop being equipped with 37 mm Oerlikon guns.*

30 JANUARY 1945

The news has arrived. Despite the general upheaval, this still comes as a surprise to us. We are leaving, but no one knows for where. Our Russian prisoners of war have to report in, so we can guess that we are going east.

We work like madmen. The protective walls go down more easily than they did before, and from the searchlight position we attract the first curious onlookers, our girlfriends of the *Reichsarbeitsdienst*,[1] whose curiosity will be satisfied once it gets dark. The atmosphere is somewhat depressed. 'Bobby' urges us to get back, for he has guard duty.

31 JANUARY 1945

The preparations appear to be complete, but there is still plenty to do, from the pumping up of the trailer tyres to the final packing of rucksacks. I take Mama's bicycle, which I had used to return to duty from my last overnight leave at home, to the Ost family and say my goodbyes there.

Isn't the truck going to come? It will soon be dark. Ah, here it comes. Working in the dark, one can quickly skip over the searchlight tasks. We say goodbye to our girlfriends on the searchlight and come back.

A woodgas-driven, museum-piece Büssing truck is standing at the battery command post. It can hardly move any longer and it takes a lot of effort to get it ready to start. It starts. The gun barrel begins swinging and goes as high as a street sign as we turn into Sandstrasse. We are loading on to a train, where bracing and wedging is carried out under arc lights. Sergeant Schumann gets us working here, Second Lieutenant Kern there. With some difficulty we find enough time to throw our kit into the goods wagon and get a glimpse inside. It looks a bit tight for thirty men and their kit, but it does have an iron stove.

1 February 1945

Midnight has gone and no one noticed. There is some straw in the wagon, in which we instantly fall asleep, all jumbled up together. The Old Man, Lieutenant Bommert (Battery Commander), and the Battery Quartermaster Sergeant (BQMS) come and rouse us in the morning. The whole battery is lined up in wagons with guns, trucks, field kitchen, office, etc., but the ammunition has yet to be loaded. Then we go for a wash. There is a standpipe in Sandstrasse. Except for 'Jonny', no one speaks to the people going past. He is good at this. Second Lieutenant Kern calls us: 'Prepare to depart, all aboard!' 'Pongo' is the last to appear. He had encountered his uncle, who as an infantryman was also waiting for a train.

We are off. The train stops again before the main station. Second Lieutenant Kern climbs down and the train goes on without him. We no longer have our officer, so Sergeant Schumann is appointed deputy troop commander. As we pass through the main station, I push myself forward to the open door. Old Weber, my former bandmaster, is standing there. I call and wave, and he recognises me. This is my last greeting from my home town.

The countryside goes past. Here and there are a few white patches, the last of the snow. The railway station signs read 'Dollbergen', 'Öbisfelde', so we must be heading for Berlin. The train stops from time to time and we even get fed, which is a pleasant surprise. Then we go on again. Karl Siebenbaum leads the singing, and a *Luftwaffe* auxiliary 'choir' forms in competition with the old hands. 'Rathenow', the name calls to mind the Berlin area, but it is dark by the time we get there, and we are in Spandau.

We spend a second night on the train and in uncertainty. Some sleep, others eavesdrop and try to discover what is going on. We move on slowly and everyone settles down in his own corner. I can't sleep. I stoke up the fire and toast a few slices of bread.

The train slows down, jerks and stops. I look out of the door once I have opened it with some difficulty. There are glows of fire and flashes on the horizon, and detonations. We are standing at a station. The Old Man comes along: 'Don't leave the train. This is Blankenburg, near Berlin. We had to get out of Berlin because of an air raid, as you can see. Good night!'

We can hear aircraft engines. I have to get out. I can't help it.

2 February 1945

I have dozed down on the bench next to the door. When I am woken up by a comrade opening the door, we are moving again and it is light outside. Slowly things come to life in the wagon. The door remains shut at first, then it starts raining again. Jonny tells us jokes. There is a stop. We are standing in a cutting between two embankments left and right of the tracks. 'Breakfast!' With many others I make my way up the embankment and behind the bushes. The ground is slippery from the rain and snow, and several slip. We have to hurry. We hear the calls to move on and can hardly pull our pants up and slide back down to the train, which is slowly moving off.

I write down my recent experiences in my diary. We stop in a crowded railway station. The sign reads 'Eberswalde'. None of us have heard the name before. Some think that it must be on the Oder. In answer to our questions, the refugees tell us that the Russians are only 80 kilometres away, so the front is quite close. I quickly write postcards to my parents, Gisela and Waltraut. A young woman on her way to Berlin takes them with her. Our Second Lieutenant Kern is back, having overtaken us on another train. Beware of the trains!

Eberswalde is behind us, and apprehension has seized us. Karl

Siebenbaum talks a lot, thinking that one can overcome this best by talking, but there is much that cannot be talked about. In all honesty, it is fear, fear of the unknown, fear that the demands upon us are not increased. We did not have these fears back in our home town, because we were at home, but here they hem us in. We don't know where we are, or whether we will ever get back home again. It is hard to shake off.

We need something to do. The train stops again in a station. Now it says 'Bad Freienwalde' on the sign. Orders come to detrain and unload. Now we have something to do! We slave away, forget and smoke. During our short breaks we chat to the few children that are on the platform, exchanging a few words and sentences. An 88 mm battery is said to have been wiped out by tanks nearby.

Sergeant Ohlsen gives the orders as usual. That idle lump! Our foursome work together: Bobby, Pongo, Jonny and myself. We get to know our drivers and their vehicles. Dear God, we get the old gas burner back. Our gun captain, Ohlsen, takes it off to the workshops.

I have lost my wallet, and look for it high and low, but cannot find it. My lovely photographs, my identity card, my Post Office savings book! It must have happened during the upheaval in Berlin or later. Our uniform breast pockets are too small for a wallet, so I always carried it under my blouse against my chest, where the belt kept it from slipping, but not this time.

After much coming and going, we sit in our trucks, tired and relaxed. The battery is ready to move off. Columns of refugees are going past with signs announcing 'East Prussia', 'West Prussia' and 'Warthegau'.[2] The wagons are wretched, the animals and people too. The war is terrible, as we can see for ourselves here, having already had some experience of it, especially during the air raids, but, as long as one is not aware of too many of its disadvantages, one is not opposed to it.

It is night. We drive off. The truck is very worn out. Its only advantage is its canopy, which protects us from the rain and shields us, so that we can eat something by the glow of a Hindenburg Light[3] that Corporal Paul Utterodt bought and has wedged in place with his kit.

We drive through a small town, where people are hurrying through the night. 'Halt!' The truck stops in front of a slope and refuses to go any farther. We have to get out and push. A couple of civilians help us. It works. Once it gets going, we can climb aboard and sit down again. It is quite cold, but we start to sweat, because we have to get out and push up every gradient. Finally another truck takes us in tow. The little town is called Wriezen.

We drive on until the Büssing is really finished. We are standing at a crossroads in front of a large crater that could well be a shell hole. There are two four-barrelled guns on the left and right, and we speak to their *Luftwaffe* auxiliaries. They come from Thüringia and only arrived a few days ago.

And then we see the front for the first time, as one sees it better at night with the tracers flying here and there. We learn something about the general situation while we wait for a truck from our battery to tow us away. Other vehicles are driving past to the front line. Occasionally one gets stuck in the crater, and we help to push it out again.

3 FEBRUARY 1945

So it continues, and daylight arrives almost unnoticed. Kleinmeier, the driver of No. 13 gun, comes to tow us away with his Opel-Blitz, all-wheel-drive, truck. But then he drives at full tilt into the crater, breaking a spring, so we have to wait all over again, and it is gradually becoming quite cold. We drag a few boards along as a make-shift cover for the hole. Eventually we are picked up and driven on a few kilometres to the front of, or back of, the village of Heinrichsdorf.

'Guns into firing positions!' In this quagmire? I am not exaggerating. Our boots remain stuck in the mud and we have to pull them carefully out after every step, and the barrel cases are twice as heavy. Sergeant Ohlsen assumes his old role, giving the orders.

We are within sight of the front line. There is no thunder of cannon, but we get to know the chirping of infantry fire, the rattling of the machine-guns and the ratsch-boom of Russian anti-tank guns.

The camouflaging goes badly. We are standing on a field close to the end houses of the village. Second Lieutenant Kern arrives. At 0730 hours we are to fire a barrage, firing in the ground-combat role for the very first time. It is as if we have been taken by a kind of fever. We don't think of our hunger any more. Smoking? Yes, as usual. The old hands pass out the cigarettes. Sometimes they are not so bad after all.

And then the spell is broken. We fire without pause. The endless practice has been of some use, and it all goes like clockwork. If only the

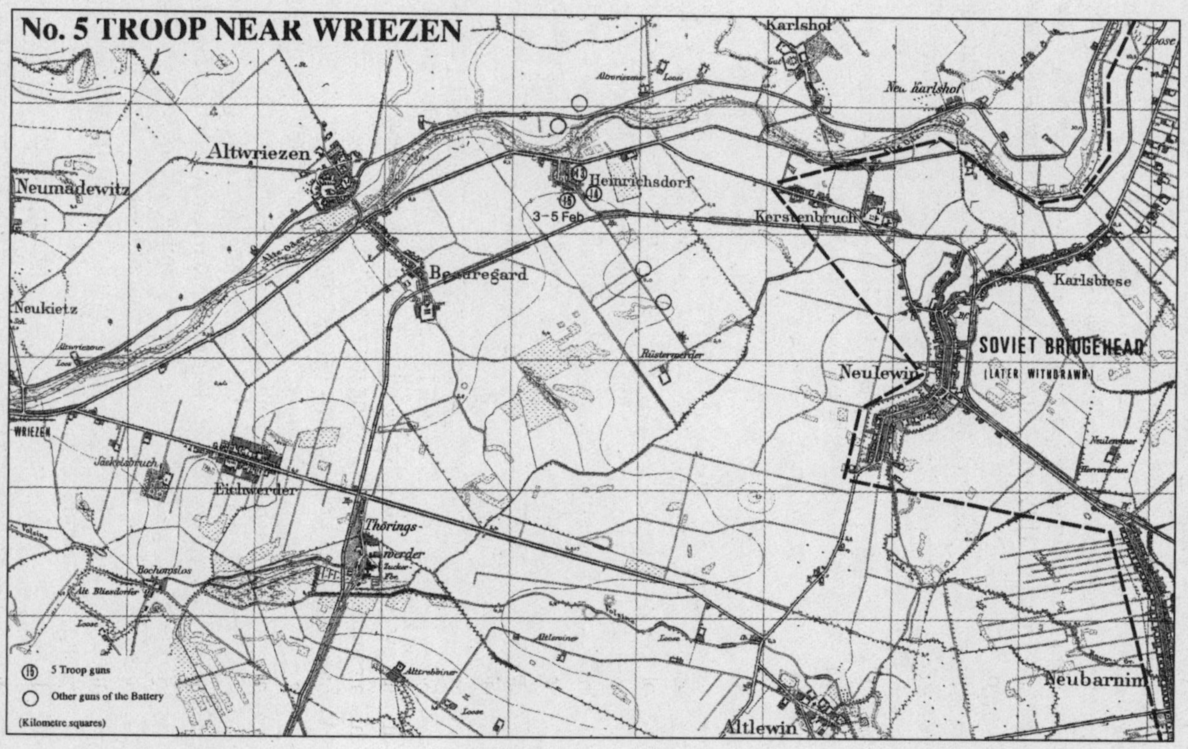
No. 5 TROOP NEAR WRIEZEN
Karlshof
Neu Karlshof
Altwriezen
Neumadewitz
Heinrichsdorf
3–5 Feb
Kerstenbruch
Beauregard
Karlsbiese
Neukietz
SOVIET BRIDGEHEAD
(LATER WITHDRAWN)
Neulewin
WRIEZEN
Eichwerder
Thörings-
werder
Neubarnim
Altlewin
5 Troop guns
Other guns of the Battery
(Kilometre squares)

ground were not so swampy. The empty shell cases sink out of sight, and our feet are as heavy as lead with clay and the straw that we have strewn around to try to get a footing.

I change over with Waldhelm in the No. 1 seat. Little Kloppenburg is indefatigable and Sergeant Ohlsen does not have to give any orders. He stands in the safest place, behind the gun, and we do everything ourselves.

The time passes, and we hardly notice. The Old Man visits us, looking pale and unwell. The BQMS is also with him. Our infantry (in fact some airmen and policemen) have suffered heavy casualties, being poorly equipped and lacking in experience and training. However, our efforts have been of considerable support to them.

It seems that we have been discovered. Suddenly, out of a clear blue sky, explosions start going off all around us. Mortars! I am fetching ammunition from the building behind us. There are a few explosions. Jonny and Flügel are also near. Flügel suffers what seems to be a heart attack and lies wailing on the ground, and our gas-burner has been hit in the engine. So we are rid of it, and get another truck in its place. With time things become quieter and reduce to a mere skirmish. We examine the terrain with binoculars. It lies open in front of us, but the mortar positions are behind the buildings in the adjacent villages of Kerstenbruch and Neu and Alt Levin, that our infantry have penetrated.

'Frieps' Köllner is runner to the local commandant, a lieutenant with the German Cross in Gold, etc., so he has the best information on what is going on and visits us often to pass it on.

The people from the village bring us something to eat. Fatigue is making itself noticeable. I even fall asleep in the gunner's seat, but when the other two guns open fire, I wake up and am ready to fire again. The number of rounds fired now is into the second hundred. We are astonished. We would not have believed this of the old hands, and all this with relatively few blockages.

No. 13 gun is silent. They are no longer able to change barrels, and apparently there has been a distortion. The gun has to be taken to Wriezen. Pongo is out of a job. Thank goodness this happened without any casualties.

We now have our first wounded man in the battery. The neighbouring battery has received a direct hit and has several casualties. However,

Flügel is out of the battle and will have to be taken care of. His nerves were not up to it.

It is getting dark. We see to the guns as best as we can, then a change of location is ordered, but only for a few hundred metres further on. But that is enough with the state of the ground. The trucks cannot get in here, so our first change of location at the front is effected with a couple of horses and a lot of effort. My carbine falls off the gun and is run over by the wheel and pressed into the ground. It is now completely dark and I am lucky to be able to find it again, but what a state it is in!

The sentries are detailed, each half a gun crew. Again we thank our lucky stars that we have three crews for two guns. The others can stretch out, but there are too many for such a small room. There is hardly room to eat. The old teacher and his wife (the building is the village school) bring us hot coffee. Then we sleep packed closely together, Second Lieutenant Kern too. Some snore.

I go outside with my comrades to relieve the sentries. Nothing has happened. One could even say that it is dangerously silent. There is not a star to be seen in the sky, and one cannot see one's hand in front of one's face. From time to time a flare goes up and then others appear, green, white and red. One ducks involuntarily. Sometimes a tracer strays through the darkness, and one hears the dull thuds of explosions. One learns to distinguish between Ivan's and our own.

We whisper among ourselves, always with one ear cocked. One learns how to do this. Nevertheless, nothing escapes us. What do we talk about? About one's impressions and of home, a cigarette glowing in one's hollowed hand, covered from the enemy. Karl Siebenbaum smokes a pipe with its bowl upturned, having learnt how to do that earlier.

'Halt! Who goes there?' It is the relief. We go back into the sleeping room as quietly as possible. It doesn't quite work, but no one wakes up. They are all used to it, the air-raid school having been good training for this. I sit down at the washing table, which is already covered over, and write until sleep overcomes me.

4 February 1945

With dawn comes: 'All out!' It is still palpably cold. There is intermittent fine rain. Even that earth which had been firm before is now soft. The guns are red with rust, and where there is no rust there is clay and dirt. The Russians are keeping quiet. I think that nobody on either side knows what and who is opposite them. Even the air activity is much less in comparison with the first LaGG 3 fighters[4] two days ago. So a good opportunity and reason to give the guns a thorough cleaning, the gunners' greatest delight. But each gun has to have an air sentry (now more a ground observer) on duty. Sergeant Ohlsen assigns me to this role several times, so I can at last have a chance to clean my carbine, and end up with frozen fingers.

Camouflaging, and then a protective wall has to be erected in front of the gun. I slip off with little Kloppenburg to the other gun, which is standing in front of a haystack, from which we can help ourselves. Straw and clay help with the construction of our wall, but give us no pleasure.

Food comes. The crew duties are shared out again, and also for the afternoon, so that we have an opportunity to wash. Bobby and Pongo are also back, having escorted their gun to the workshops. I hadn't noticed this with all that was going on, and hadn't missed them.

Then I go for a wash. I am about to go through the door behind which Sergeant Ohlsen has disappeared, when another door opens and an old man calls out that I can wash in his place. I take my things from my rucksack and follow him in. A musty warmth confronts me. At first I can hardly identify anything, then slowly discover that I am in a longish room about five metres long and three metres wide. A bed, unmade and with a check-patterned, filthy covering, an old iron stove with a damaged door, an old cupboard, and a metal washstand with a basin, fill the room in such a way that one can hardly see the torn stone floor with the earth showing through in several places. Only a tiny window with dirty panes lets a little light into the room. The old man pours some hot water into the basin. He looks like many of the people that we have seen around here. He has a tangled shock of grey-blond hair around his head, and his nicotine-stained moustache has long been untended. What can I say about his face? It is old and creased with wrinkles. His feet, over which crumpled socks are tucked into his trousers, are stuck into wooden clogs. There is another pair in the corner where I undress. I almost hesitate to use them. Is there nothing clean in this place? But I too am dirty, so have to get on with it. The old man sits on the bed and puts a few pieces of wood into the stove. 'Yes, it will soon be warm here,' he says.

I wash myself. Who can appreciate how good that feels? Today is like Sunday. The man tells me something about his life. I listen with only half an ear. How good it is to have clean clothes. I also change my shoes, so that the felt boots can dry out thoroughly. I thank him and go out and breathe the fresh cold air, which causes my warm skin to prickle. I go back to the gun. The BQMS is there, and I tell him of the loss of my papers. He asks me about the circumstances, etc. I get no telling-off, for Second Lieutenant Kern is standing there.

We are going to fire again. German aircraft, Ju 87s,[5] appear in the sky. We can see them clearly as they dive to the ground, and, according to the map, they must be attacking a bridge. The Russian flak is efficient, but no way as good as ours.

Washing has made me hungry, but I am interrupted while eating. It is already getting dark when we have to resume a small bombardment of the old targets until the advent of darkness brings it to a close. The sentries are detailed off. We have been allocated another room for the night, but it is not much better and still very tight.

We are not quite asleep when someone bursts in: 'Alarm! Everyone outside!' We grab our carbines, Second Lieutenant Kern issues some brief instructions, and then rushes outside, with us following.

It is pitch dark outside. Second Lieutenant Kern speaks to Siebenbaum, who is on sentry duty. The atmosphere is so tense, one hardly dares breathe. Everything seems too loud. Our corner is supposed to have been fired on by a machine-gun, so a runner is sent off to inform the local commandant.

We wait. All is quiet. There are some flares in the distance, a few dull shots, otherwise nothing. It is cold, and we have only put on the basic essentials in our hurry, so the fine rain is that much more uncomfortable.

It was probably an error by one of our own machine-guns. The matter is not resolved. I can't hear anything. At last we are dismissed: 'Back inside! Sentries keep a sharp lookout!' I think that everyone is happy that this delicate situation has been brought to a rather harmless conclusion. I sleep until Hesse summons me for sentry duty, which passes peacefully. A new day dawns over Ivan.

5 February 1945

We are back to work, erecting walls, mounting a lookout, and cleaning, with something to eat between whiles. As soon as one stops, the hunger returns. While one is digging in mud, one doesn't notice it. They still haven't given us any cigarettes, and so the Old Man, who looked in at noon, was given some poisonous looks.

Then orders come to prepare to move. We have to leave immediately. Everything is packed up in haste, although we have to remain prepared to open fire. We can leave the gun one at a time to put our things in order, and people are sent off here and there, which is how I get to go through the village for the first time. Running past, I see people, children, in rags, clay houses, all marked with the same dirt. I make my way with an effort and difficulty through the mud of the village street, which has been churned up beyond recognition by the trucks.

It is late afternoon before we are finally ready. Two half-track armoured personnel carriers pull us out of the dirt. It is a pleasure to see how resolutely these things make their way across the field, where we can hardly move on foot. Behind them are the guns, hardly recognisable as such, and all full of dirt. Now we are standing on the street with our cannon and our kit. Then come the trucks to take us away. Hitching up is quickly done. Two guns, three trucks, three gun crews, three sets of gun accessories. There is trouble. Second Lieutenant Kern is very angy with the stubborn No. 13 gun crew, who want to keep their truck for themselves alone. We climb on to No. 15's open truck and drive off into the approaching night in slowly falling rain.

Villages that we recognise from our arrival appear like shadows. There is the crossroads with the hole. We take a sharp bend. We are not going into Wriezen, but to Letschin, as we can read from a sign by the truck's dimmed lights. Then the column stops and we stand around in the rain and wait. Slowly we become uncomfortably wet and one part of the body after another goes to sleep. On the other side of the road is a horse-drawn supply column. Occasionally motorcyclists go past. If only we could have found a better spot.

The Old Man comes along and we can hear him talking to people in the other vehicles: 'We have to stay here. I have no other orders. There are no buildings in the vicinity. Two sentries from each troop!' There is general grumbling. He gets back in his car.

But then we start. The Old Man is to blame, of course. Couldn't he have left us where we were if he had no other orders? He comes back again: 'Fasten your tent-halves together[6] and pull them over the struts!' Nobody answers or moves. 'Stubborn lot!' he snaps, and goes off. At least we have the satisfaction of his being angry. I stop trying to improve my un-comfortable position, hardly feeling anything any more, and sleep comes in spite of everything.

6 FEBRUARY 1945

There was no pleasant awakening this morning. It took some time for me to climb down from the truck and start walking about. Now we are moving on again. We drive through Letschin, a clean scene at last with broad streets, simple, two-storeyed buildings and a statue of Frederick the Great. We leave all this behind and drive east out of the town. Then we separate from the others of our battery and go on a short distance to a farmstead.

The gun is to be deployed behind a hedge in a small front garden, which gives us all plenty to do. First we have to hack through the bushes and hedge with axes. Our gun then practically vanishes inside. It doesn't go so quickly with No. 15. We can't move it on the muddy road, so Second Lieutenant Kern brings along a tracked tractor that makes short work of it. The tractor belongs to a 37 mm Army Flak unit[7] deployed among the nearby farms.

But we are still not finished. Each gun has to have a shelter wall as high as the hedge, then ammunition has to be moved, mud shovelled and branches cut. Each gun crew sends two men to take over the accommodation allocated to them. Finally the trucks are emptied of unnecessary ballast, such as empty ammunition boxes. Second Lieutenant Kern divides up the gun crews, which is an easy matter with two guns and three crews. We enter the buildings. The farm is a dependency of a manor farm, as we discover. Did they really house people in rooms like this? Little Kloppenburg has already made a good job of clearing them out, but one can see what they looked like before. The kitchen: a front room with a bricked-in oven, a cupboard that has lost all its paintwork, and the barest of essential cooking utensils. The floor: naked stone. In the next room are two double beds, a table, a kind

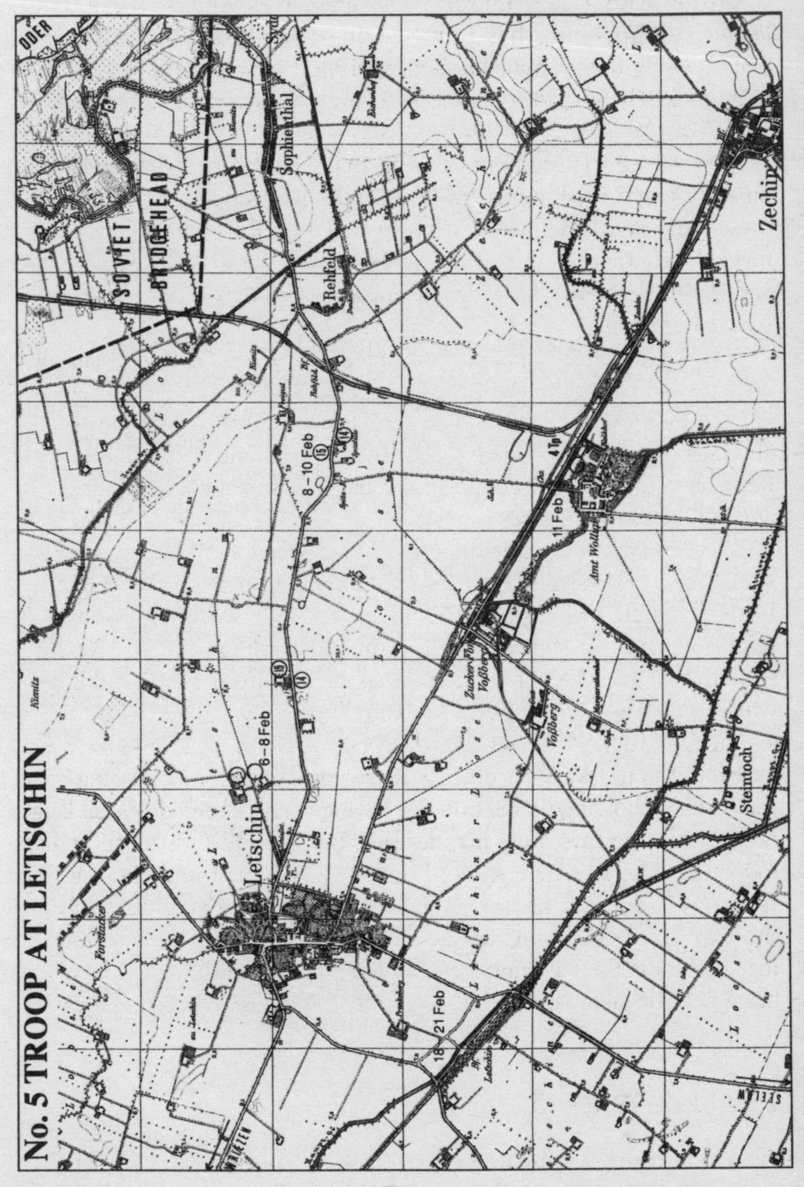
No. 5 TROOP AT LETSCHIN
ODER
SOVIET
BRIDGEHEAD
Sophienthal
Rehfeld
Zechin
8–10 Feb
11 Feb
6–8 Feb
Letschin
Voßberg
Steintoch
21 Feb
18

of dresser with a large mirror, two night tables, chairs, and a *chaise-longue*. Kloppenburg has removed the feather-bedding to a small neighbouring room, in which there is another bed, but none of us want to lie on it. The very idea makes us itch involuntarily. The door is quickly closed.

Now we are allocated our sleeping spaces. Sergeant Ohlsen will sleep on the *chaise-longue* against the wall. Feddern, Kippert, Waldhelm and myself take the beds, lying on the mattresses. Kruse and Kloppenburg make themselves a nest of straw on the floor between the windowed wall and the beds. Now quickly to eat, for my two hours of sentry duty will soon be here.

Nothing much is happening outside. We clean, polish and shovel. I go across to No. 15 a few times. Pongo is also there already. They have got the best rooms, even a radio, but no electricity, plum mousse and all kinds of things for cooking. The truck drivers and Second Lieutenant Kern have the best, of course. They have even slaughtered something and will be having rissoles tonight.

The Old Man arrives with Second Lieutenant Kern. We have to do something. Orders to dig shelter and ammunition trenches. Everything has to vanish underground. That is enough work for today and tomorrow, and, of course, there is some grumbling. But first we eat – something that is different from what we get from the field kitchen, which is well hidden, or at least we can't see it.

The first artillery fire, and how the shells roar! The explosions are not so far away from us. We hurry outside. Karl Siebenbaum comes running out of the darkness holding up his trousers, having been disturbed. We all laugh, but I have to go myself ten minutes later. But generally it is quiet, perhaps too quiet. The flares are some distance away. There must be a mortar battery[8] not far from us, and from time to time its rockets go screaming through the darkness. As always in quiet situations, we slept huddled together under thin coverings; interrupted only by guard duties. The cold is bearable. One takes nothing off. Nightshirts? Pyjamas? What are they?

7 FEBRUARY 1945

Even today cannot bring us anything new, except that there is a fantastic meal, for a ram has been slaughtered. We have to work as usual. I prefer cleaning carbines or being look-out to digging shelter trenches out of the root-clogged earth.

The food was good. We have not seen or eaten such fat for a long time. I even get heartburn. I rummage through the house for some sodium bicarbonate, but do not find any. However, it wears off in time.

An officer from the mortars comes to visit us, a nice chap. He explains things to us, which makes a change.

8 February 1945

During our free time I rummage around the farm with Jonny, Bobby and Pongo. The barns are full of wheat. There are only a few cattle here. There is even something to read, and I take a twenty-pfennig novel with me back to the gun.

In the evening come the orders to change location. Everything is packed in the greatest haste. Jonny and I fill up our sweet jar with plum mousse.

Kleinmeier has to pull us out, all in the dark. Second Lieutenant Kern flashes his torch around. There is a row over the schnapps issue. We reckon that Übersreuther and the driver have been cheating again, but we are used to that. We drive off eastwards. We stop. Then comes the beloved voice of the Old Man: 'Unlimber!' We can see that we are next to a farmstead. Down into the dirt, which is the same everywhere. No. 15 gun goes on the right with us on the left of the position. 'Dig in!' The wall grows slowly and one piece of clothing after another is hung on the gun. Sergeant Ohlsen doesn't need to divest himself, for he is only giving orders as usual. We take bundles of straw from a nearby stack so as not to have to shovel so much, and spread dung over it from a heap nearby.

We go inside the house. It looks cleaner than those we are accustomed to. I have to go on sentry duty, and when I have finished I have to report to Second Lieutenant Kern, who gives me a cognac and congratulates me on my birthday, as midnight has just passed. Pongo must have told him that I am sixteen today.

9 February 1945

When one is on sentry duty one sees more in the bushes than is really there. One also hears the sound of aircraft. They must be ours, for they are flying eastwards and then one hears explosions. We must not look up in the daytime, and the crew have to sneak around the gun by roundabout ways.

The farm is well laid out in a rectangle, everything apparently in order, clean and well looked after. Jonny has to see to the animals, of which there are all kinds: turkeys, geese, calves, sheep, pigs and a cow.

Today we have meat soup with peas. We turn back the supply section bringing the food from the field kitchen. We hardly need to explain ourselves, for artillery fire starts and the supply section promptly disappears.

Behind our house is another, like a small villa with barns, which our foursome also visits, except for Bobby, who has sentry duty. There was another unit there but it left today. The men had slaughtered a pig, but were unable to take it with them, so we make our neighbourly claim and take it over to our kitchen, keeping the liver to cook ourselves. Why should their lordships always get the best bits? Attracted by the smell, Sergeant Ohlsen asks for a small piece. Others do too, but we are not so obliging.

Jonny finds a bottle of wine next time. Pongo and Bobby have gone with a truck back to our old position to fetch some coal, so we wait until we are on sentry duty to drink it, for it is clearly my birthday wine. I have duty with Waldhelm and the other three join us. The bottle does the rounds, but nothing is said.

10 February 1945

The Old Man has been again. There is not much for him to grumble about. Second Lieutenant Kern sends me off to the farm opposite with orders to keep under cover. It is certainly a former gentleman's residence, possibly of a noble military family or something similar.[9] There are Russian snipers in the farms beyond it. I carry out my task, checking our camouflage on the way back. Up to a hundred metres off it looks just like a dung heap and only our steel helmets need some camouflage.

The airmen are busy today and there are some dog-fights overhead. We can only distinguish friend from foe with difficulty, and the recognition books are thumbed through frantically. The Russians all look the same to us, but that one must be a LaGG 3 and that one an Airacobra.[10] This is confirmed at the highest level. A few minutes later an He 111 wanders calmly over to the east, drops its bombs unperturbed by the flak, which comes up far behind, and flies back home again. Shortly afterwards a Ju 87 does the same thing. What? Only one Ju 87? We are thinking of Rudel, about whom so much is said.[11] We even have to open fire ourselves a few times.

We find another bottle of wine in the house next door and drink it up straight away. Better now than never. There is also some pudding powder for the kitchen, but we see nothing of the pudding later on.

The place has become too small for us. Kippert and I lie on the bed in the side-room without using the feather bedding. We lay our tent-halves on the mattress, for prevention is better than cure.

Before sleeping we warm ourselves from the heat streaming from the tiled stove that can be found in every house here and is often located in the passage. We sing songs with Karl Siebenbaum. The only ones missing are the sentries and No. 15 gun crew, who have their own place. Flügel grumbles something about sleep from his corner in the wardrobe, but doesn't raise his voice, having had enough from the last quarrel. Pongo, the poor chap, is ill, but there is still some spark in him.

Our snores are disturbed in the middle of the night. A runner brings the beloved orders to change location. There is swearing as we resume our favourite task, but Second Lieutenant Kern does not give us much time for it, and he is right, for we would never have believed how deep into the mire our gun has sunk. It is a right mess. Jonny works like a madman, while Sergeant Ohlsen thinks that he need do nothing himself. Kleinmeier can only pull us out after we have built a corduroy track and winched the wheels out of the mud. Sachte estimated that it cost us six hours' work.

It is time too, for the morning cannot be far off. We hardly have enough time to put our own things together, so it is just as well that we have kerosene lamps to hand, and we take them with us. Jonny thinks of everything: geese and turkeys are stuffed into sacks and thrown on the truck, followed by a slaughtered calf. And then we are off.

11 February 1945

It is getting lighter. We drive past some positions through Letschin, after which we rejoin the battery, ending up in a manor farm. Surging life meets us on the capacious square; soldiers, civilians, vehicles. The yard is so big that it is difficult to take it all in, but we hardly get a chance as Second Lieutenant Kern starts issuing instructions. The guns have to be driven under some trees and now stand next to assault guns, radio trucks and so on. We are getting a rest day in Amt Wollup, but No. 4 Troop has to go into position in front of the farm.

So let's get on with our rest day. First we are given our quarters, which are in a room a little small for us, but everyone gets a seat at the long table. We eat, read and write, then go for a wash. It is bitterly cold, but who cares?

I make a tour of the farmyard, which has roomy stables, clean and light, and large barns smelling of hay and grain. I am astonished by the sheep shed. I have never seen so many sheep in one space. I have to call Jonny to continue my tour with me. Many animals are standing ready for collection, and ewes are tending their lambs in small enclosures, one licking the blood from the wet coat of a newly born.

In the centre, well and strongly fenced in, are the rams, real mountains of wool. They look so threatening, we daren't go near. A few dead animals are lying in the passage, new-born lambs and some a little bigger. We read the tally '1,500' on a board – 1,500 sheep here, in an area of healthy heat and bright light, with a fine smell of animals and their dung, and the animals themselves bleating out a concert in various tones, while the war is only a few kilometres away.

Outside some pigs are wallowing in the dirt, but I have never seen pigs like this before. They are mountains of fat – that is all that one can say. Their eyes have disappeared and their sharp ears stick up cheerfully. Jonny reckons them to be between 5 and 6 hundredweight and still not fully grown.

We come to the cow barn, where there are almost as many humans as cows, of which there are seventy-two. Milking and filtering is going on. Everything is spotlessly clean, cleaner than the houses that we have been sleeping in. There is a feeding trough and a sewage trough worked by oxen, of which there are about twenty standing outside. All the cows have boards with their names and all their data.

We speak to one of the officials responsible for the many Poles and Russians. They are all well-behaved and hard workers and want nothing to do with Stalin, unlike our own former prisoners of war. Only when they have been drinking are they difficult to control, for there is a distillery on the farm. We take due note of this.

That the men and women here like their schnapps, I have already seen for myself. When one of No. 4 Troop came with two bottles of schnapps in his arms and mess tins in his hands, wanting to obtain some milk, a shrivelled-up old woman busy milking said: 'First hand over the drink.' He handed her a bottle and never saw it again, for it vanished like lightning under her dress. Meanwhile he had been surrounded by other men and women, and held the other bottle high above his head. Had he not done this, a hand would have grabbed it and the bottle would have gone. His mess tins, filled with milk, were pressed into his hands and they all went back to work. In all honesty, I didn't think to help him for a moment. Why not? I could only laugh at the sheer cheek and stupidity of it all.

We went back to get mess tins for collecting milk and water bottles for schnapps. Pongo met us in the quarters with a request to keep a look-out outside the door while he and Bobby went into the bakery. There did not seem to be much to take, and they soon came out again, but a Frenchman had seen this and cried out. A woman came running up, as round as a ball, a living 2½ to 3 hundredweight. And then the show began, with Jonny talking his way out with his glib tongue, but in the end there was no bread to be had.

Consequently, although a calf is slaughtered to make rissoles, they fall apart from the fat because there is no bread in them. We finally got some milk and schnapps, but it is so strong we have to water it down. It must be 90 per cent proof potato spirit.

So it goes on until evening, and we look for places to sleep, but hardly anyone settles down. We drink, eat, sing and tell stories. I even have to play the piano until I can play no longer. We haven't been so relaxed for a long time.

Then I have to do sentry duty with Jonny. Why? It's nonsensical. I creep around half asleep. We have hardly settled down in the straw after being relieved when we get: 'Change location!' We are supposed to leave at midnight, but it is 3 o'clock before we do so. The rain drips monotonously on the truck canopy. The poor chaps from No. 15 gun that have to sit on the open sides of their Borgward truck! It slowly becomes lighter. We are already through Letschin and it starts to snow.

12 FEBRUARY 1945

Morning has arrived. We can tell because of the light between the swirling snow. Our truck is alone. We stop and can hear infantry fire, which is not very comforting. We cannot see anything, and know even less. We pull on our camouflage jackets. The gun goes into the hedged-in rectangle of an unattractive house. The building is nothing, just naked and empty. We have no bread, so I unpack the last of my crispbread and share it out. It has stopped snowing and we can see another house on the other side of the road with a track leading off to a manor farm.

Along with 'Frieps' Köllner, I go to collect our rations from the crossroads where No. 2 Troop is located. We take one of the little infantry sledges that are lying around everywhere. Then Jonny and I visit the house next door and find a few edible things. In the evening No. 15 gun also arrives and is deployed at the manor farm, from where we collect some straw.

We now discover where we are. Our house belongs to Alt Tucheband, which lies behind us and is where the supply section and Nos 1 and 4 Troops have established themselves. The place in front of us is called Manschnow and is occupied half by us and half by the Russians. Beyond it is Küstrin on the Oder.

Here we have lain for a week without firing a shot. Nevertheless we have had some exciting moments. We can only leave the house through a window, as the door is overlooked by the enemy. Jonny and I have visited the house next door as often as possible, for there are some brickettes there and we have been able to wash our underclothes, and once we made a milk pudding and even some coffee. Kleinmeier brews himself some liquor, using aromatic herbs and schnapps from Wollup. I have tried it myself, but it doesn't taste of much.

One day we have an inspection by the battalion commander. I was already over in the other house and he noticed. We now have to fill the space between the gun and the hedge with a wall and excavate anti-tank holes in the roadway.

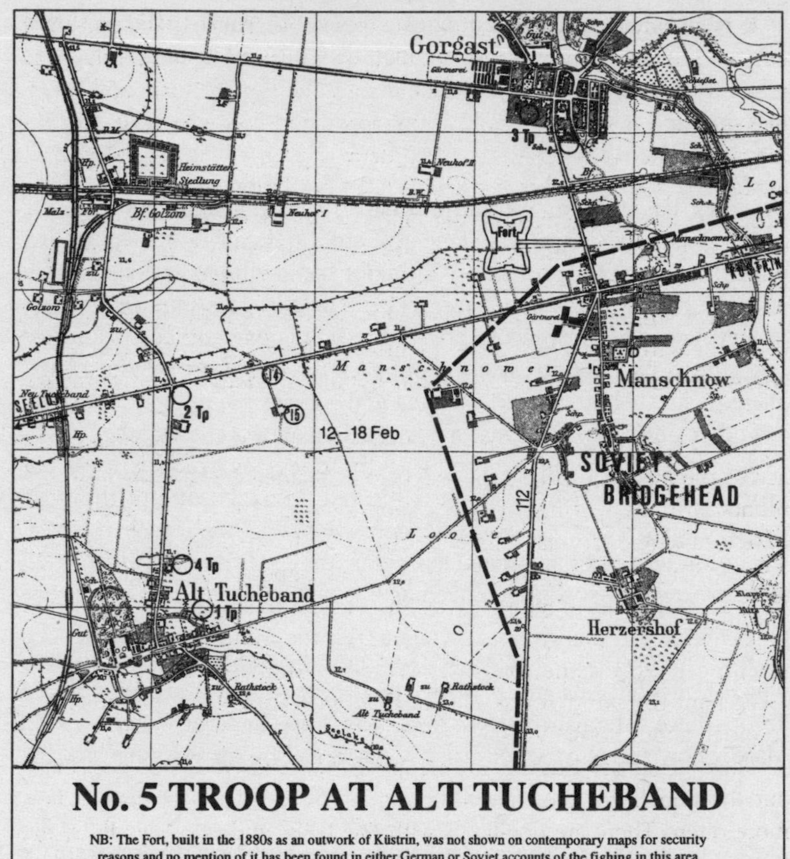

No. 5 TROOP AT ALT TUCHEBAND

NB: The Fort, built in the 1880s as an outwork of Küstrin, was not shown on contemporary maps for security reasons and no mention of it has been found in either German or Soviet accounts of the fighing in this area although it must have played an important part. It was later found to contain a stockpile of panzerfausts.

We have not seen much of the Russians. One day a sentry reported something suspicious at the farm in front of us. We could make out something faintly through the binoculars, a dark hole and a couple of figures relaxing and smoking, but we were not allowed to shoot.

Second Lieutenant Kern sends me to see Lieutenant Weiss, who has turned up again here as the local commandant. He is a fabulous chap, and is said to have been wounded twenty-seven times. Yes, that is a Russian anti-tank unit in front of us, but we can be sure that it will soon disappear.

It is already dark when I make my way back. There is the sound of engines and air activity. At first I think from the 'pot-pot' sound that it is a boat on the Oder. Searchlights illuminate the sky and here and there, like shooting stars, come tracers from above and to and from it. Second Lieutenant Kern says that it is an 'Orderly Officer' or 'Sewing Machine', as this old double-decker is called.[12] Then our ration party returns quite upset, for one of the machines dropped its bombs right in front of their noses and caused them to tumble into the ditch with the food canisters, but no one was hurt.

Next morning our unpleasant neighbours have vanished and the area is swept with extra heavy rocket fire. I am on sentry duty and the splinters whistle low over us, the hits coming within four or five metres from us.

Later I have to return to the local commandant and on my way come across the fins of a rocket, about 13 cm in diameter. The Poles from the manor farm are leaving. I make a short visit to No. 13 gun crew, who have it much better than ourselves. They even have some wine.

Feddern has also taken note, and when he goes to collect our rations from there, he fails to return. Finally he staggers in singing, with the food on his back. He was given a fair amount of the fruit wine and has been sleeping it off on the roadside. We once drank some with Second Lieutenant Kern until it was all gone. Why? Because we had been talking so much about home.

There are many Russians in the air by day, and we are able to make out the pilots, but they haven't found us. No. 4 Troop behind us fires more often. There are dog-fights with Me 109s, and once five Il-2s, the Butchers, attack Seelow, but within a short while the 2 cm guns nail two of them and the rest make off.

We sometimes come under artillery fire, and behind us Alt Tucheband has taken quite a hammering.

Those who stayed behind in Hanover have now arrived, including Schumacher. We are relieved of our long-nosed Sergeant Ohlsen, but have received another instead: Sergeant Brendl, the former commander of No. 4 Troop. ('He'll soon size you up!' Sergeant Ohlsen said.) The first thing he does is to consume a whole pig's trotter in front of us until he can eat no more and then offers Flügel a few scraps. Brendl was transferred because he had let his own crew down. They say that he is a frightful egotist.

A 105 mm flak gun has drawn up behind us and is firing at Manschnow church tower, in which there is supposed to be an artillery observer, and after a couple of shots the tower tips over. We learn later that it is a gun from a Hanoverian battery, perhaps from Buchholz.

Second Lieutenant Kern and Siebenbaum have to go off with the Old Man to reconnoitre new positions. We will soon be off again and the trucks have already been brought up.

There are often German aircraft in the sky at night, and then one sees the glow of fires in the east. There is said to be heavy fighting near Küstrin, with the Russians using lots of tanks. At night the mine-layers go along the roads cutting holes in the surface. The situation is extremely tense.

18 February 1945

It is Sunday. We get ready but do not move off until Monday. We pass through Seelow, meet up with the other units and drive to Letschin, where we are deployed to protect the station from air attack. There is also an armoured train with 88 mm and four-barrelled flak guns present. Preparing the position here is difficult because of the heavy clay. We have thrown our kit into a dugout. Soon the first LaGG 3 appears. We are ready for action but do not get to open fire.

Our accommodation is some distance from the guns. Some are in the station waiting room, but we have a lovely railwayman's cottage and have never had it so good. The whole day and the next are spent on preparing the position, but not without interruption. The telephone cable had only just been laid when the 15 cm battery and the 88 mm flak near us started shooting, which brings a reply and for the first time we find ourselves under an artillery barrage. The impact is devastating and strips people of their masks. Sergeant Brendl is the first to vanish without any consideration for the others. The *Luftwaffe* auxiliaries, especially little Kloppenburg, acquit themselves extremely well. We would not have believed it of him. The explosions are damnably close, but nothing happens, only the tracks and the armoured train are damaged.

More and more aircraft appear. We have to keep throwing our spades down to shoot, and once an aircraft passes very low over us. Was it a Russian or a Messerschmitt? We didn't shoot. It was a Russian, which made us angry. (We once opened fire in Friedenau, back in Hanover, and

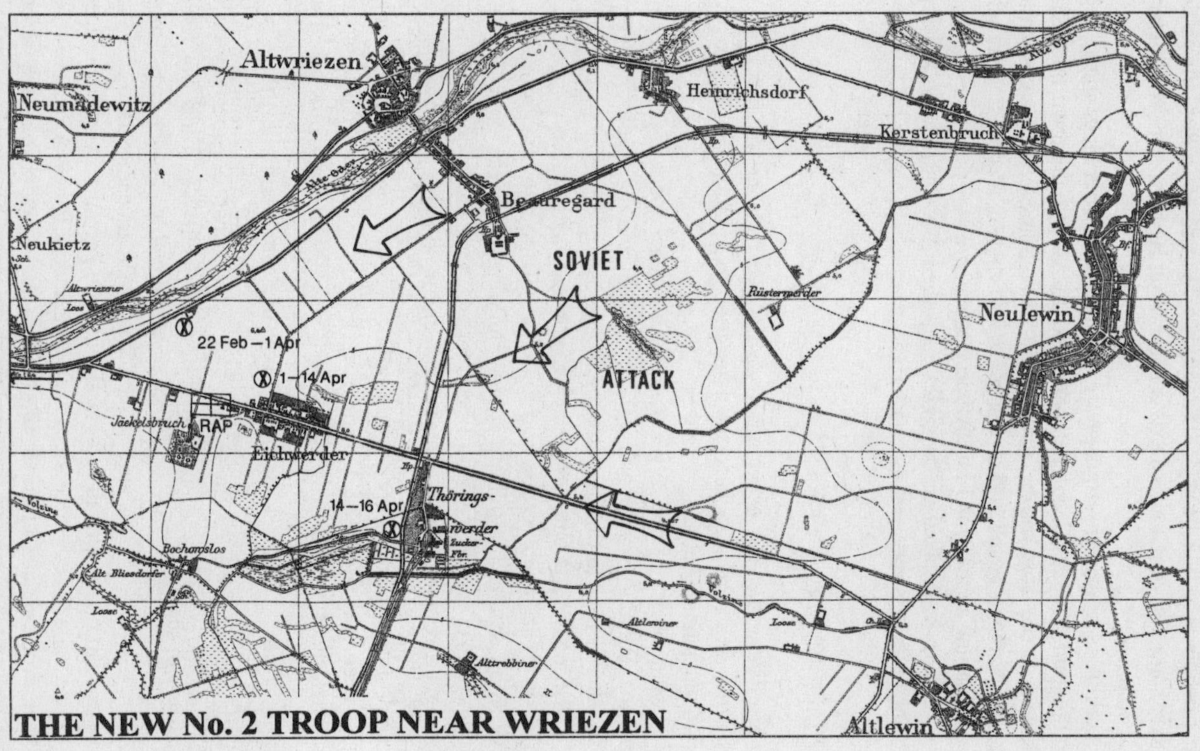

THE NEW No. 2 TROOP NEAR WRIEZEN

it turned out to be an FW 190, and not a Thunderbolt.) But better safe than sorry, for shortly afterwards a Focke-Wulf is shot down by our own 20 mm flak.

There is a feverish atmosphere around. The weather is warm and quite muggy. Second Lieutenant Kern lets me go into the town once, for I want to see what can be done about my missing Post Office savings book. Nothing. I can't find a post office and there is no one that can tell me anything about it, so I hardly speak to anyone.

Feddern has milked a cow. (Next day there was only the hide left.) None of us feels very well.

21 February 1945

This Wednesday was especially exciting. We had one air attack after another with bombs, rockets, machine-guns and cannon, and Pongo was credited with several hits.

I went to the quarters to get ready, as we were supposed to be pulling out that evening. It was a little quieter outside, and the 20 mm flak crew was already back in the field chasing rabbits as if nothing had happened.

Heaving the gun out of the clay was another real slog. No. 13 gun was also there. Each gun needed two trucks hitched to it to pull it out. Then we stood around the railway station buildings until we moved out at midnight. All the bridges had been prepared for demolition. Some men brought a couple of sacks of sugar with them, so I checked through the wagons with Jonny again, but there was nothing much worth taking.

Then we were off. The journey was interrupted once, but it was not until we had moved on again that we discovered that Tatge had been run over. The drivers had been celebrating Kleinmeier's birthday and were quite drunk. The truck had got stuck in a ditch and the driver had stupidly given it too much gas. When the gun was pulled round it had gone over Tatge's pelvis. He had already been taken away. We were really angry with the driver's intemperance.

22 February 1945

We return to an area we know. On the right is the well-known fork in the road where we heard and saw our first shots in the front line.

It is misty, but not raining. The Old Man indicates a ploughed field for our next location. It is obvious that we can't send the trucks into the field, so we have to wait until No. 4 Troop have finished using the farmer's four horses. and then it is back to the old theme, pushing, but it is next to impossible to move the gun. As we are about to move the second gun we hear a loud argument on the road. It is some high-ranking person, apparently our new battalion commander. Orders come to stop work, so out we come again. It gets worse. I search for a toilet at a nearby house. There are a few girls standing around, and Kleinmeier is with them, of course. Eventually a three-axled Henschel truck pulls us out. And now? We have to go into the next field, as if that is any better! A Bulldog tractor now becomes available, but only after we have stopped pushing the gun along on planks, and having gone all of seven metres in 35 minutes. But even the tractor gets stuck after 20 metres. The gun is now hardly visible any more. With an effort we get it back on to some hard ground.

At a distance of 500 metres further on the Old Man is looking for a site in another field, this time not ploughed. But first of all we take a break. We are absolutely bushed and have nothing to eat, but then the supply section comes along and we are allowed to go into the farmer's barn to eat. We immediately start looking around for eggs, and find some.

Then the Old Man comes back. This time it goes better and soon the gun is in position. But now we have to dig, and that goes slowly as there is clay here too, and we can only go down a fraction at a time.

Evening comes. Our quarters are 200 metres away in a farm labourer's cottage beside the road. We have a room, a kitchen and an attic. When we go inside there is already straw in the room, and Second Lieutenant Kern has partitioned off a corner for himself. We lie down closely packed together, Flügel complaining as usual.

I have to go on sentry duty. It is very dark, and we stumble across the field. It is all very strange. The Russians seem to be having a rest. Will we get one too? A small counter-offensive is said to have taken place.

We are now supposed to stay in this position until the middle of April. (Much happened during this lengthy period of course, but I have lost my notes about it.) The major soon arrived and found fault with our accommodation, and we had to dig dugouts near the guns. These were large and had electric light. We even had a radio. The guns were camouflaged with wire netting. We slaughtered an animal from time to time, even though it was forbidden, and we took eggs from the farmer's straw. There was some flirting with the girls from the house, but they were nothing special.

A few soldiers went off to Küstrin[13] and we got some *Luftwaffe* auxiliaries from there that were difficult to understand, two from Guben and one from Stettin, a real dour Pomeranian, although I got on well with him. The motorcyclist Kreuzmann also joined us and we were often together, but Bobby, Jonny and Pongo remained a bit standoffish. There was also an officer cadet with them, but he was soon exchanged. We called this little show-off 'Spatz' and laughed about him.

There was a duty roster and training programme just like in barracks. After we had fired a few times without success, we were forbidden to fire so as not to reveal our position, and the dear Russians were able to fly over us scot-free as they busily took their photographs. Even the Tommies came over as far as us in their raids on Berlin, which we could see well from where we were.

Our field hospital was installed in the sculptor Arno Breker's farm,[14] so naturally everyone wanted to see it. I modelled two naked women for Second Lieutenant Kern, but the clay soon cracked and I gave up. We also had to go to the hospital for inoculations, and once I was ill afterwards. The doctor was very young and very sympathetic, and was easy to talk to.

We received our first mail here. On one occasion I got twenty-five and on another fifteen letters.

Then we had to dig fire trenches. When you had completed your metre, you were allowed time off. Apart from this, it was real army life, not front line stuff. Soon we even found ourselves in front of a court martial for having taken a farmer's hut for the construction of our position. There were also some infantry attack exercises organised, in which we twice got Sergeant Brendl completely exhausted, for he always wanted to win.

In the evenings we would sit in our dugouts and play Pontoon, but I stopped playing after I had lost 60 Marks. We chatted, wrote letters and curled up in the straw whenever we were not on sentry duty. Then we would stand in the entrance and listen very quietly to Soldatensender 'Calais',[15] being quite cunning about it.

Firing practice with carbines and machine-guns was also on the programme, the best shots getting leave passes to Wriezen, but I never made it.

Meanwhile all the *Luftwaffe* auxiliaries were promoted to the rank of Gunner and sworn in. That is all except myself, being the only one born in 1929. I might even have been able to go back home, but who knows where I would have landed up.

Just before Easter it was announced that we would be changing position to just a few hundred metres away. This made us terribly angry as we saw no sense in it now that we had got everything in good order, in this weather and over Easter too. But it was no good. Within eight days we had prepared a model position, a proper little fortress with six corners in each of which was either a gun or a bunker, and all below ground.

Our life continued this way for a short time. From continually lying in straw with its terrible dust, I had got a sort of scabies and often had to visit the hospital. My mother would have said that it came from not washing often enough.

We even went hunting. No. 4 Troop shot a deer, Sergeant Brendl a rabbit. We were now called No. 2 Troop, as the old No. 2 Troop no longer belonged to our battery. No. 1 Troop also had a second lieutenant now. We knew him without being aware of it, for he had once crossed our paths dressed as a *Luftwaffe* auxiliary and asked us questions. This was called counter-intelligence.

Our attention was now directed more to the Russians. We were told that they had fewer troops in front of us, but we were still a little restless. From the radio we learned that the enemy in the west was pressing farther forward, approaching Hanover. Second Lieutenant Kern was looking depressed, for the enemy had already reached Neustadt an der Haardt.

There was regularly air activity at night. A 'Sewing Machine' would fly to and fro over us and drop a few bombs without causing much damage. A few bombs even fell on Wriezen. We also came under artillery fire again after a long time.

On 11 April our gun crew were supposed to have a pass to go into Wriezen. From listening to 'Calais' the night before we had heard that white flags had been hoisted in the suburbs of Hanover. The Old Man was reluctant to give me a pass, as I had no photograph in my paybook. I had lost everything, but 'Frieps' Köllner had one that would do. While we were in the battery office we heard the *Wehrmacht* report that Hanover had fallen after heavy fighting.

Then we set off for Wriezen with our carbines slung. Anti-tank ditches were being dug everywhere and demolition charges placed under bridges. The scene was very warlike, but we went into a cinema to see the love story of a doctor. We would really have liked to see some young girls, but that didn't work out, as there were none, so we drove back to our position on a tractor.

Next day there was some hefty shooting. In the beautiful weather the Il-2s and LaGG 3s came over in swarms. We fired efficiently as their bombs fell fairly close. Sergeant Brendl made himself scarce.

On 13 April Schütz and Aue left for an officer cadet unit, and on 14 April we had to provide anti-aircraft cover for an infantry regiment on the march. That morning I was sent as a runner to their commanding officer, a young captain, who was really nice, and easy to talk to.

Then the guns were dug out, although we still had to fire from time to time, even from the trailers. Then we set off at top speed. Our kit was to follow. We were all very excited and sang as we drove past the people from our old quarters. We stopped on the road under some trees in Eichwerder and waited as the Russians roared overhead, firing like crazy. Two eight-wheeled armoured cars were standing near us firing their 20 mm guns, which were faster than ours.

The Russian artillery fired from 6 until 7.30. We were still waiting. The Russians were supposed to have broken through somewhere.[16] Kleinmeier had found a young girl with whom he was flirting. Naturally we were jealous.

There was a cherry tree in bloom in front of one of the houses and we said that we would return when the cherries were ripe. Then came the order to set up our guns in the old position of No. 1 Troop, which had gone further forward. The whole project had come to nothing.

So we went back to digging, in spite of the Russian aircraft. It was soon dark. The position was near the sugar factory and its bunkers were terrible and small. The second lieutenant of No. 1 Troop had had his wife from Berlin with him here. I wonder if she got away in time.

Meanwhile we had obtained a few new 'old hands'. One of them, Urbanitsch, also had his wife visit him from Berlin once, and she took back three of my films to be developed.

15 APRIL 1945

It is Sunday again. It is quiet, dangerously so. We make some raids on the sugar factory, finding coal but no sugar. Many workers are going past us. We orientate ourselves: we are right between a manor farm and the sugar factory,[17] and nearby are a 150 mm artillery and an 88 mm flak position. We get an issue of schnapps.

16 APRIL 1945

I have just finished sentry duty, the armourer having let me go. I can hear a 'Sewing Machine' and bombs dropping, then it is quiet. But then at 4.30 a.m. it starts, a real bombardment, and when our neighbours start firing back too, the fun really starts. This continues until 7.30 a.m., then the artillery and aircraft take over from each other. We cannot fire properly, because of the mist. We get a few bombs quite close.

We have no idea what is happening in front of us. There are supposed to be some tanks in front of us, so the officer cadet and Köllner go off with a panzerfaust, but are soon back again. It was only a rumour. The Old Man comes, the major too. Then come the Stalin-organs. At first we don't know what they are, but soon recognise them. One salvo lands on our position, lasting seconds, the rockets landing quite close together, but there are no hits. Requardt gets a splinter in his back and runs over to the farmyard. Hesse can stay here with his injured finger, Schumacher too.

There is news from No. 1 Troop, which has been overrun. The second lieutenant and some of the crew come back, but the others are dead or have been taken prisoner, including Sergeant David. There is an earnest discussion. In front and to the left the view is obscured by the road and sugar factory. The front line seems to be getting closer. We can see a few tanks, but they are not moving. Some soldiers are running back. What's wrong? The major comes to our gun. A few are running off across the field. 'Shoot!' The major pulls me out of the seat, aims the gun and shoots at them. One falls. Is he wounded? Do we agree that we should fire on our own men for leaving us in the lurch? Even Second Lieutenant Kern poses this question. Have they gone through more than we have only to be put at our mercy?

One of them comes straight towards us and we pull him into our position. Second Lieutenant Kern asks him: 'Why are you running away?'

'They were firing so . . .'

'And not on here?'

'Yes, of course, but my rifle doesn't work.'

'Of course not, there is sand in it! How long have you been a soldier?'

'A few months.'

The scene reminds me of the story of Flügel when we first reached the front and came under fire, for he too is no longer young, he is the father of a family, far from home, and his nerves have gone. He stays with us. I have to take the carbine to the armourer, who with Sergeant Brendl and the others (apart from Mucho and the other chap from Guben who are with me on the gun) are behind us in the trenches. As I get up another salvo arrives, one shell exploding near us. I get a pain in my right lower jaw, feel it and pull out a splinter. It doesn't bleed, at least not at first. I don't feel any pain either. The spot is only badly swollen and we put a plaster on it. I now qualify for an award. Many of us have dreamed of getting awards, even me, but then I am a volunteer, even if for various reasons.

Some men are running across the field in front on the right towards a farm. That is roughly where No. 1 Troop had been. We get worked up again. Are they Russians? 'Yes,' says the major. 'There are none of ours left there now, so fire!' It goes like clockwork and they are all lying down over there.

It is getting dark. The artillery pulls out with what they have left. The guns have to be blown, as they have sunk into the mire. There is a demolition team in the sugar factory in front of us. We can hear the cries of: 'Hurray!' I cannot describe the feeling that gives. Then we hear what seems to be German coming from loudspeakers. They must be the voices of members of the Committee for a Free Germany.[18] 'Come over to us! You have lost everything!' and similar expressions. They have been well used as propagandists. The 'Russians' are said to come from Turkestan or somewhere like it.

We prepare to change location. Pongo returns from the hospital, where he has been cut and bandaged up. We now discover that Kimme Brandt was killed on his way back to the manor farm by what seems to have been a direct hit from a tank and is barely recognisable. Pongo almost went right past him.

The Russians appear to be in the sugar factory or nearby. Flares, as light as day – 'Stand still!' Then we can carry on. Ten o'clock. This pattern continues until one o'clock. According to a rumour, the Russians should have attacked at midnight. The trucks come up quietly and without lights. The guns are pulled out with ropes, then the ammunition has to be moved, mainly carried in our arms. We drive off at two o'clock. Thank goodness, we made it. We stop at the manor farm, which has been completely burnt out by Stalin-organs. It is gradually becoming light in the east as we drive out of the still-burning manor farm on the road to Wriezen. Is everyone here? No, someone is missing, but who? It is morning, but what a morning! Only the ground-attack aircraft are missing. Today is 17 April 1945.

The last days of the war were naturally the worst. The retreat now began without any significant pauses. I believe that we only took up firing positions in properly prepared positions once or twice. (According to my school comrade Heini Döpke's timetable we were first east and then south of Schulzendorf on 17 April, and west of it on 18 April, when he shot up three T-34s, as I recall having heard.)

I still remember 19 April well and will never forget it, although not our location. It was early evening and already a bit dark when the order came to collect the rations, so the supply section was still somewhere near. I was detailed for this with Utterodt and Urbanitsch, but then immediately recalled, as being No. 1 on the gun, I was needed to ensure its readiness to open fire. So Köllner took my place, and that was the last time we saw him alive. Meanwhile it had become dark and, as usual, the duty 'Sewing Machine' arrived, flew right over us and shortly afterwards there were a few explosions quite close. We waited for our food, which still did not come. Finally two or three of us set off with torches along the route and soon found it. I can still remember the cooked ham full of splinters, fragmentation grenades being a speciality of the 'Sewing Machine', which often switched off its engine before dropping them. We also found the three dead ration carriers. 'Frieps' lay on his stomach, but one could see right inside him and his ribs from behind. Our already reduced fighting morale was at its lowest. But next day, Hitler's birthday, Goebbels pulled us out of this depression with: 'The Americans and British are uniting with us against the Russians; a relieving army is on its way, V-weapons of the latest kind will ensure our final victory, etc., etc.'

But the retreat continued. Once, I do not know where, the BQMS went crazy. He stormed out of the building during an artillery barrage singing psalms and reciting incomprehensible religious texts. He must have belonged to some sect or other. But what happened to him after that, I have no idea.

At Oranienburg aerodrome, where the latest models of Focke-Wulf, Heinkel and Dornier aircraft stood around, no longer able to fly, there was a depot with food and clothing. Together with the refugees, we took it in turns to help ourselves to what we needed. I took a complete leather suit, which I still had until my return home, when I exchanged it with my father for a British military jacket, and two blue woollen blankets, out of which I made my first winter overcoat. However, before then, these things caused me to sweat, for the spring was warm and the summer hot in 1945.

I am confused about where we went next, but can remember Joachimsthal and the Schorfheide, where Hermann Göring's hunting area was protected by SS units, also Gransee, Zehdenick and Wittstock, especially the water and the flames from burning buildings. Once we were quite close to Berlin at Bernau, where we often had to dive into the ditches because of ground-attack aircraft. Sometimes they were German types and we waved cloths at them and pointed at the street, but they fired none the less, which made us think that they were captured aircraft either flown by the Committee or by Russians, for they even fired on the refugees. By then Berlin was already surrounded or taken, even though we heard that we were supposed to have entered it.

Then we came to the Mecklenburg lake plateau and I read signs for Neuruppin, through which I think we drove, and Rheinsberg, then past others for Schwerin and Neustrelitz with kilometre distances. I recall seeing 'Mongolian' Vlassov soldiers[19] with their panje carts taking big bites out of lumps of margarine. In no way did they want to fall into Soviet hands.

This was the last time that we received a full issue of rations and cigarettes from the supply section. From then on we had to fend for ourselves from abandoned farms, if there was something available. We still had some stuff on the truck, and had previously eaten well from it. Round about this time I was told that I should take some matches to keep my eyes open if my relatives were to be able to recognise me again. I can still hear the mooing of the cows that had not been milked. Our unit was no longer intact and some stragglers had tagged on to us whom we took along with us in the truck.

It must have been near Parchim that we took up a firing position for the last time, the gun only unlimbered and ourselves in sleeping holes excavated nearby. The Russians attacked in the morning. The supply section, which had stupidly camped in front of us, and some other comrades were either killed or captured.

We now had only one aim: not to fall into the hands of the Russians, but to make it to the Americans, who must be behind us. We were between two fronts. That morning or afternoon we met up with the Americans – or they with us. We were standing on a long, dead-straight road blocked with military and refugee columns in the warm sunshine. The first American tank drove past us without taking any notice of us, or our gun. They were going to meet the Russians near Parchim. So we assumed that we were now prisoners, fully armed, and were sent westwards towards Ludwigslust. Alongside the road we saw some concentration camp prisoners who had been shot, as somebody told us. Then we came upon some living and surviving ones. They were pulling the medals off soldiers and swore at us, for we still had our gun.

When we came to a wood the whole column of trucks and soldiers on foot was stopped by SS officers and sent back to face the Russians. That is, all from the truck except myself, being No. 1 on the gun once more, the driver and Second Lieutenant Kern, and those of the dogs still remaining. I was later told that the whole effort proved to be a failure, for one after another they all slipped away, some even getting home without being captured.

The next chance we had, we drove our gun aside into some woods and put a demolition charge in the barrel, as we had been taught. Now we were safe from SS games. We drove on up to the American front line, which was at the Elbe, but already on the east bank.

At some point we were ordered off the truck and rounded up. Many still had their handguns. The stupid ones like myself had thrown them away or lost them, but those who had kept them, especially pistols, had capital that they could exchange later in the camp for food or cigarettes. However, our main concern was whether we would be sent over the Elbe or handed over to the Russians. Rumours swept through the area. I had to put all my English together and ask an American. The answer was: 'Maybe, maybe not.'

We were amazed at the Americans' perfect equipment, their almost sporty clothing and their uniform vehicles. What a contrast to our last motley assembly and our woodgas-burner!

Eventually we found ourselves in a vast camp, in fact a large open area incorporating some potato fields. It must have been near Neuhaus an der Elbe, but I did not see any signs of habitation. But it was really big and some 17,000 men were assembled there.

We were in a group of about twenty soldiers, but few of my close comrades were among them. I can still remember the young medical orderly with whom I had an argument over my nail-clippers, which he said belonged to him, but I kept them. We were fortunate in having a large tarpaulin that we had taken from the truck. With this and some branches taken from the wood, we were able to make a large tent, and so were much better off than many others, who had to dig holes in the ground from which they had to flee when it rained, which happened from time to time. But in general we had beautiful May weather.

I had my place at the entrance because of the dogs that had stayed with me when nobody wanted them. It was a bit narrow, but dry, and the dogs kept me warm in the cooler nights. During the retreat we had taken a pair of silver-black cocker spaniels from their owners on the truck with us. The male was later run over, but the female, who was well fed by us, produced five or six pups in the truck and, as I was the only one remaining in the rear of the truck after the SS round-up, she had stayed with me with her one remaining pup, the others having perished in the upheaval. Thus I had become an unwilling dog-owner. I had had some experience with our neighbour's dogs, one of whom was a cocker spaniel, but now the mother wanted to eat so as to suckle her pup.

The Americans took no interest in the camp. They only came to swap pistols, binoculars and medals. They were not interested in my telescope that I had brought with me. They expected the German officers to run the camp, but I never saw any of our own officers in this camp again.

I had hardly anything left from my pack. What I possessed would fit into a gas mask case, including my last letters from home, my breadknife and the nail-clippers.

A few brief recollections. As *Luftwaffe* auxiliaries we had to give the 'Hitler Salute' with an outstretched arm, which we had found a bit of an insult, but after the assassination attempt on Hitler of 1944, everyone had to use it. Now in the camp we had to learn how to salute our officers, and as this could not be done with the Nazi salute, we had to practise saluting in the camp by bringing our hand to our cap. This was simply absurd, and made us angry with the officers, who were on special rations. I once had a biscuit ration taken off me because I had failed to salute a German officer correctly.

Every day we had to share out between ten men a '24 Hour Ration Pack' intended as cold rations for two Americans. This was very difficult with some items. I always exchanged my cigarettes for something else. Among the items were about ten tasteless crackers, of which as a juvenile I got thirteen or fifteen. Three or four horses were slaughtered every day to make a thin soup for I do not know how many soldiers, but we seldom saw any of the meat. I often went to try to get something for my dogs. We did not starve, but were always hungry and no one put on any weight.

Once I made an excursion and met some of my old comrades, but I have forgotten whom. Once there was an address by a general, the camp commandant. Then there were plays and variety concerts. We discovered a field that had been planted with potatoes and went out at night to dig for them. Once we pretended to be guards and chased the others off so as to be able to dig ourselves.

A small river ran through the camp. One could stand in it, and I found some mussels, which I cooked in my mess-tins without salt, using sand instead. We collected twigs and birch from the wood for burning, but the wood was soon swept clean. There was nothing to read or to write with, but the dogs provided something of a diversion. I had toothache but there was little enough to bite into.

We stayed here for about a month.

Then came a move, we had no idea where to. We went north by rail, truck and much marching. I stuffed my belongings into my pockets, hung the gas mask case over my stomach and put the pup inside, just like a kangaroo. Somewhere along the way I saw one of our drivers beside his truck, ran across and handed over the animals to him, for he would be able to look after them better than me.

We ate sour apples and stinging nettles on our way, landing up in a group of about a hundred on a farm in Holstein at Nienhagen, near Grömitz and not far from Neustadt. Here we also met up with our old officers, including Second Lieutenant Kern and our 'beloved' Old Man. We were quartered in the barns, the officers in the farm.

Life here was almost unbearable for me. Every piece of newspaper was fought over, first as reading material and then for the toilet, which we first had to construct. Water had to be collected in a tanker from a pump in a field and then hauled back manually. The food was less and less, and worse with it, the water too. After a while nearly everyone became red and thin from a kind of dysentery, but I escaped it.

We could move around freely and once I set off to see the sea and collect some mushrooms, but turned back after going two or three kilometres, having only just heard the sea, or at least I thought I had. I cooked the mushrooms with my last letters. Goodness knows how many times I had read them, but I still did not know them by heart.

We discovered that we were interned by the British in a wide area around Eutin, which had some lovely names that I knew something about.

My neighbour in the straw beside me got lice, went off to be deloused and came back with a shaven head, but next day the lice were back, crawling all over his bald head. Fortunately I did not catch them.

The discharges started. I believe that they were based on home town and profession. I thought that I would be discharged early as a juvenile, but then came 'Action Barleycorn', discharge to help with the harvest. Second Lieutenant Kern saw to it that my name soon appeared on the list. Another month had gone by, and I felt weak and miserable. My reserves of fat had been burnt up, but I was not thin, just bloated.

At the beginning of the last week in June I was sent off with a group to a tented camp close to the Eutiner Lake. Cards were played up to the last minute, even for watches and wedding rings, but I was excluded because of my lack of skill and something of value to gamble with. We went through delousing and were given our discharge papers. One or two nights later we were given two days' rations for the journey, which nearly everyone, including myself, consumed immediately we got on the truck. The results soon made themselves known, for now I had diarrhoea.

I remember going through Lübeck and recognising the Holsten Gate from our geography book. We ended up at the Arminia Sports Grounds in Hanover. Again we had to spend a night mainly standing up, as there was nothing to lie on except the ground. In the morning the Hanoverians were sorted out and taken to Ronnenberg. Fortunately we had fine, warm weather, even shortly to become too warm. We were all issued with a yellow triangle, rather like the Star of David patch the Jews had had, but this triangle denoted Agricultural Labourer/Barleycorn. Our papers were taken off us and we could go home, but had to report back in the morning for detailing to work.

So I made my way alone at noon from Ronnenberg to Linden. I was sweating. Fortunately I had little luggage, just my gas mask case again. From time to time I rested on the roadside. No traffic went by. Dust, sun, heat.

I reached home on 27 June 1945, the day before my mother's thirty-ninth birthday. They had heard nothing of me since about the middle of March.

'Harvesting?' asked my father. 'I've already booked you into school!' I don't think that was true, but the first thing was to obtain ration cards. This was done, but I don't know how. Then I had to get used to this new kind of life that those that had stayed behind knew well. At first I went as co-driver with my father on his truck. As the Waldorf School was due to reopen ahead of the state schools, I reported there, my parents having left the choice to me. A few teachers from the old school, including my last class mistress, were there again, which influenced my decision. My father helped with the reconstruction of the school at the former youth hostel on the Masch Lake by making several deliveries with his truck of school furniture, roof slates and stone for the walls.

The school started in October/November with old and new friends, but with quite a few interruptions at first for work commitments.

Friedrich Grasdorf went on to qualify as a teacher and specialised mainly in teaching physically and mentally handicapped children. He married a Swiss woman and later became a Swiss citizen, eventually working and settling near Lugano in Italian-speaking Switzerland.

NOTES

1. The state labour service, pre-military for men, became compulsory for women in 1939, when they were employed mainly in agriculture and in assisting in the resettlement of German families in the east. The drain on manpower from the Home Defence Flak during the course of the war resulted in first the employment of schoolboys as *Luftwaffe* auxiliaries on the guns and searchlights, and later the girls taking over searchlight and communications tasks.

2. An administrative area incorporating the districts of Posen, Hohensalza and Lodz (Litzmannstadt) annexed by the Reich in October 1939 from former Polish territory. In order to help Germanise the area, Baltic Germans and other Germanic groups (*Volksdeutsche*) were compulsorily resettled here. The whole area reverted to Poland in 1945.
3. A development from the First World War consisting of a small paper cup containing candlewax and a wick, rather like a night-light.
4. Largely made of wood, this fighter was armed with a 20 mm cannon firing through the propeller hub and two 12.7 mm machine-guns in the wings. It had a top speed of 350 mph.
5. The famous 'Stuka' dive-bomber.
6. German soldiers were issued with a waterproof sheet that could either be used as a raincape or, when buttoned to another, serve as half of a pup tent.
7. The anti-aircraft artillery (flak) was essentially a *Luftwaffe* preserve, but there were also some Army units (see Diary of Defeat, page 75).
8. In addition to conventional mortars, the Germans also developed Nebelwerfer (smoke-throwing) mortars that were essentially highly effective rocket launchers for area bombardment, their only disadvantage being the amount of smoke released upon discharge to attract counterbombardment.
9. Seemingly 'Freigut' on the map.
10. The Bell P-39 Airacobra, with a top speed of 385 mph, was delivered in considerable quantities to the Soviet Union on Lend-Lease. It had a 39 mm cannon in the propeller hub and fuselage-mounted .30 inch and .50 inch machine-guns.
11. Highly decorated Lieutenant Colonel Hans-Ulrich Rudel specialised in tank-busting with cannon-equipped Stukas, often working at turret height, and was credited with 519 Soviet tanks destroyed and 800 damaged, as well as the sinking of a cruiser and the severe damaging of a battleship.
12. The Po-2 was armoured against infantry fire and was used extensively for night bombing behind enemy lines. Many of the crews were female. The observer would drop clusters of hand grenades or light bombs in First World War style.
13. This fortress town was under siege from the end of January 1945, the population being gradually evacuated, and the garrison told to hold out to the last man and last bullet. Nevertheless, its Waffen-SS commander and the last of the garrison abandoned the position on 28 March.
14. Arno Breker's statues for the Olympic Stadium so pleased Hitler that he was showered with public commissions, including the heroic 'Party' and 'Army' figures that flanked the main entrance to the New Reichs Chancellery.
15. This was a highly successful British propaganda radio station aimed at German soldiers. Despite the draconian punishments for listening to enemy broadcasts, its effect could not be curbed.
16. Preliminary to the main offensive to come two days later, the Soviet 47th Army that day conducted a reconnaissance in force in the form of an attack supported by ten tanks that breached the German front line near Gieshof and penetrated as far as Neu Barnim.
17. Seemingly 'Bochowlos' farm and Thöringswerder respectively.

18. The National Committee for a Free Germany was a Moscow-organised group of German prisoners of war opposed to Nazism. The members were initially used for disseminating written and verbal propaganda encouraging German soldiers to desert, but later also for the spreading of false orders among retreating troops in order to entrap them, and also in actual combat against them. They were generally referred to as Seydlitz Troops by the *Wehrmacht* after the Vice-President of the Committee, General Walther von Seydlitz-Kurzbach, who had been captured at Stalingrad, and who in fact disassociated himself from all except propaganda purposes, and for which he was exonerated by the German authorities after the war.
19. Captured in May 1942, Lieutenant General Andrey Vlassov became the leader of an anti-Stalin movement among captured Soviet troops in Germany. Eventually in November 1944 he was allowed to raise the Russian Liberation Army (POA) from prisoners of war and forced labourers working in Germany, which finally amounted to about 50,000 troops divided into two divisions, one of which fought near Frankfurt on the Oder, and the other he led into Prague, defeating the SS troops defending it, made contact with the Czechs and unsuccessfully attempted to turn Czechoslovakia over to the Americans. He was arrested by the Soviets, tried and executed.

COUNTERATTACK

HERMANN KOCH

Professor Hermann Koch was a Second Lieutenant commanding the 2nd Platoon in Lieutenant Alfons Jenewein's 6th Company of Panzergrenadier Regiment 119, 25th Panzergrenadier Division. I had the privilege of being invited to visit the battlefield described below with them both in April, 1993.

I awoke to a frightful din. It was the thunder of guns and shells exploding in the immediate vicinity. I was in my quarters in the Friedersdorf schoolhouse, south of Seelow. The little glass vase with snowdrops that Frau Pursch had put on the bedside table for me was dancing, so great was the vibration from shell impacts nearby and in the distance. I now realised what had been happening during the night and early morning. Since the beginning of February the Russians had been able to form two bridgeheads on the west bank of the Oder, the first near Gross Neuendorf and a second south of there, near Reitwein. These two bridgeheads were separated by an open corridor leading to Küstrin on the east bank of the Oder. Several days previously our regiment had been deployed on the southern side of this corridor, and what we had already feared had now taken place; the Russians had closed the corridor, uniting their bridgeheads and isolating Küstrin.

Sleeping with me in the same room was an older officer who was responsible for soldiers' graves. As we were discussing the situation, a runner appeared. 'Second Lieutenant Koch to report to the company commander!'

I quickly shaved and then reported to my company commander, Lieutenant Jenewein, shortly afterwards. Jenewein wore the Iron Cross First Class, and I saw in him the ideal of a German officer.

Counterattack

'You are to drive to the regimental command post in Werbig straight away and pick up the orders for our battalion!' A car and driver were already standing by. We drove through Friedersdorf northwards to Seelow, the road running along the Seelow Heights, from where one could see right out into the Oderbruch valley. Large columns of smoke stood above Küstrin, and there were also fires in the villages of Gorgast and Golzow west of the Oder. Shells continued to land on the road and on either side. Torn-off branches littered the way. The inhabitants of Seelow, a small town, were highly excited. People were standing around in groups, talking to each other with anxious expressions. As we drove past girls and women, we were aware of what would happen to them if they fell into the hands of the Russians, and to me it was quite clear that we had to save them from such a fate.

At the regimental command post in Werbig I was obliged to wait. Then I was given a sealed envelope, which I knew contained the orders for a counterattack.[1]

When we got back to Friedersdorf, the intensity of the artillery bombardment had increased. A radio truck standing close to the schoolhouse was attracting the artillery fire and I had to seek shelter in a trench near the school.

That afternoon at about 3 o'clock we drove in broad daylight in trucks and some cars and motorcycles to the assembly area for the counterattack. I had not experienced such a move before. On the roads to the north, to Werbig, and also on the little side roads, a large number of vehicles of all kinds was moving forward; even tanks could be seen. The Russian ground-attack aircraft flew in from the east and dropped their bombs. Our truck stopped and everyone jumped off and looked for cover. Despite the attack, which was made at a low level, we suffered no casualties.

My company, the 6th, assembled on the southern edge of Werbig. The high rise of the Seelow Heights was broken here by a small gully running east–west. We could see that the heights had been strongly fortified with trenches and dugouts.

Our soldiers stood around, hardly anyone saying anything. Our company commander, Lieutenant Jenewein, was summoned to an orders group. At about 4 o'clock we were given some warm food, but none of the soldiers ate anything. When I asked them why, they said that a stomach wound became worse if one had eaten beforehand.

Then Lieutenant Jenewein returned from the order group, looking very earnest. The radio section got a telling-off because their set was not working. Then he gave us the orders for the attack, explaining them to the platoon commanders with the aid of a map. 'Our regiment is to attack along either side of the Werbig–Küstrin railway line. The objective of our attack is the Alte Oder stream.'

This was a westerly branch of the Oder on the eastern edge of Gorgast. I can still visualise clearly the line of attack shown us on the map. With the map's help we would be able to direct artillery fire on the enemy.

Then at about 5 o'clock on the afternoon of 22 March 1945, we set off on our counterattack. This was the first undertaking of this kind for me, and I had no idea of what a shattering experience it would prove for the company, Lieutenant Jenewein and myself. From this point on we were held in a vice from which we were unlikely to escape.

My platoon, the 2nd, was already correctly deployed. Panzergrenadier Regiment 35 was supposed to be attacking on our right, but neither on that day nor during the following days did I see anything of our right-hand neighbour. This was dangerous for us, for our right flank was open. I led the platoon carrying a panzerfaust and a sub-machine-gun. Lieutenant Jenewein led on my left, riding a motorcycle. It was a real spring day at the end of March; the earth was dry and the seedlings beginning to emerge.

Tanks were rolling along the causeway to our right and even a couple of Me 109s raced across towards the east. It slowly became dark as night fell. It was quite quiet in front of us, with no sounds of fighting. Only the conflagrations could be seen.

At about 10 o'clock we reached the Annahof, which formed the forward edge of the assembly area. From then on we could expect enemy action. We continued eastwards. Lieutenant Jenewein had left the motorcycle behind and was now walking alongside me. Neither of us was wearing a steel helmet. Once we heard the rattle of tank tracks ahead of us and the tension grew. Then out of the darkness of the spring night appeared some German armoured personnel carriers. They had obviously lost their way. Once we had sorted things out with them, we left them behind.

It became unnaturally quiet. My company commander said to me: 'Koch, now we put on our helmets.'

Then a railway embankment appeared in front of us, which carried the line running north–south from Golzow to Neu Tucheband and was about six metres above normal ground level. To our left, on the other side of the embankment, a hop factory was on fire to the northeast. It was so quiet, we could hear the crackling of the fire. As the company, more than one hundred men strong, reached the embankment, the silence was suddenly ripped apart in the most frightening manner as shells fell right and left. Explosion followed explosion and flashes lit the night. The cries of the first to be wounded came through the din of the bombardment. I lay down in a furrow, the exploding shells dazzling me as iron sped through the air, then the voice of my company commander came through the inferno: 'Koch, I've been hit!'

I jumped up and raced to him through the fire, steel and dust, and over the soldiers lying on the ground. He lay stretched out on the earth. It was only later that I discovered that he had been severely wounded in the left arm. He said to me: 'Take over the company. Here's the map. You know the objective – the Alte Oder. Long live Germany!'

I no longer know if and how I said goodbye to him. I hurried back to my platoon and shouted: 'Lieutenant Jenewein is wounded! I am taking over the company. We will cross the embankment!'

Our objective was certainly the Alte Oder, but it was obvious to me that we could only get through this hellfire if we could get away from the embankment as quickly as possible, and I ran up the embankment. From this point on, the company runner, a young Austrian called Hofmeister, was constantly at my side.

As I reached the top of the embankment, I found a very fat sergeant major, whom I did not know, standing between the rails. He shouted to me: 'What are you doing here? Go back immediately! This attack is pointless!'

I shouted back to him: 'I am commanding this company! Get out of my way!'[2]

Once we had the embankment behind us, we were really out of the artillery fire. The shells howled over our heads, striking the embankment as before.

I went on ahead, with Hofmeister staying close. About twenty men were still following us, including two NCOs and Sergeant Heilig, who said: 'I'll bring up the rear!' So he went back to the rear of the group. The hop factory was burning on our left and there were also some individual fires in Golzow.

It had quietened down again. Once I saw six steel monsters appear out of the night in front of us. They were German tanks. I recognised them from the thickening of the gun barrel forming the muzzle brakes. I went forward to identify myself and climbed on a tank. A captain was standing in the turret hatch. About one hundred metres further east, a farm was visible. I asked him: 'Is that farm free of the enemy?'

He replied: 'We came through there an hour ago. There were no Russians to be seen.'

I told him: 'I am going to advance there with my group.'

We approached the farm, where the buildings were set out in a hollow square, the front of the farmhouse itself facing south. In front of the farmhouse was a large garden surrounded by a thick hedge. I crept up to the southern side of the farmhouse and lay down beside the hedge. All the sounds of fighting had died down, and even the artillery had stopped firing. Then I saw a tank standing in the garden, barely three metres away. Its side was set half obliquely to me, its guns pointing southwest and its turret hatch open. I recalled what the tank captain had said and was so surprised that I could hardly take in that there was a Russian tank in front of me. I rushed back to the tank unit and asked if it could be a German tank in that garden. The captain replied: 'If there's a tank there, its Russian!'

When I went back to lie down again on the southwest side of the farmhouse with Hofmeister, all doubts about the nationality of the object in front of me vanished. The five side wheels over which the tracks ran, the lack of a muzzle brake on the gun, all indicated a Russian T-34. It is really quite true that up to this point I had not been at all scared. One of my soldiers took up position with a machine-gun at the corner of the building, then I stood up, raised the long sight of the panzerfaust and took aim at the tank.

As I steadied my aim, something totally unexpected occurred. With a loud crash, both halves of the door in the centre of the southern front of the farmhouse flew open and out tumbled about seven Russian soldiers close together. What I then did was entirely due to basic instinct. I swung the panzerfaust round and shot at the Russian soldiers before they could fire at me. There was a flash as a monstrous din tore the night apart. The Russians were simply blasted away. At the same moment the T-34 rolled back out of the garden in an easterly direction with a damaged track, as I later discovered. We all jumped up together shouting: 'Revenge! Revenge!' the battle cry we had been ordered to use. What we had heard of the Russian soldiers' cruelty to the German civilian population of Goldap in East Prussia made it a cry from the heart. I was as if intoxicated by it.

As I was crossing the garden with my men, we fell into a communications trench about a metre deep, and I saw that it was occupied by Russian infantry. They fired at us with their sub-machine- and machine-guns. They were the tank's escorting infantry, as we were to discover later. I climbed out of the trench and charged with my men, throwing hand grenades and firing at the Russians. They were so close that we could make out their steel helmets in the muzzle flashes from their machine-guns.

Then I got a hammer blow on the left side of my helmet, which sobered me up. I felt my helmet and found the dent of a bullet.

Hofmeister shouted: 'Sir, you have captured a tank!'

'No!' I called: 'It's over there in front of the trench!'

But Hofmeister showed me a second steel object parked alongside the farmhouse's southern wall. It was an assault gun, a tank with a fixed turret.

Meanwhile we had occupied the trench for a length of about 150 metres, and posted a machine-gun on our right flank to secure it, and the noise of battle had died down again.

I had to establish contact with the company that had been fighting on our left flank. With Hofmeister at my side, I rushed through bomb and shell craters to the group of buildings in front of Golzow that we could see on our left. I came across a unit of our battalion and asked the company commander what he intended doing. He said that it was impossible to advance any further. The place was full of Russians. They were even in the next building. His company would therefore establish a defence here.

I hurried back to my soldiers with this information, deciding on the way to do the same thing. So we stayed in the trench and prepared for defence, tensely watching the east.

Then we heard the clanking of tank tracks again from behind. It was the German tank captain with his six tanks. He drove his tank up to our trench. The tank stopped and the captain poked his head out of the turret. 'Who is in charge here?' he demanded.

I stood up, reported and said: 'I am, sir.'

He addressed me gruffly: 'Don't you know what the objective is? Keep up the advance with your men, or I'll have you court-martialled!'

I understood what he was threatening me with, but was not lacking in courage: 'Sir, the 6th Company, which I command here, consists of only twenty men. The company on our left cannot advance farther because of strong resistance. Worst of all, there are no German troops at all on our right, so my small group is in danger of being cut off if we advance any further!'

He shouted back from his tank: 'The objective is the Alte Oder! Advance immediately, or I'll have you court-martialled!'

During this heated exchange his tank had started firing, and a shell must have hit a barn or a big haystack, for the battlefield was now as light as day from the big conflagration. Without another word, the captain retreated with his tank.

When morning came we counted about fifty Russian tanks within about 1,000 metres of our sector. It was hardly light when Russian snipers began firing at us. One could scarcely lift one's head above the parapet without a bullet whistling past, and our position came under constant artillery and mortar fire. Sometimes we thought that our own '*Volksartillerie*' must be firing short and hitting our trenches. Russian ground-attack aircraft were in the air all day long dropping bombs. When I saw the Russians marking their trenches with Very lights, I used the same to keep them off.

That day I examined the Russian assault gun that stood right next to the southern wall of the farm. It was undamaged and stuffed full of bedding. The most important thing was the map case that I found in the tank. It must have belonged to a high-ranking officer, for the plans for the main offensive on the Seelow Heights and for the encirclement of Berlin were drawn in crayon on the maps. I had the maps sent back to the battalion command post that day.

To the right of us, on Reichsstrasse 1, which led from Berlin to Küstrin, all day we could see Russian tanks advancing as far as the railway embankment and then being shot up. A tank second lieutenant, Giese, shot up sixteen tanks that day.

We were very afraid of being ordered to resume the attack towards the Alte Oder, for by day we could see and sense how strong the Russians were in front of us, and knew that it would be a suicide mission.

Three days later, on 25 March, I left the trench in the approaching darkness in an easterly direction with three men. We wanted to blow up the tank that lay in front of our trench, but then discovered that the Russians had towed it away in the dark. So we went on and came across a drainage ditch running east–west that was full of dead. Low voices could be heard, but because of the proximity of the enemy positions, we could not ascertain whether the dead and perhaps the living were German or Russian.

When we got back to our lines, we came under heavy mortar fire, and I went into a ditch that came up to my hips. A bomb exploded on the edge of the ditch immediately to my left, the blast of the explosion throwing me into the bottom of the ditch, at the same time splinters hitting me in the back and face. However, the worst was, as the doctor later told me, that my middle ear had been displaced, which was to prove much worse than the external wounding.

I reported my injuries by telephone to the battalion commander, who ordered me to hand over the company to an NCO and to return to the dressing station. At dawn I took leave of my soldiers who had experienced and suffered these days of combat along with me. I know of only two of them being still alive. All the others, including my good comrade Hofmeister, were killed near Kunersdorf when the Russian offensive began on 16 April.

The departure from the company was the beginning of an odyssey of ever-increasing pain for me to Schwerin in Mecklenburg. I came so close to death that the doctors and nurses actually gave me up for dead. But that is another story.

NOTES

1. Instant counterattack was the German Army's standard reaction to any enemy attack. This counterattack of 22 April having failed as described by Koch, a major counterattack was launched five days later using reserves Hitler had intended for mounting an offensive from Frankfurt an der Oder on the east bank of the river. This too failed, primarily due to the minefields the Russians had been able to lay in the meantime.
2. Another instance of the so-called Seydlitz Troops in action.

FIGHTING IN THE ODERBRUCH

COLONEL HELMUT VON LÖSECKE

This report was kindly supplied by Dr Fritz-Rudolf Averdieck, then serving as regimental signals sergeant of Panzergrenadier Regiment 90 of the 20th Panzergrenadier Division, and comes from his commanding officer's diary.

The regiment was transported in three trains. Coming through Berlin, the last train nearly became involved in an Anglo-American air attack. Nevertheless all went according to plan and we detrained southwest of Küstrin. The regimental command post found accommodation in Döbberin, the 2nd Battalion in villages northeast of there. Accommodation was a problem, as all the villages had long been filled. Company training was begun as soon as possible.

On 22 March we were put on alert and marched north to take up quarters in Werbig. Because of strong enemy air attacks, the battalions stayed out in the fields east and southeast of the village. I was given the task of exploring the road system with a view to a possible attack to the northeast, as a result of which I found myself caught in an uncomfortable Russian night air attack on Alt Langsow, in which numerous phosphorous bombs were dropped but without creating damage, all falling on the fields. Despite parachute flares, neither the village nor the roads on which all sorts of vehicles were standing were hit. The bombs burned brightly in the damp meadows of the Oderbruch. The nightly nightmare was over and I could get on with my task.

On 23 March we took up a reserve position in the Pismühle area, 1,500 metres southeast of Seelow, but had to march back to Werbig in the early morning. At noon I was summoned to Divisional Headquarters. This sunny spring afternoon drive made one think of times of peace, although noise of combat could be heard in the distance. From Division I received the task of sending a battalion that evening to northwest of Alt Tucheband and, in combination with Panzergrenadier Regiment 76 on the right and another infantry regiment on the left, of attacking the enemy positions at Manschnow and pushing forward as far as the Alte Oder east of that village and, if possible, establishing a bridgehead east of the Alte Oder. In order to minimise the effect of the enemy air and artillery capability, one could only attack at night.

During the drive to the assembly area my APC drove into a soft, clayey field and stuck fast. As all the radio communications equipment was on this vehicle, I could not leave it and had to wait. It was an unpleasant delay. The 3rd Battalion's assembly area northwest of Alt Tucheband was shared by Panzer Battalion 8, which had been allocated to my support. As the tank commander had better radio communications with Division and the artillery, I climbed in his tank, and my APC followed close behind.

At the beginning of the attack we crossed the railway embankment forming the forward edge of the assembly area. We moved smoothly at first and soon crossed the road leading northwards from the eastern end of Alt Tucheband. The battalion broke through the first enemy positions. Shortly afterwards the tanks reported a minefield and stopped. The leading company of the battalion reached the western outlying farms of Manschnow and came up against strong enemy resistance. While our right-hand neighbour was advancing only slowly, the left-hand one did not even appear to have left its assembly area. As a result of its brave attack, the 3rd Battalion had become a wedge thrust into the enemy front line and was now receiving fire from both flanks. The enemy artillery started bombarding the whole of our assault area, while our own artillery only fired the odd shot into Manschnow. As the enemy minefields could not be cleared in the dark, the tanks had to remain where they were. Despite all the courageous endeavour, the attack had stalled and casualties were mounting, and the exceptionally brave Second Lieutenant Zwanziger, commanding the 9th Company, was seriously wounded.

Just before dawn I decided to curtail the taking of casualties by withdrawing the battalion to the start line without waiting for instructions from Division. The attack had been carried out with insufficient means to shatter the strong enemy bridgehead west of

Küstrin and had foundered. I set up my regimental command post in the buildings of Neu Tucheband. Shortly afterwards the Divisional Commander, Colonel Scholze, arrived with another colonel and I made my report about the battle, holding nothing back and describing the weak support from our own artillery, the strength of the enemy's defensive fire, the difficulty with the fire from the flanks and the consequent heavy casualties sustained by the battalion. To the question why I had withdrawn the battalion, I explained that in the completely flat and open countryside daybreak made all movement absolutely impossible and consequently the withdrawal of the battalion had been a tactical necessity. To some quite sharp comments from my side about the higher command that could order such an attack with inadequate means, neither of the gentlemen responded. They were apparently convinced of the correctness of my conduct. Shortly afterwards they excused themselves and climbed silently into their vehicle. While I had been addressing myself principally to Colonel Scholze, I had paid little attention to the other officer, but as my adjutant informed me, this was the Corps Chief of Staff, who had been listening attentively to my account of my conduct and my views on the battle. Nevertheless, I am of the opinion that neither he nor Colonel Scholze had been responsible for giving the orders for this attack. This had come from the highest level.

Soon after this encounter we packed up and overtook the brave soldiers of the 3rd Battalion on their march back to Werbig.

The Oderbruch, the fruitful, open plain west of Küstrin, looked like a large garden with many small villages and individual farmsteads giving the countryside its own character. Brooks and wide drainage ditches, often with willows on their banks, extended throughout the whole depression, flowing from west to east. The Seelow Heights bordering the plain in the southwest provided a good view eastwards over the countryside, but now war had taken over the whole area. The peaceful inhabitants had fled to the west and everywhere one saw soldiers, headquarters personnel, vehicles and weapons clinging close to the farms or whatever cover there was in order to keep themselves out of sight of the enemy. Ruined buildings, fallen trees and bomb craters bore witness to the enemy air attacks, and artillery activity betrayed the immediate vicinity of the front.

Following the great Russian breakthrough on the Vistula, the enemy had driven forward over the Oder without encountering any worthwhile opposition, taken Küstrin[1] and formed a bridgehead west of the town, which our attack of the previous night was supposed to have driven back. The strong enemy defensive fire from artillery units of all calibres, mostly coming from the Neu Manschnow area, had negated our initial success. This Russian bridgehead could not be attacked again unless the enemy artillery could be suppressed by our own artillery fire and simultaneous air attack.

As there were still some isolated German units in action between Alt and Neu Bleyen, once more orders came from the highest level to launch an attack on the enemy bridgehead. This was to be from the Heimstätten settlement by the troops stationed there, from Golzow by Panzergrenadier Regiment 90, from north of Golzow by Panzergrenadier Regiment 76, and from north of there by the 'Müncheberg' Panzer Division with its new tanks. I was given the task of driving hard south out of Golzow as far as the Strom ditch, then on southeast to the sports field one kilometre northwest of Gorgast, and then to attack Gorgast itself. Panzergrenadier Regiment 76 was to attack via the Tannenhof to the sheep farm two kilometres north–northeast of Gorgast and then to press on in a southeasterly direction. The 'Müncheberg' Panzer Division was tasked with a sweeping attack north of the Tannenhof and the sheep farm to attack Alt Bleyen from the east and to take this hamlet. There they were to join up with the fighting German units and attack southeastwards in the direction of Kietz. This attack was intended to prise the Russians out of their bridgehead. As no significant participation by the *Luftwaffe* could be expected, the whole attack would have to be conducted at night.

I went with the battalion commanders on a reconnaissance of the terrain to be attacked across, which we viewed from a building due east of Golzow. The countryside was completely open and flat, dropping a little away to the north towards the brook, along which there were a few trees and bushes. The farmstead immediately south of the bridge 500 metres north of Golzow was still in our hands,[2] while the other farmstead east of Golzow was occupied by the enemy, although north of the brook. In the distance one could see the colourful roofs of Gorgast, the greenhouses on the western edge and the tall clump of trees in the manor park.

I decided to split the regiment into widely separated echelons to advance in the order 2nd, 1st, then 3rd Battalions. The 2nd Battalion would lead the main attack and was given the task of going via the sugar

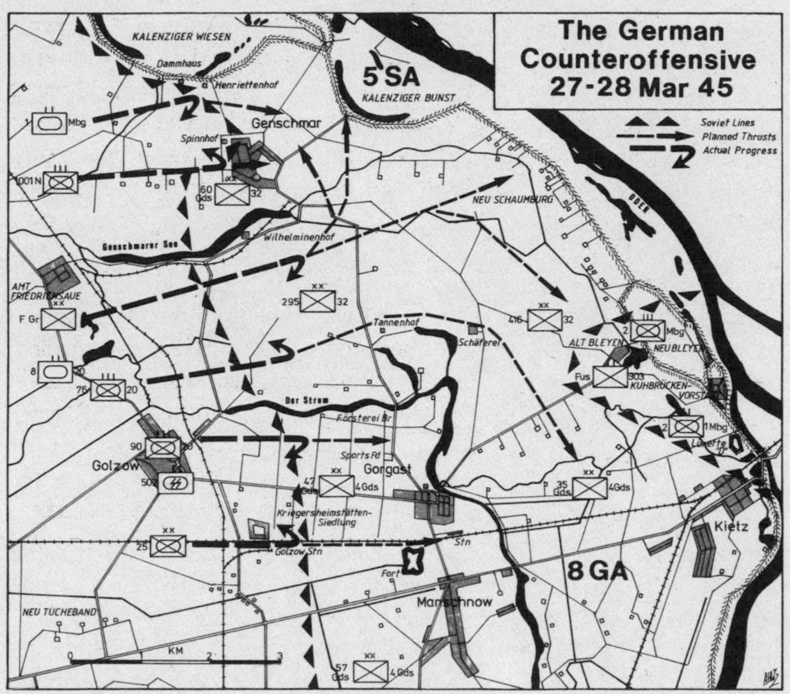

factory and the farmstead south of the bridge 500 metres northeast of Golzow, attacking in an easterly direction, of taking the farmstead near Point 11.5 (1,000 metres east of Golzow station) and the 'Am Strom' farmstead two kilometres east of Golzow station, and then of securing the Fösterei Bridge 1,400 metres north of Gorgast in order to enable a continuation of the attack southeastwards on Gorgast. The 1st Battalion would follow, deployed to the right, while the 3rd Battalion would remain in its assembly area west of Golzow at regimental disposal. A 'Tiger' battalion would be available to support us in our attack in cooperation with the regiment. The forward observers of the Infantry Gun Company and the 2nd Battalion, Artillery Regiment 20 were also given their tasks on this reconnaissance so far as the artillery had not been given their own targets on divisional orders. Several artillery units would work on Gorgast, for which an allocation of 1,000 shells had been made.

On 26 March the regiment moved forward into the area west of Golzow. The move took place at night in order to conceal the preparations for attack from the enemy, and by morning everything had disappeared into the few farm-steads and barns.

On 27 March the 2nd Battalion moved into the assembly area east of Golzow station while the 1st Battalion remained on the western edge of the village ready to follow deployed to the right. The 'Tiger' Battalion rolled forward at 0300 hours and the attack began. I had my command post in the building immediately east of Golzow station. It was the most practical from a communications point of view, as from here I could best reach all parts of the regiment, as well as the artillery, the tanks and Division, while combat was in progress.

Our artillery bombarded Gorgast. Infantry weapons opened up. Soon came a message from the 2nd Battalion that they had broken through the first enemy lines. Further reports said that the right-hand company of the 2nd Battalion was engaged with the enemy in a strongly defended farmstead 1,000 metres east of the railway station, and the left-hand company was under heavy enfilade fire from the sector north of the brook, where Panzergrenadier Regiment 76 were attacking. One could hear heavy fire coming from there too. Finally the right-hand company of the 2nd Battalion took the farmstead, where the tanks remained in position. The left-hand company also were unable to advance as the enemy north of the brook were firmly ensconced in their buildings and were maintaining a constant enfilading fire on the regiment's whole attack front. Our own tanks could not progress further because of enemy mines. The fighting came to a halt.

In answer to the clearly nervous calls from Division, I could only repeat that enemy resistance had stiffened to such a degree that one could no longer expect a breakthrough before dawn. This gave me great concern for the 2nd and 1st Battalions; the latter, having been drawn into the fighting meanwhile and having taken part in the assault on the farmstead, needed to be got back under worthwhile cover so that they would not be exposed with the coming of day to enemy fire in the completely open ground without protection of any kind. However, I could not withdraw my troops without the tanks as the tanks could not stay there without infantry protection.

The day began to dawn and what I feared occurred. As soon as the morning mist lifted, the enemy began to shoot at the stationary tanks, which presented an easy target on the plain. At 1100 hours a bombardment by all calibres began, including 'Stalin-organs'. The soldiers, receiving no support from either their own artillery or the *Luftwaffe*, began to leave their positions, at first individually and then in groups. It was a panic. I stopped them near the command post and led them forward once more and in a short while the old front line was regained. The enemy had not followed up. In the evening we shortened the line so as to start making a line of defence. The tanks were towed away during the night of 28/29 March and the enemy artillery fire died down.

Our futile night attack of 27 March had exhausted all our possibilities of removing the Russian bridgehead on the west bank of the Oder. Night attacks in previous years had been conducted with well-trained soldiers and proper leadership for only limited goals, attacks on this scale being begun shortly before dawn and then secured with the arrival of daylight by the engagement of artillery, *Luftwaffe* and tanks against the target area. Here, where both artillery and *Luftwaffe* were lacking, we were obliged to attack at night. It failed. Unfortunately orders to withdraw the attacking troops were not given, with the result that the high cost in casualties was even further increased by the overwhelming artillery fire next day.

Thus during the night attacks of 24 and 27 March, first the 3rd Battalion and then the 2nd Battalion of Panzergrenadier Regiment 90 sustained very high losses in officers, NCOs and men. The loss of many brave soldiers was lamentable, but especially painful was the loss of irreplaceable leaders. Each failure further shattered the confidence of the troops. The responsibility for this was not to be found at Division or Corps, but rather at the highest level, where at their map tables they often no longer felt a responsibility for the fighting soldier. If one complained about this, the only answer that came was: 'Führer's orders!'

We still had the task of reinforcing our position. Our right wing rested immediately northwest of the Heimstätten settlement. Northeastwards it went out as far as the farmstead that had been so hard fought over in the night attack, with the enemy finally being driven out. Then it carried on in a northwesterly direction to the farmstead at the bridge, 500 metres northeast of Golzow station. The 1st Battalion was on the right and the 2nd Battalion on the left of this sector. The regimental command post was still in the house east of Golzow station, where we were installed in a vaulted cellar that was quite dark. Captain Oryvall's 2nd Battalion's command post was in the farmstead by the bridge. One could reach it by day and have a really good view from its ground floor. Located there alongside the battalion staff in the cellar was the Battalion Medical Officer, Dr Killian, who was also the Regimental Medical Officer.

Every moment at night was spent visiting the trenches. Although the battalion had been severely weakened in the night attack, an enormous amount of work was in progress and the position visibly improved. As not all the company positions could be reached by day, my main activity began at nightfall. Going via the 2nd Battalion's command post, my way led to the farmstead furthest east in our positions, 1,000 metres east of Golzow station. It had been a massive house and its cellar was still intact and occupied by one of the companies. The company commander reported the progress in developing this position, while the company sergeant-major reported to the second lieutenant the state of the supporting supply unit and on all the important questions of clothing, equipment, defence stores, supplies and ammunition. The individual platoons then received their rations. There was a constant coming and going. Despite the bad conditions at the front, discipline was excellent. I spoke to nearly every soldier that came to the command post, and all were upright and in good order, none sullen, even though duty in the positions went on almost without a break day and night.

Then I carried on into the night, where the positions were full of activity everywhere with reinforcing and carrying forward material from ruined buildings that was to be used for constructing bunkers. Out in no-man's-land were sentries, for every company had to send out a standing patrol at night. Occasionally one heard rifle and machine-gun fire flaring up and dying away again in devilish music, and here and there came the dull thump of exploding mortar bombs. Everyone would freeze when a light rocket tore the night apart for a few seconds, illuminating the landscape with a ghostly light.

By the time I reached the forward company on the regiment's right flank, day would already be beginning to dawn, and I and my escort, the regimental runner, would wearily make our way back to the regimental command post, where a new day of unending work would await me after a few hours of sleep.

Notes

1. Küstrin had been surrounded and cut off, but did not fall until 29 March 1945.
2. This was the same farm that was so vigorously defended by Captain Horst Zobel's tanks of the 1st Battalion, Panzer-Regiment 'Müncheberg' on 23/24 March, as related in 'The Bridge at Golzow' in *With Our Backs to Berlin*.

MUSKETEER

Günther Labes

I found Günther Labes's name in the visitors' book in Seelow Museum and wrote to him, as a result of which he sent me this report.

Formation of the unit

After volunteering, my six weeks of basic training as a Panzergrenadier, i.e. of running behind or sitting on top of tanks as an infantryman, ended on 31 March 1945, so that I reached the Eastern Front's rear area at Müncheberg with my training unit at the beginning of April 1945. I can no longer remember the various staging points I passed through until I arrived in the front line on 14 April. My interest in these matters was then very little in view of my prospects of facing a 'hero's death' shortly before the foreseeable end of the war.

Shortly after the arrival of my training unit in the Müncheberg area (perhaps in Müncheberg itself?), it was split up and individual elements sent to reinforce units depleted by enemy action in the front line, while other elements, including the section to which I belonged, were sent to rear area posts in the surrounding villages. Sometime during the second week in April we unwanted newcomers met up at an assembly place with two or three of our comrades who had been sent forward and had already been lightly wounded and since recovered, who told us they were among the few (four or five) survivors of an originally 100-man company that had escaped the pandemonium, and that the 4 per cent chance of survival could be taken as the mean for the forth-coming fighting.

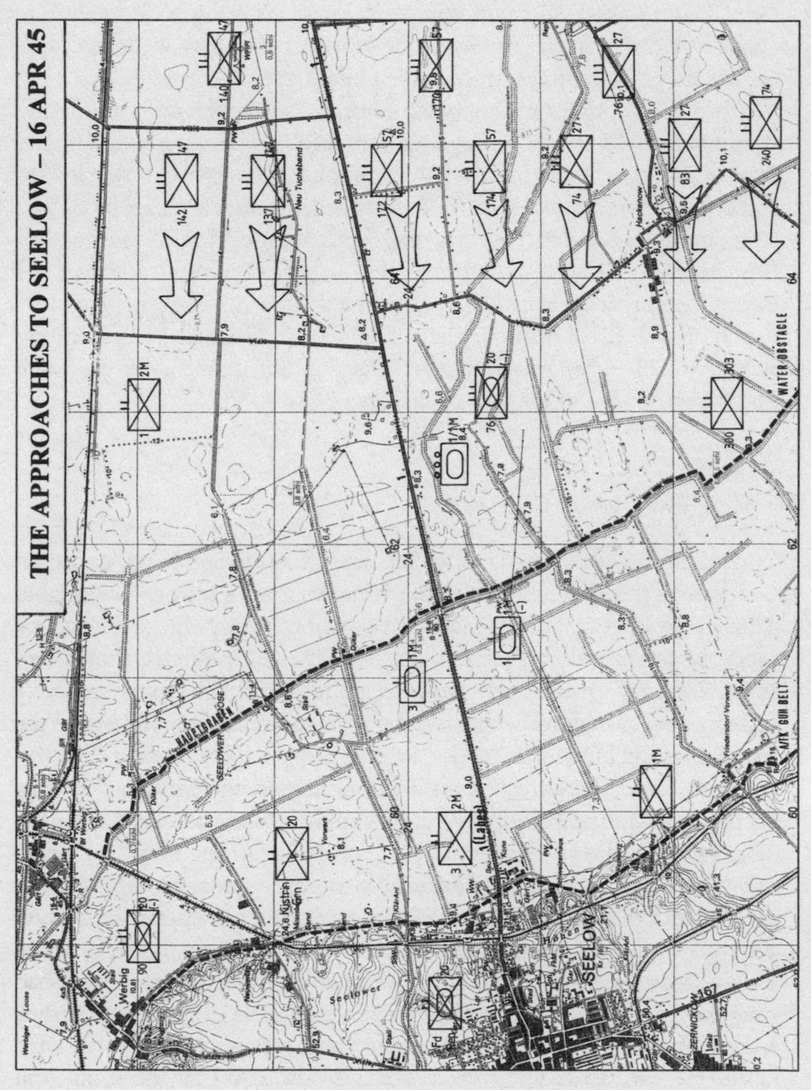
THE APPROACHES TO SEELOW – 16 APR 45
SEELOW
WATER OBSTACLE
A/TK GUN BELT
HAUPTGRABEN
Neu Tucheband
Hackenow
Werbig
ZERNICKOW

Together with the 'stragglers' from other units that had joined us earlier and with some provisionally patched-up wounded, we were formed into an 80–100-man company. This was done so sloppily that apparently not even the names of the individual soldiers were recorded, so that after the war it was impossible to trace them.

Once the company had been formed, we received a company commander, who led us into a large barn and had us parade in an open square. He then gave us his name, Second Lieutenant Kalliczec, or something similar, and said that he had been allocated to us as our company commander. He said that he demanded total commitment from us, and drew his pistol, loaded it in a demonstration of his determination, and warned us that he would shoot any of us personally that he came across without their weapon. He finished by saying that should any of us become separated from the unit, they should be aware that they belonged to the 2nd Müncheberg Division.[1]

CALM BEFORE THE STORM

During the night of Saturday to Sunday, 15 April 1945, we occupied positions in the trenches about 60–70 metres east of the Seelow Heights in the Hardenberg Line. This Sunday was a sunny day without any excessive fighting.[2] The section was divided up for sentry duties, my stage beginning in the afternoon and lasting until the early evening. I had to patrol the centre section of about 20 metres of the 50-metre long trench, which ran north of the Reichsstrasse 1, between it and the Seelower Loose.[3] Despite good visibility, no enemy activity could be seen without binoculars, but none were available, for binoculars were then more valuable than mere lives.

Without binoculars I was also unable to see the Russian snipers, who kept firing at me in vain as I patrolled the trench. I became aware of their activity, which for me was life-threatening, through the occasional sounds near my head. A comrade, whom I met on my patrol, told me what they meant. The gentle hisses were the sounds of projectiles from a sniper's barrel and I would be advised to keep my head down a bit lower! He was right. The trench was only about 60 cm deep and the parapet of dug-out earth in front only 30 cm high, so that walking upright only 50–60 per cent of my 188-cm-long body was protected by the earth. To remain under cover, I would have to move about on all fours, and I could not do my job properly like that!

As the Russian sniper had not yet hit me while walking about the trench, or could only hit me with difficulty, I surmised that the zigzag line of the trench was my saviour, for this changed the rhythm of my regular pacing in his aim, and he was unable to estimate my speed and hit me.

THE FIGHTING

Fighting began in the early hours of Monday, 16 April 1945, with the firing of Stalin-organs. I was off duty when the artillery barrage began and was fast asleep in the relatively small and shallow earthen bunker, which was covered only with wooden planks. The shell-fire failed to wake me, as I was dreaming of being back at home in the air-raid shelter listening to the explosions of British bombs, which closely resembled those of Stalin-organs. It was only when a near hit caused the plank ceiling of the bunker to jump up that I lost my dream. I woke up and was immediately brought back to reality. My comrade, No. 1 on the machine-gun, naturally failed to understand such a deep sleep, as he had not experienced the nights of bombing that I had in Hamburg in 1943. He accused me of being late, but I countered with the question whether he believed that the Russian infantry would run into their own fire, which ended the debate.

At that time, about 0500 hours, there was nothing to be seen of the Russian infantry attack that our training had taught us to expect. Despite a fine mist, visibility from our trenches gave a firing-field range of 400–500 metres, and the daylight from a cloudy sky, which I have since heard was reinforced by 143 Russian searchlights, produced a light that was fully adequate for all kinds of infantry work. At a distance of about 500 metres from our trenches, vision was obstructed by a thick wall of fog, which was apparently thickened by rocket propellants and artillery fragments mixing with the early morning mist and, as a result of the light easterly wind, was slowly moving towards us. As it was only at the end of the artillery attack that I looked over the parapet, I cannot confirm whether the 143 Russian searchlights had in fact 'blinded the German lines', as is claimed, before the wall of fog developed. At the time I prepared for action, which was as the Russian infantry attack began, they could not possibly have blinded our positions because of the fog.

There were about 10–15 minutes after the artillery bombardment before the shadows of Russian infantry began to appear on the horizon. It really was a ghostly spectacle that opened up before our eyes. As if from behind a milky glass screen, black human shadows arose and fell back shortly afterwards, seemingly on the same spot, against the impenetrable wall of fog. This spectacle can be attributed to the artificial light behind the Russian infantry, as well as the moving wall of fog, producing a three-dimensional effect. Under these circumstances we aimed at the third dimension, firing at the shadows that appeared like figure targets.

THE WEAPONS

The effect of our fire cannot be measured either against modern standards or indeed against the standards then valid. Due to the lack of suitable raw materials, such as copper and zinc, the cartridges for our rifles and machine-guns were no longer being made of brass, but of normal steel. The unprotected steel would normally have soon rusted but, as no soldier in the German *Wehrmacht* could have rust on his arms and ammunition, the Aryan masterminds of the remains of the Greater German Reich had come upon the solution of dipping the cartridges in transparent lacquer to prevent rusting. One would surely be overestimating the intelligence of those responsible for this decision if one accused them of sabotage! The effect this measure had on the fire power of our troops is almost indescribable. The 98 Carbine then on general issue as an infantry weapon was meant to be used as a repeater, but as a result of the lacquering of the cartridges, the ejection of empty cartridges after firing by means of lifting and pulling back the bolt was only seldom possible, and even then only within half a second of having fired. Usually the short time it took to reach for the knob of the bolt was sufficient to enable the cartridge to burn fast in the breech. When this occurred regularly, it was not very clever to present oneself as a target to the enemy while trying to clear the breech under cover. The rifleman therefore had to go back into the trench with his unusable weapon each time after firing and by hammering the knob of the bolt with either a hefty kick or a blow from his bayonet, pull back the bolt and force the empty cartridge out of the breech with his ramrod, providing it was long enough. Sometimes a hard bang of the stock on the bottom of the trench sufficed.

As a No. 2 on the machine-gun, I also had to use my ramrod on the spare gun barrels as the last cartridge regularly burned fast in the breech after a burst of fire, and consequently the barrel had to be changed after each burst and a fresh belt of ammunition fed in to prepare for the next burst.

Looking back, I cannot help thinking that the musketeers of the Thirty Years War with their seventeenth-century weapons had a faster rate of fire on average and consequently greater fire power than we infantrymen of the twentieth century with our modern automatic weapons, but lacquered ammunition!

Despite this greatly reduced fire power, our defensive measures from the trench north of the road still hindered the advance of the Russian infantry units within our field of fire more than those in the trenches south of the road. According to rumour, this section of trenches was defended by *Volkssturm* units that were partially equipped with light sporting weapons, which would explain the relatively short time it took the Russians to break through there!

From the poor arming of the German combat units north and south of the road, one can doubt whether the army command really wanted to defend this part of the Hardenberg Line! Perhaps the soldiers deployed there were only intended to be be visible and so attract the Russian artillery fire upon them-selves and allow themselves to be buried economically. Soldiers deployed like this are known as 'cannon-fodder'.

THE RETREAT

The breakthrough by the Russians into the positions south of the Reichsstrasse presumably caused our company commander to issue the order to evacuate our section of trenches. While the wall of fog produced as a by-product of the Russian artillery, sulphurous, stinking and really thick, with under ten metres' visibility in the middle, had now reached our position, the Russian infantry north of the road were only 200 metres from us. For this advantage of distance – a retreat when the enemy were on top of us would have been difficult – we certainly had the wall of fog and the 143 switched-on searchlights to thank, for its dazzling light made a completely impenetrable wall from the eastern side, which the Russians, with few exceptions, were obviously not entering. One can compare this to the case of a driver using undipped headlights instead of yellow foglights to drive in fog along an unfamiliar road, knowing that it will end in either a wall or a cliff edge. For the Russian soldier the cliff edge was the enemy trenches, whose location he certainly could no longer determine. Apart from this, during the course of their attack, the Russian infantry had some painful and deadly experiences as a result of the illumination from behind, which had turned them into figure targets for us. There is no question that these circumstances had hampered the rapid advance of the Russian troops. They could not see us and therefore were unaware that we were in the process of clearing the trench. They were more concerned with their experiences so far, with aimed shots coming at them from unknown directions and, apart from some individual courageous exceptions, were being especially cautious.

How limited the visibility in the fog really was can be shown from the position of two dead soldiers that I saw during our evacuation of the trench. They were lying about three metres apart, close to the trench north of the Reichsstrasse. They had first spied one another at short distance and immediately shot at each other. Both lay with their heads towards the road and their weapons in the aiming position, the Russian with an automatic assault rifle, and the German with a carbine.

The dense fog was also the reason that our section leader, an officer cadet and new to combat like ourselves, who had made a reconnaissance of the area the day before in good visibility, could not find the trench exit at the critical moment. Unfortunately, he was also lacking in intelligence and did not appreciate that the trench was only 60 cm deep and provided little cover when moving about upright in it to effect a retreat. The best and only real protection the troops had from enemy action was the dense wall of fog. The shallow trench could have enabled even the weakest soldier to climb out and join the retreat, and much valuable time could have been saved. Of course, everyone would have had to know the direction to follow, but this information had apparently been denied us from the beginning for obvious reasons. Even the section leader only knew this route from the trench exit, or he would not have been looking for it so desperately. In his frantic search for the trench exit, he made one mistake after another, leading the section in the wrong direction southwards to the Reichstrasse, on the other side of which the Russian troops had already forced their way into the German positions. Recognising his mistake there, where I saw the dead soldiers, instead of ordering an about-turn, he turned around and led the section back on itself to the north, the men looping round behind him, obliging the moving part to walk along the parapet, as there was no room to pass each other in the narrow trench.

Such a crazy thing has to be seen and experienced to be believed! During this chaotic retreat further time was lost in which the Russian infantry were able to advance on our defence positions without any resistance from us.

TAKEN PRISONER

By the time the trench had been evacuated the Russians were close on our heels as a result of all this loss of time, and so occurred what I had always feared. I was physically too weak to keep up with my section while carrying the pack of a No. 2 on the machine-gun (two spare barrels, my own rifle, two boxes of 500 rounds of machine-gun ammunition each, 120 rounds of ammunition for my own weapon, and two egg hand grenades). My call for assistance from those of my comrades within sight remained unanswered, and so I alone was captured somewhere in the relatively small area between our abandoned position and the eastern foot of the Seelow Heights.

I do not know what happened to the rest of the company.

Günther Labes was released by the Russians in July 1945, having been graded unfit for physical work. He then returned to Hamburg, where he took a degree in engineering.

NOTES

1. The designation of this unit has been identified as the 3rd Battalion, 2nd 'Müncheberg' Panzergrenadier Regiment, 'Müncheberg' Panzer Division.
2. The Soviet 'reconnaissance in force' was carried out on 14 and 15 April, but was virtually completed on the first day in this sector.
3. Reichsstrasse 1, now known as Bundesstrasse 1. The Seelower Loose was the open ground immediately below the Seelow Heights here.

LUFTWAFFE INFANTRYMAN

HERBERT BÖKER

I was born in Westphalia on 16 February 1927. After two years at a commercial school in Bünde, Westphalia, I went on to the Business School at Freiburg-im-Breisgau. I was called up in 1944, following seven months as a *Luftwaffe* auxiliary in Freiburg and Karlsruhe, where we were trained on 37 mm anti-aircraft guns, both German and captured Russian. In the autumn of 1944 I had three months of labour service in the Bayerischen Wald, then did my basic training at Oschatz Airfield in Saxony. I should point out that I volunteered for the *Luftwaffe* because of my anger at having to watch helplessly as the Anglo-American terror bomber units drew their white condensation trails across the sky. I specifically wanted to be a fighter pilot and fly an Me-109 among them. I announced this wish when I was called up and was told that unfortunately we no longer had sufficient fighter aircraft.

As a result of my educational background, I was advised to report as a potential officer, which is how, after completing my basic training at Oschatz I was sent to the *Luftwaffe* War School in Berlin-Gatow. The course ahead of me was still using the old 'Bücker' and 'Arado' training machines. We were to be the next course to learn to fly. The joy for me as a seventeen-year-old was tremendous, the dangers of no significance.

On about 11 April 1945, we were suddenly told at night to pack our rucksacks, and our course, which was in about company strength of 120–130 men, was marched off towards the Oderbruch. At first we went by barge, travelling eastwards on the water, presumably the Spree. Towards morning on 12 April we disembarked and went on by foot. It must have been along today's B1, which took us to Müncheberg. One of my jolliest comrades – we were all the same age – who came from Bavaria remained quiet the whole day while we were on the march. In answer to my question, he replied: 'Once the fighting starts, I won't survive the first day.' And that is what happened, but I will come to it later.

Our destination was the Oderbruch, which was criss-crossed with drainage ditches lined with trees and with isolated farms among the fields. The whole valley bed was quite flat. Then we received orders to dig ourselves foxholes in the open field. There was a road not far off, which must have been south of Seelow, and beyond it was a small wood with a football pitch inside it. It was a warm, sunny day, and after we had dug our foxholes we stood around chatting in the field. Suddenly a Russian aircraft appeared above the wood and explosions started up frighteningly close to us. We rapidly took cover, as we had been trained, and only then heard the aircraft. It had shot three of us like a hunter chasing rabbits. We had been warned.

We had each been armed with a captured French rifle, which must have been of the 1870 pattern with a very long barrel, and five rounds of ammunition. We also had two egg hand grenades. There were also a few out-dated machine-guns. I had seen only one 'Tiger' tank in our sector.

At 3 o'clock on the morning of 16 April we heard a frightful thundering in front of us that went on and on. We were spared the artillery fire at first, but it kept coming closer until the salvoes were falling right in our sector. The foxholes in our open field made us uneasy, so we withdrew to the tree-lined ditches. There was an old farmhouse in the field on our right that was occupied by our people with panzerfausts. Our sector was being bombarded unendingly by shells and salvoes of 'Stalin-organ' rockets. The ditch had a small bridge for the farmers' and harvest wagons to cross and pipes of about 30–40 cm diameter for the water to flow through, but too narrow to crawl through. As the bombardment became unbearable, one of our comrades lost his nerve and shouted to me: 'Let's run over the little bridge!'

I shouted back: 'Wait till the salvo's exploded!' But he jumped up and ran past me, and was already on the bridge when the shells exploded. He had a wound about 30 cm in circumference and his rear was completely torn away. We laid him in a tent-half[1] and two comrades carried him off to the rear, but he could not have survived. He had slept in the bunk above me in barracks, and came from Düsseldorf, but I do not remember his name.

The other comrade from Bavaria was lying about five metres away from me when a tank shell hit the tree above him and he was riddled with splinters. I crawled across to him and turned him over. His face was chalk-white and grey. He looked at me and said: 'You see, I was right!' He died on the spot.

At about 10 o'clock rifle bullets suddenly started flying over our heads. I shoved my steel helmet on a stick briefly above the edge of the ditch and it was immediately riddled with machine-gun bullets. A quick glimpse over the edge of the ditch showed that the situation was hopeless: T-34 tank after T-34 tank with Russian infantry in between.

Towards noon on 16 April the order filtered through: 'The remains of the unit back to the edge of the wood!' The Russian tanks had a hellish respect for us. They came hardly any closer, although we were only armed with rifles. In crawling back I suddenly noticed that the safety cap of one of the egg hand grenades on my stomach was hanging off. I immediately threw it away and it exploded in the same moment. I was lucky not to have been torn apart. In contrast to my Bavarian comrade, I always had the feeling that nothing would happen to me and that I would return home unscathed, which is indeed what happened.

As we luckily reached the road with several comrades, I saw our company commander sitting completely apathetic and spiritless, leaning against a tree. He was in shock and was not responding. He had obtained his Iron Cross First Class as a fighter pilot and ground combat had finished him off!

I also met there my barrackroom comrade Karl-Heinz König from Hamburg, who had trained as a youngster with Heinten Hoff, the European heavyweight champion. He remarked: 'We have all aged a year today.' I met him again by chance years later while visiting Hamburg.

Of the 130 men of our unit, only 60 still remained at the end of the first day, all the others were either dead or wounded. The advancing Russians shot the wounded at the dressing station. We streamed back to the little wood as ordered. Many soldiers, including some from other units, were going straight across the football pitch. I said to my two comrades: 'We'll go round through the trees. The Russians must have the football field under observation.' I had hardly said this when the 'Stalin-organ' rockets started landing on the pitch. Arms, legs and bodies flew through the air. I have never seen anything so frightful. We ran back across a cemetery, hiding behind hedges, as the leading Russian tanks kept pace with us. Thanks to four bouts of basic training, I was reasonably fit, which was what presumably saved my life.

Suddenly there was an older comrade lying in front of me with a stomach wound. He had one of the modern quick-firing rifles with a curved magazine over his shoulder and a map case with an Ordnance Survey map in it, and presumably was an officer. As he died shortly afterwards, I took his gun, ammunition and map for myself. Equipped thus, we went across the countryside.

A defensive position had been prepared on a small hill near Müncheberg on which stood one or two houses, and we were directed there by the military police. We were a colourful mix of all elements of the Armed Forces and SS, with some old hands among us. Once more we waited for the enemy, sleeping through the night. At dawn we discovered that the old soldiers had gone and only we young officer cadets remained. Again we had the same picture of densely crowded Russian tanks with the infantry following. Then the show started: bombardment with shells, 'Stalin-organs' and machine-guns. I lay my rifle across the trench, heaved myself up and ran up the slope, dropping every five steps, jumping up again and running in a zigzag. A fat officer with a drawn pistol above us ordered us to counterattack towards the tanks, which we did, but turned round the first barn and went off in another direction. We might have been young, but we had enough sense to know that we could not hold up the tanks with our bodies alone.

On the retreat to Berlin we picked up from a radio in an empty house that the Russians had thrust past the south of Berlin and that their tank spearheads were turning north. It was obvious to us three that the Russians would close the ring around Berlin in the north, so we would have to march northwest if we were not to be caught.

Meanwhile on Hitler's birthday, 20 April, we were given a rosy report on the situation from the leadership, and then heard again the appeal from the traitors on the Russian side, the Free Germany Committee, calling on us to go over to the Russians, and promising us wonders, etc., ending with the words: 'And now follows an organ concert' as the 'Stalin-organs' started up.

Roosevelt, the American president, died on 24 April, and Goebbels took this occasion to prophesy in his leaflets that fate would now change its course. 'Hold on for a few more days longer and the wonder-weapons will come into action', etc., etc.! The Jew Ilya Ehrenburg in Moscow was meanwhile urging the Red Army soldiers on with his leaflets: 'The only good German is a dead German! Take your revenge on the Germans, take their women, kill everything that moves, etc.!'

North of Berlin we saw prisoners in striped uniforms for the first time. They were singing and happy about their forthcoming liberation, and must have been from Sachsenhausen Concentration Camp. None of us knew of the existence of these camps. We were directed to an airstrip, where units were to be formed, and taken into surrounded Berlin by air. We kept ourselves discreetly in the background and made off at dusk, for which the map proved useful. Somewhere east of the Elbe we passed a sunken road through which Wehrmacht lorries towing 88 mm guns were driving. We sat on the guns as they drove over poor tracks and so reached the Americans, who directed us into a meadow. A few hours later we saw the Russians and Americans shaking hands.

The rest is soon told. We unloaded several trucks on the assembly area and stacked the ammunition, slept in the meadow at night and drove next day in the empty trucks over a pontoon bridge across the Elbe to another meadow. After a few weeks we were handed over to the British at Munsterlager on Lüneberg Heath following a two-day march. There it was announced that release was imminent. First came miners and agricultural workers. My paybook showed my profession as 'student', so I took a pen and inserted 'landw.' in front, indicating that I was an agricultural student. I was registered as such, and on 16 June was informed of my release.

I do not know what my unit was called or to which formation we belonged in the Oderbruch, but presume it was a parachutist one.

NOTE

1. German soldiers were issued with tent-halves, which also served as individual rain-capes.

DIARY OF DEFEAT

DR HANS-WERBER KLEMENT

Dr Hans-Werber Klement was the Signals Officer of Army Flak Battalion 292 of the 25th Panzergrenadier Division. His Battalion consisted of three batteries, Nos 1 and 2 with 6 x 88 mm guns, and No. 3 with 20 mm Vierlings (four-barrelled guns) and 37 mm Zwillings (two-barrelled guns).

Once more a front line was established out of nothing, and once more the flood from the east was checked. When the Russians reached the Oder river either side of Küstrin with weak forces in early February, there were only a few combat teams available to meet them. They were unable to prevent the formation of bridgeheads, and reinforcements coming from the west were unable to clear them either. So a front was formed that held, and the enemy was forced to redeploy and commit their reinforcements.

The enemy started preparing for their main offensive on the Reich's capital, preparations that gave some indication of the scale of the battle to come. We looked to the future with concern; would our front be able to withstand the onslaught? How often was this question the topic of conversation, and how often the talks ended with a definite 'No', and yet no one thought that this was the lead-up to the finale, for there was still hope of a major change in the situation. The few happy hours that we enjoyed from time to time now seem as if we were dancing on the edge of a volcano.

In the middle of March the day of the big offensive seemed to have arrived, as we waited quietly after two days of preparation for an as yet undisclosed task. The counterattack saw our division back in the Seelow area, which had become a second home to us during the past few weeks.

But after several days the situation calmed down again as the expected main offensive did not occur.[1] The Russians had widened their bridgehead and Küstrin fell. The enemy's preparations entered their final stage after the fall of the fortress.

Meanwhile the enemy had invaded in the west and crossed the Rhine, striking at the heart of Germany. There was hardly any chance of establishing an organised resistance. Now we believed that we only had to stop the enemy in the east from getting any further into the Fatherland.

As the enemy had yet to start his main offensive, we remained in Army Reserve, undisturbed by events in the west, but now farther north in the Wreizen area, near Trebbin at the Burgwall settlement. Meanwhile spring had started and the fruitful countryside lay under peaceful sunshine, with hardly a shot to be heard. It seemed as if this colossal event had forgotten us. But our worries had increased, for the enemy in the west was approaching our lines of supply. How would our supply system function during the main offensive?

16 April 1945

Captain von Rippen called me during the night; an attack by Russian shock troops indicated the beginning of the main offensive.

At 0440 hours: a thunderous din along the whole front. The earth shakes and the buildings seem to sway. The long-awaited moment has arrived.

We are lying immediately in front of the second line, which is occupied by a *Luftwaffe* officer cadet regiment, all inexperienced volunteers. When the first rounds of the bombardment begin to fall, they still do not realise what is happening. I feel sorry for these youngsters; they will sustain heavy casualties.

The bombardment lasts about three hours in undiminished strength, and then gradually changes over to harassing fire. Ground-attack aircraft have been attacking the roads and villages since dawn. A vast cloud of smoke and dust hangs over the Oderbruch. Wounded are being taken to the rear. No good news arrives from up front.

There are still no orders for us, and it is not until noon that we change position to a wood near Kunersdorf, where we have to wait for further orders. Here I discover that bomb splinters have wounded two men from my telephone section that I had sent to the rear. It is completely quiet for the moment, but suddenly there is a sharp roar and we are being bombarded. I lose my Sergeant Donder with the last shells from a severe wound to the head. Two men have been slightly wounded, but can stay with us.

The front is pushed back today, but is still holding.

17 April 1945

Night brings another change of position to Marienberg farm, where there is no possibility of accommodation, so we move the command post into a little wood west of Möglin. The division has been deployed in 606th Division's area.[2]

Here in this wood I see an old woman from Burgwall again, sitting on the grass with her dog and several hens, not knowing what to do. We have her taken further back.

A tank alert causes us to get our panzerfausts ready and to prepare ourselves against being taken by surprise. However, nothing happens, only some harassing fire during the course of the afternoon.

That evening orders come from Division to redeploy our batteries, which had been sited in the ground-fighting role, back to the anti-aircraft role. We know that from tomorrow onwards we are going to have a hard time. Captain von Rippen issues the necessary orders.

Part of the control post moves back to Marienberg farm in order to be closer to the batteries this evening, as the Russians conduct air attacks on the roads and villages.

Despite having made further territorial gains, the enemy has still not broken through today. Our forces adjust quickly; all our reserves have already been committed, for there has been no relaxation of pressure.

18 April 1945

Strong harassing fire is laid on Marienberg farm during the night, and the Russians have set up loudspeakers calling on us to give up the fight.

At the same time a Führer Order has been issued ordering us to retake the front line. With what? Have those above any idea of what is going on? Apparently not.

Soon after daybreak swarms of ground-attack aircraft appear. One of the first of them takes us on, dropping bombs and firing directly at Marienberg farm. It seems that the Il-2s are methodically tackling every building and wood.

The commanding officer orders the command post into a small tunnel under the road near Schulzendorf. Apart from constant harassing fire, the afternoon is comparatively quiet once more.

Here General Busse's Order of the Day, as commander of the 9th Army, reaches us, first as a rumour, and then in writing: 'Only two more days, and then it will be done.' What does that mean? No one can understand it.

There is no time for reflection. Ground-attack aircraft reappear. Second Lieutenant Matthé reports by telephone that there is strong artillery and mortar fire on the gun positions. First comes a bombardment of all calibre of weapons on our area, then 'Boston' bombers for the first time, laying a bomb carpet. The Russians seem determined to force a breakthrough here. The whole area is covered in smoke and dust through the constant bombardments, bombing and strafing.

Major Daeschler, Division Chief of Staff, telephones for a situation report, and I give it to him. The commanding officer and adjutant are on their way. In a second communication, I have to tell him that the situation is gradually becoming untenable for me. The infantry are pulling back, and I have to get our vehicles out.

We race over the open fields. There are innumerable squadrons of aircraft above us, and we are under artillery fire. Can we make it? I meet Lieutenant Wahrer in front of Lüdersdorf, and he instructs me to set up the command post in a wood further on for the time being.

Ground-attack aircraft and artillery are now hammering at the woods and villages, and the dead are lying on the roads. At last I get the vehicles into a wood on a hill, from where we can see far over the countryside. Everywhere is fire, smoke, dust and explosions, a cruel picture of the German countryside being laid waste by war, so it is gratifying to see a Pe-2 dive straight into the ground in front of us.

An order from Captain von Rippen summons me back to Lüdersdorf.

Meanwhile Lieutenant Wahrer has been severely wounded, apparently mortally. The batteries are redeploying here. The command post is to go back to the Haselberg area. During this order group in the open we are under constant shellfire.

I get the radios working again in a hollow west of Haselberg and wait for the commanding officer. It gets later and later. Then I hear from a passing officer that Captain von Rippen has been badly wounded, so I drive to Division. It is true. Captain Götz has taken over the battalion. I drive back to the command post at Haselberg during the night.

Lieutenant Wahrer has died, and Lieutenant Fromme and Second Lieutenant Matthé have been wounded this evening.

The *Wehrmacht* Report of 19 April still fails to report the extent of the enemy attack. A breakthrough is still being prevented, but our forces cannot withstand this pressure for much longer.

19 April 1945

The batteries take up new firing positions near Haselberg, and the command post is set up on the Haselberg–Steinbeck road.

Here I learn that my Signals Sergeant Richter and one of my signallers were killed while in action with our supply section, and another signaller wounded.

The fighting at the batteries is hard, and there are constant reports of losses in men and guns.

There is the sound of fighting in the rear near Steinbeck this afternoon. There is no more traffic on the road. The Russians must have broken through in the neighbouring sector. Danger threatens us from the right and behind, where there do not seem to be any of our troops any more. I take safety precautions. The commanding officer is on the move. Darkness falls and still no orders. The situation is critical. At last Second Lieutenant von Schuckmann brings instructions to bring the command post close to the divisional command post.

The Russians have achieved their first breakthrough. The division is to pull out of the threatening encirclement and engage the enemy again farther to the west.

20 APRIL 1945

As usual I lead the command post vehicles to the next location. Shortly after leaving, I come across the divisional staff heading in the opposite direction and about to drive into the Russians, having been misdirected by a military policeman. While we are stopped in the moonlit night, two bombs are dropped close by from the ground-attack aircraft flying ceaselessly above us. The drive goes on relatively smoothly, although I wonder why the road further back seems dead. Once a civilian tries to direct me into the nearest village, but I drive on, using my map.

A horrifying but beautiful sight lies before us at Heckelberg. The whole countryside is brightly lit by a vast fire in the village.

The road widens beyond Heckelberg. There are several ground-attack aircraft above us, shooting up the area. I drive faster in order to open up the column more. A Volkswagen comes from up ahead, and a man waves at us energetically to stop. It is Lieutenant Protz with our motorcyclist. Both are highly excited, for the Russians are less than 100 metres further on. They have captured our Senior Medical Officer, Dr Kühling, who had gone ahead with his driver. The escorting motorcyclist was able to escape, and was picked up by Lieutenant Protz.

I have everyone turn around and ask the battery following me to take up firing positions on the southern edge of Heckelberg. Nevertheless, one of our batteries is captured. Then I drive with Lieutenant Protz and the commanding officer, who has arrived in the meantime, to Division at the Kruwe Farm. Our report hits them like a bomb, and we are ordered to make a reconnaissance of the immediate area.

But this proves to be no longer necessary. We meet a signaller from No. 1 Battery, who had been captured with his battery but managed to escape. He reports that they had been misdirected by a sentry in parachutist uniform. Now, as observed on the march, it is obvious that enemy agents have been at work. So we report back to Division, where we meet the general and his chief of staff in a simply furnished room. They have no idea where the individual elements of the division are, apparently due to a whole series of misdirections.

Nobody says so, but we all know that this means that it is now impossible to stop the enemy breaking through from the east. The fate of Berlin and the outcome of our battle have been sealed only two days after General Busse's Order of the Day.

The fate of our division is also decided this night. The breakthrough is occurring to our south, consequently we will not be pressed back on Berlin but can slip off to the northwest.

We spend the whole day gathering our badly battered battalion near Beerbaum and fixing those weapons that are repairable. Second Lieutenant Gudenus, who was wounded the previous evening, is taken away. During the morning Dr Kühling's driver appears, having managed to escape. Dr Kühling was beaten half to death by the Russians and is probably dead.

Evening brings orders for a move in a northwesterly direction for the first time, to Finow. On the way the consequences of being overtired begin to show in me. I have hardly slept at all since the beginning of the main offensive.

21 April 1945

We have a few hours rest in Finow, having got away from the enemy's main line of advance. Here we experience for the first time something that is going to give us acute concern – lack of fuel for the vehicles. I spend half the day finding enough to ensure that we will be able to cross the canal in an emergency.

Forming our front line to the south, the canal enables us to take a hot bath and get a few hours' sleep. We no longer have to defend Berlin, but to cover the area north of it, in order to prevent the troops fighting on the Oder there from being encircled.

22–24 April 1945

The command post is in Buckow Manor Farm. We are here until the afternoon of 24 April and have quite good rest, being able to sleep for two whole nights. Only one question refuses to go away; can we overcome the fuel problem?

24 April 1945

We receive orders for a change of location to the Neuruppin area, where we are relieved in order to cover the southern flank further west.

The move takes place before dusk through the most beautiful part of Mark Brandenburg, the Schorfheide.[3] The countryside goes past us incredibly peacefully. An especially painful feeling grips me at this point; we are an army no longer capable of saving our country.

On the way we receive new orders to wheel to the south and take up positions in the Löwenberg area.

25–27 April 1945

We wait in Lindow for definite orders to go on to Teschendorf, from where attacks to relieve Berlin are to be directed from Oranienburg during the next few days, and so have a relatively quiet time.

During this period we are joined by a young *Luftwaffe* auxiliary who, having brought his grandparents from Berlin to Rathenow, is unable to get back to Berlin, so I take him on in my Signals Platoon.

We follow developments in Berlin and on the Lower Oder river with concern, for we are in danger of being encircled should the Russians break through, both from Nauen in the west and Stettin in the north. We are not surprised to receive orders on 27 April to move north to the Neustrelitz area in order to throw ourselves against the enemy advancing from Prenzlau.

28 April 1945

On our way to Strelitz we overtake refugee columns in indescribable distress. Among them are columns of concentration camp inmates, foreign workers, prisoners and deserters. At Strelitz these columns go past us again. This is the beginning of the end.

Our command post is ordered to Hohenzieritz, where we find Queen Luise's castle and a village that has as museum-like an appearance as the castle. Even these tradition-filled places will be taken by the enemy, and again I am filled with a sense of leave-taking that remains with me.

This evening a liaison officer from Corps strays to us. We discuss the situation and he informs us of the views of the staff, giving us the first clues as to the purpose of our recent actions. The troops must be withdrawn from the Russians to surrender in the west in order to save as many lives as possible. Orders to attack have only one purpose, and that is to cover the retreat and withdrawal of the refugee columns. There is no effective government any more.

29 April 1945

The morning of 29 April sees us moving towards Gevezin, near Neubrandenburg. Soon the amount of air activity shows that we are in contact with strong enemy forces again.

I drive off in search of motor fuel, which has become the most important item.

The situation becomes confused towards evening. Two of No. 3 Battery's troops are missing. It is said that elements of the 281st Division have been throwing their weapons away. Major Fellmann, commanding officer of Panzergrenadier Regiment 119, arrives and says: 'It is all over.' Lieutenant Kersten, commanding officer of Artillery Regiment 25, coins the phrase: 'We are covering the retreat of deserters.'

Before we move again this evening, I tell my NCOs what was said at Hohenzieritz the evening before. The men have to know what lies ahead.

The move takes us to Vossfeld Manor Farm, where we get a few hours' sleep.

30 April 1945

We have to leave Vossfeld during the morning. I go ahead with the command post to Deven to an abandoned Schloss, where again we experience urgent fuel problems. When the grenadier regiment's command post moves back, we move too, Division having ordered us to Jägerhof.

Jägerhof is a small farming village, overflowing with refugees, and lying in particularly exposed ground, so we do not stay there long. By chance, I overhear a conversation between the general and Lieutenant Proell, the commanding officer of Panzergrenadier Regiment 35. There is another move of the command post during the night.

1 May 1945

The tracks across country that we have been using as usual are blocked, as a result of which the Reconnaissance Battalion company that should be covering our right flank is still behind us. However, all goes smoothly. Near Kirch-Grubenhagen we come across a massive counterflow of columns fleeing west. Fortunately, we seldom have to use the main roads, as they are all blocked like this.

In the middle of all this traffic, I meet Second Lieutenant Müller, my training officer from the officer cadet course at Rerick.

At our next command post location at Peenhäuser some vehicles have to be pumped dry to supply No. 2 Battery, which needs the fuel.

Before we set off on our usual evening change of location, we can see our infantry in action on our level to the east. Our route at dusk once more takes us through the wonderful Mecklenburg countryside with its lovely lakes.

As we are setting up the command post at Zehna Manor Farm, someone asks us why we could not have notified them by telephone of our arrival in advance. The people here are still unaware of what awaits them, and that the end is in sight. One consequence is that our moves are becoming more frequent and longer. It is difficult to tell the people the truth.

2 May 1945

We move on again this afternoon. More holding lines are being planned, the last being at Schwerin, but we have heard rumours that the Americans are already there.

These rumours are confirmed at Rothen Manor Farm. We now know that the next 24 hours will decide our fate.

Rothen is one of the finest farms in which we have stayed, but we only stay two hours here, during which I have a chat with the squire, Herr von Oerzen. We talk about Hitler: how things had to end this way, for the man had no standards of behaviour, like all impostors.

The von Oerzen family have no intention of leaving their farm, Frau von Oerzen being particularly determined not to leave their property in the lurch. What should we advise? Finally they decide to flee on horseback. Their labourers are bitterly disappointed at the decision.

The von Oerzen family are sheltering the mother and sister of the famous flying ace Manfred von Richthofen,[4] who are refugees from East Prussia. I take the baroness and her daughter in our vehicles, as I cannot let these women fall into the hands of the Russians.

These hours at Rothen are the final farewell to free German soil for me, from the German traditions that I feel here once more.

3 May 1945

On our next move we come upon a column hopelessly blocking the road to Schwerin, and have to drive over the open fields in order to reach the next location for our command post in a small woodland Schloss. To the right and left of the road one sees an unusual picture; soldiers sitting at campfires, and discarded arms and equipment lying everywhere.

With dawn we can see the chaos. The column has moved on and is coming towards us: refugees, foreigners, prisoners, liberated concentration camp inmates, deserters, groups of soldiers, dead horses, and ammunition exploding as units blow up their weapons. Rumours abound, as no one knows for certain what is happening even a few kilometres away.

We push ourselves into the stream before Pinow, which lies a little to the side of the road. We set up our command post in the village and try to establish contact with Division. The first American sentries are said to be only 1½ kilometres to the west. It is also said that some concentration camp inmates have armed themselves and are shooting at the troops trying to get them through safely to the west. We wait tensely for a long time, not wanting, as proper soldiers, to anticipate Division's orders.

At last Captain Bruness arrives from Division. He is excited: 'I have the following orders for you: the troops are to destroy their arms and equipment and flee to the west in their vehicles immediately!'

So it must be. Captivity in the west is the most favourable end awaiting us, but we are still deeply shocked.

I have my men parade and tell them that we are going into captivity, that after five years the war is lost, that it was all in vain. This is the most difficult moment I have had in front of my platoon.

We drive along the tracks to the west, destroying all our equipment on the way. We keep our handguns as security, for armed concentration camp inmates are likely to be encountered. Now the Americans; a patrol with a vehicle, which simply lets us drive on to the west.

The division gathers at Hof Göhren. We do not know what is to happen next. Later in the afternoon we have to drive on again in our own transport. Near Warsow we are directed on to a meadow, which is to be our prison camp.

This evening the commander awards me the Iron Cross Second Class.

4 May 1945

There are supposed to be considerable elements of the division near Schwerin, especially our supply column with its vehicles. These are to be released to us, as apparently the Americans want to keep us together as a formation. Above all we need our field kitchens.

I drive off with Captain Geyer, the military police officer, and an American sergeant, who is to assist us in this business and prevent us from being detained.

There is a big field full of captured German soldiers near Schwerin, from which we extract those members of the 25th Panzergrenadier Division, but we still do not have our vehicles and field kitchens. At last, after many difficulties, we have a whole line of vehicles ready to drive off. Then I hear loud voices coming from behind me. I turn round. There is a truck with a Soviet star, and a Russian second lieutenant is climbing off. He comes towards me. What should I do? The American sergeant is not around. I salute the Russian and he salutes me back and goes past. A Russian soldier is sitting in our Volkswagen, wanting to drive off. He demands the ignition key. I try to explain to him that the vehicle belongs to the American. The latter comes just as the Russian second lieutenant also reappears. I explain to him that we are working for the American, translating between the two, as they cannot understand each other.

Then I have to tell them about two of our drivers, whom the Russians are taking away. The situation quietens down and I work on our vehicle, while the Russians go off to look for other vehicles until an American officer sends them back across the demarcation line.

NOTES

1. The 25th Panzergrenadier Division was involved in the fighting connected with the Russian unification of their bridgeheads on 22/23 March 1945 and in the German counterattack of 27/28 March 1945 that failed to reopen the Küstrin 'corridor'.
2. The 606th Infantry Division virtually collapsed on the first day of the Soviet offensive, 16 April 1945.
3. Reichsmarschall Hermann Göring had his 'Karinhall' residence here.
4. The 'Red Baron' of the First World War.

DEATH WAS OUR COMPANION

MAJOR GENERAL RUDI LINDNER

Rudi Lindner was born in 1923 and started his Reichsarbeitsdienst *service in 1941, working at Orly Airport outside Paris and then on the occupied Channel Islands of Jersey and Guernsey, where he recalls laying barbed wire on L'Ancresse Common golf course. He went on to do his military training in France, being posted to Infantry Regiment 106, which was transferred to Russia in February 1943 and fought on the Dnepr Front. During a counterattack east on 21 November 1943, he was shot in the left upper arm and bayoneted in the chest, as a result of which he needed fourteen operations in various hospitals before his return to active duty in January 1945.*

The Fahnenjunker-Grenadier-Regiment to which he was finally posted was one of several raised from officer cadet schools with an establishment of 25 per cent officer cadets, 25 per cent soldiers and NCOs, and 50 per cent Volkssturm.

FAHNENJUNKER-GRENADIER-REGIMENT 1241 'WETZLAR'

I was posted from my holding unit to Fahnenjunker-Grenadier-Regiment 1241 at the Wezlar Officer Cadet School near Marburg, where we were accommodated in hutments, issued with new equipment and weapons, and given instruction on the new assault rifle 44.

In undergoing the latter we had a tragic experience in which three of our comrades were severely wounded. We had paraded in front of the hutments for instruction on the new assault rifle with the instructor standing in front of us. He called for a rifle, intending to demonstrate the

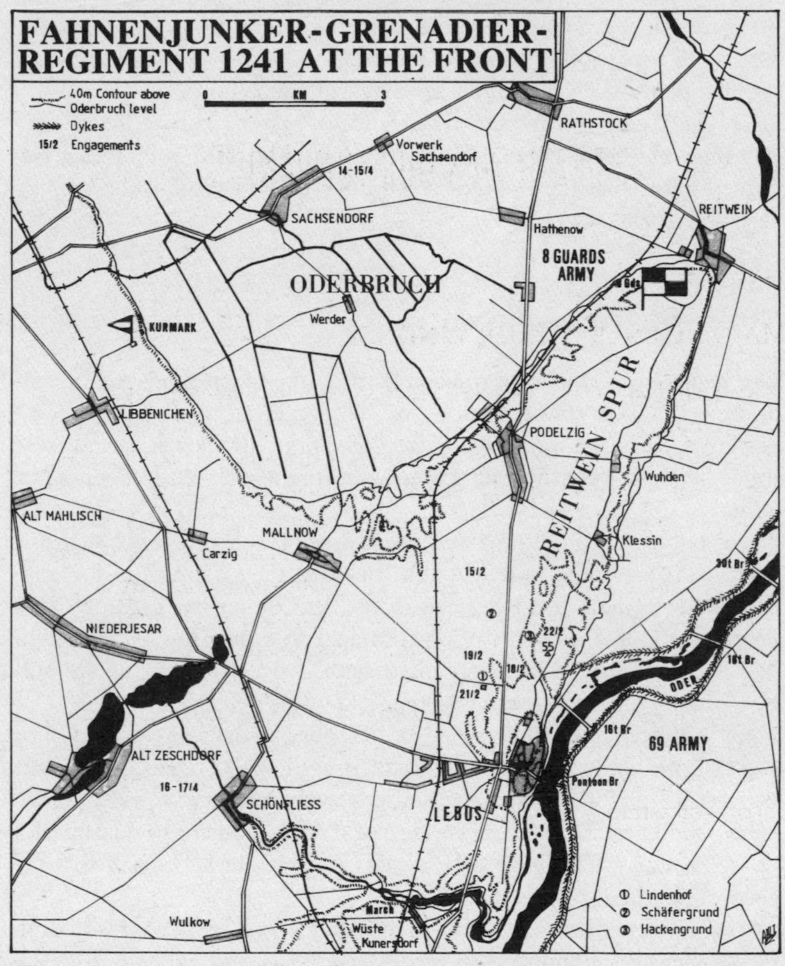

handling of it. In doing so he made a serious error by not checking the state of the weapon and whether or not it was loaded. Believing there was an empty magazine in the weapon, he cocked it and pressed the trigger, firing a burst of live ammunition into our ranks.

Everything had to be done in a hurry, which is why he had not noticed that we had started off with magazines filled with live ammunition that should have been in our ammunition pouches and not in the weapons. The consequences of ignoring basic military security precautions were three severely wounded comrades.

Several young recruits saw what horrible wounds looked like for the first time and heard the cries of pain coming from their comrades. They had no idea what they would have to live through during the coming days and weeks.

THE LEBUS BRIDGEHEAD

Our regiment assembled at the Frankfurt-on-the-Oder goods station and at the Schönfliess railway station over the period 15–17 February, being assigned to the Panzergrenadier Division 'Kurmark', and was immediately involved in the defence against the Russian bridgehead at Lebus.

For many young officer cadets, as well as for those regulars that had spent their service in orderly-rooms, this was their baptism of fire and, unfortunately, also cost many casualties. Already on the evening of 15 February the first elements of our regiment to arrive, the 1st Battalion, had been committed in battalion strength between Lebus station and Podelzig in order to plug a threatening gap in the defence.

Once the remainder had arrived, on 18 February the regiment was given the task of conducting a counterattack with the support of the 2nd Battalion of the Panzer Regiment 'Kurmark' with the aim of constricting the Lebus bridgehead. The orders for the attack read: 'Thrust down both sides of the Podelzig–Lebus road as far as the crossroads in Lebus and split the enemy bridgehead.'

The main point of attack was set east of the road, which is also where the tanks were committed. The order of advance was as follows: in the first echelon, west of the road the 1st Battalion, east of the road the 2nd Battalion with the 2nd Battalion, Panzer Regiment 'Kurmark'; in reserve, one company of the 1st Battalion behind the 2nd Battalion; the direction of advance was south towards Lebus.

Preparation for and support during the attack was implemented by the mass of the Panzergrenadier Division 'Kurmark's' artillery and mortars, as well as a squadron of Me-109s.

On 18 February, following 30 minutes' artillery preparation, our regiment, together with the 2nd Battalion, Panzer-Regiment 'Kurmark', went into the attack and immediately ran into a massive barrage from the Soviet artillery that forced our infantry to dig in after having gained only a little ground. East of the road, the tanks managed to push through to within 1,500 metres of the northern edge of Lebus. Support for the attack from our own low-flying aircraft had only lasted 30 minutes.

The infantry had become separated from the tanks as a result of the artillery barrage, and the tanks ran into a strong enemy anti-tank artillery belt. In these circumstances, the divisional commander, Colonel Langkeit, called off the hopeless attack and had the tanks return to the start line.

That evening elements of the Russian 69th Army in regimental strength conducted a night attack from the northern edge of Lebus on our regiment, which had gone over to the defence. The attacking Russian troops were able to make a breach in our defences, occupy the Lindenhof and effect a breach along the road running north.

Early on 19 February, the divisional reserve counterattacked and forced the enemy back to the track fork two kilometres south of the Schäfergrund. However, the counterattack came to a halt here when the enemy committed new forces.

This was the baptism of fire for our regiment, involving high casualties. These were needless victims to no tactical advantage; on the contrary, there had been loss of ground.

From IX SS-Panzer Corps under SS-General Kleinheisterkamp then came the order for the Panzergrenadier Division 'Kurmark' to launch another attack on the Lebus bridgehead on 22 February.

In this attack the left wing of the regiment was assigned to the northern edge of Lebus, east of the Podelzig–Lebus road. An attempt by a storm troop from the regiment to improve the situation at the Lindenhof on the evening of 21 February failed.

At 1015 hours on 22 February, following an artillery barrage and with direct support from ground-attack aircraft, the division's armoured group attacked from the Hackengrund through the lines of the 2nd Battalion, Panzer-Regiment 'Kurmark', north of Point 55 and the left wing of our regiment. The attack came abruptly through the southern exit of the Hakengrund and reoccupied Point 55. The enemy responded immediately with massed artillery fire, putting down a heavy anti-tank barrage over the area under attack. Their numerous, well-camouflaged

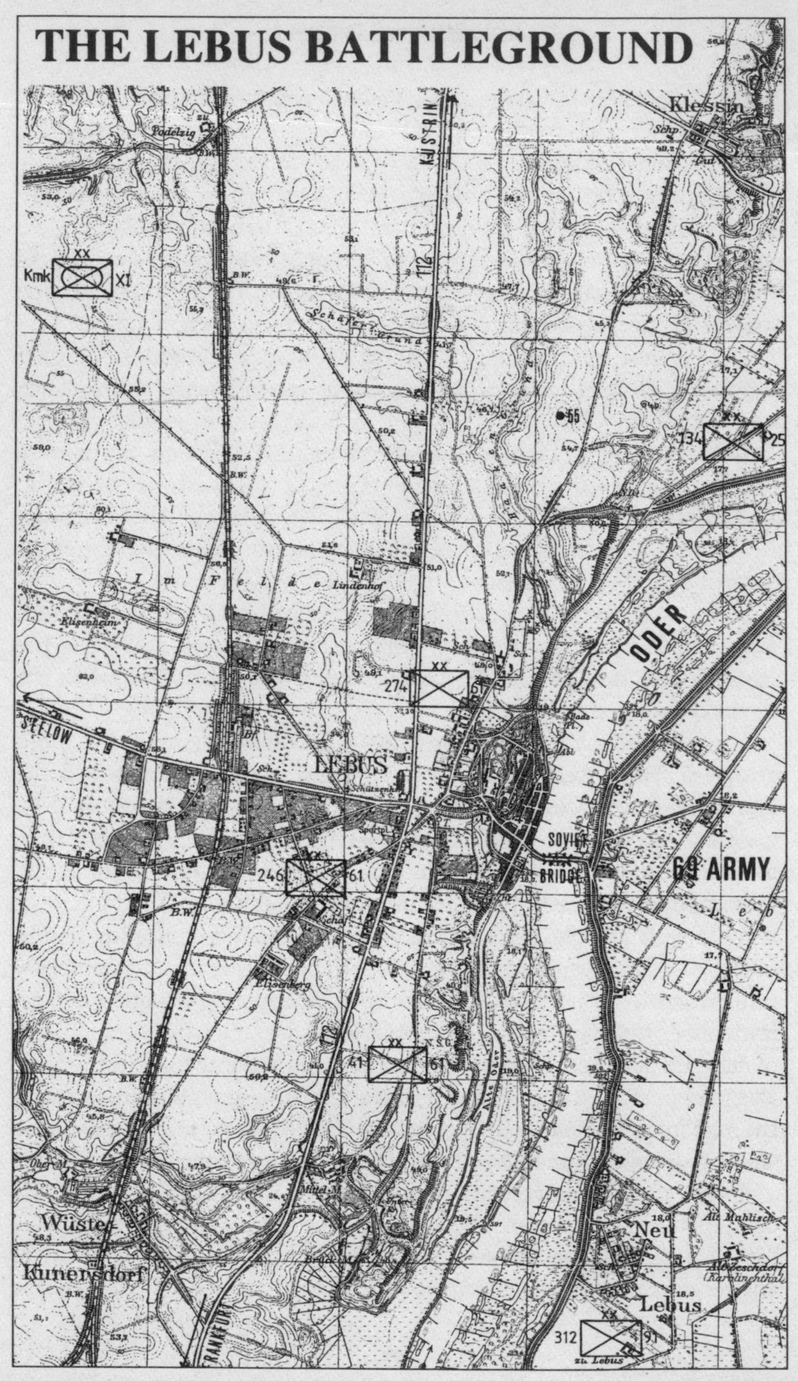

THE LEBUS BATTLEGROUND
Klessin
Podelzig
KÜSTRIN
112
Kmk
XI
Schäfer Grund
55
134
25
I m F e l d e
Lindenhof
Elisenheim
ODER
274
61
SEELOW
LEBUS
SOVIET BRIDGE
69 ARMY
246
61
Elisenberg
41
61
Alte Oder
Wüste
Kunersdorf
FRANKFURT
Neu
Lebus
312
91
zu Lebus

anti-tank guns opened up a concentrated flanking fire into the advancing wedge of our armour. Apart from this, another anti-tank belt joined in the fight north of Lebus.

In view of these overwhelming factors, the divisional commander decided to break off this attack as well, and to establish a defence on the seized Point 55, but these heights were retaken by Russian troops a few days later. The senselessness of this attack and the high, unnecessary losses involved, were quite obvious.

While the enemy opposite Regiment 1241 and Panzergrenadier-Regiment 'Kurmark' had only gained a little ground in the Podelzig area, with an attack in divisional strength they had been able to force a breach five kilometres by four in the Panzergrenadier Division 'Kurmark's' northern sector.

WÜSTE KUNERSDORF

Because of its special role as divisional reserve, at the end of March the Panzergrenadier Division 'Kurmark' was concentrated in the second defensive strip, but the grenadier regiments remained in the front line.

During those last days of March, as the 69th Army increasingly tried to enlarge its Lebus bridgehead, part of Regiment 1241, the 2nd Battalion, had to be deployed in the Wüste Kunersdorf sector in order to relieve the greatly weakened units there. In this sector the 69th Army had been able to establish a narrow bridgehead and set up their defences in the former German front lines. Separated by a narrow strip of no-man's-land that was secured with minefields and barbed wire, the Germans and Russians lay opposite each other here in well-built trench systems. Because of the unfavourable terrain on the east bank of the Oder and the more favourable conditions in the Lebus bridgehead, there was no expectation of major attacks in this sector at this time, although smaller attacks could always be reckoned with. On the German side, the possibility of regaining the old front line through local counterattacks resulted in a constant wearing down and weakening of the units committed there.

Artillery and mortars kept up a barrage around the clock, and well-camouflaged snipers took their daily toll. Despite the well-constructed trench system, casualties were relatively high, and measures against the enemy snipers were demanded.

We thus were given the task of constructing several large bunkers in the front line facing the enemy. Each bunker had a firing slit, a table with a sandbag, and two stools. The entrance from the trench was covered with blankets so that it was fully dark inside, enabling concealed observation and well-camouflaged firing. These preparations were for the deployment of our own snipers, but also intended for other purposes. Once the bunkers were ready, two sniping teams were installed in our sector, each consisting of an observer and a sniper. Only one shot was fired from any bunker, leading to an immediate move to the next one. Within three or four days these snipers had bagged nine enemy snipers through observation. For a while we had a rest from enemy snipers, but the fire from other weapons was increased.

Along the Oder between Frankfurt and Küstrin the deceptive peace lasted until 10 April. Apart from the daily artillery duels, mainly one-sided from the Soviet side, and the storm troop and reconnaissance tasks day and night in the individual sectors, no special engagements marked the days from the end of March. From the German side the constant reinforcement of enemy forces and equipment could not help but be noticed. More and more Soviet artillery were deployed, more and more batteries fired themselves in, and hitherto unknown infantry units appeared. Vehicle traffic on the known Oder bridges steadily increased, while on the German side it was hardly possible to move.

Apart from our own infantry units, the majority of which were improvised with many inexperienced soldiers, our own artillery and heavy infantry weapons remained silent under their camouflage, the ammunition situation still enabling them to engage the attacking troops at least for the first day of the anticipated major offensive.

All available time, especially at night, was used to improve the positions. The majority of soldiers had no idea of the deadly danger awaiting them, knew nothing of the preparations on the other side. They had no idea of the vast number of enemy tanks prepared to destroy them, of the gun-barrel-to-gun-barrel deployment of the Soviet artillery, so packed together that there was hardly enough room for the crews in their gun positions. However, more and more each day they sensed that something was about to happen that would be far worse than anything yet experienced in this war, and began to realise that it would be a final battle of life and death, man against machine, individual against overwhelming technology, and that the prospects of survival were slight.

The Soviet artillery fired at our infantry positions more than usual with their attritional fire, but this did not develop into an attack, at least not in the Frankfurt–Küstrin sector.

On 14 April local attacks in battalion strength were conducted in the form of a reconnaissance in force in order to uncover weak points in our defences, to reveal our fire system, and to make the German side release, bring forward and deploy its reserves.

On 15 April these attacks were resumed with limited objectives, 32 battalions being involved. East of Seelow the enemy was able to close up to the Heights' positions and breach our lines in various places, but these breaches were cleared by deploying reserves.

SACHSENDORF

In this connection, our regiment was allocated the task on the evening of 14 April of conducting a night counterattack on Vorwerk Sachsendorf to try to stop the enemy that had broken through and clear the breach. The attack was to be supported by four self-propelled guns. The move to the battlefield was made at night in complete silence and without artillery support.

We split up into firing lines and moved towards Vorwerk Sachsendorf. It was pitch-dark and we had problems maintaining our direction and contact with the neighbouring company, so that we had to stop several times to re-establish them. Meanwhile we had become accustomed to the darkness and reached our start line for the counterattack before dawn.

The outlines of the houses in Vorwerk Sachsendorf appeared and our advance became more cautious. Our counterattack had yet to be discovered, but all hell could break loose at any minute. Only the odd Very light rose in the heavens, causing us to stand still, and the usual unaimed firing of infantry weapons could be heard. Where was the enemy, where were their weapons, and when would they discover our counterattack?

We advanced by bounds, using every bit of cover. Suddenly an anti-tank gun opened fire on our self-propelled guns. The enemy had spotted us, and the signal for the counterattack and firing on the enemy in the houses came through the dawn, although precise targets could only be identified with difficulty due to the poor visibility. But it was quickly becoming lighter, so that we could soon recognise details. The enemy also used this improvement, being in the more advantageous position of the defender. We were plastered with machine-gun and mortar fire and were soon suffering considerable casualties. Consequently our counterattack came to a halt short of Vorwerk Sachsendorf at dawn under concentrated Russian artillery, mortar and sniper fire, and we were obliged to dig in with heavy losses. The snipers in particular exacted many casualties and many officer cadets who had no entrenching tools had to scrape out shelter scoops in the ground with their bare hands in order to get minimal shelter and protection. As I had landed in a shell-hole, it was not difficult for me to transform it into a halfway reasonable foxhole.

Now we used every gap in the firing to tend to our wounded comrades in their scoops, shell-holes and foxholes, but, because of the heavy enemy activity, it was unfortunately not possible to evacuate them from the fire zone all day.

Our supporting self-propelled guns were forced to withdraw during the morning. We were not able to do this ourselves until the evening, and then again with heavy casualties.

SCHÖNFLIESS

On 16 April, the day the main Soviet offensive began, the enemy managed to effect a breach in the 712th Infantry Division's sector at Schönfliess, so the Panzergrenadier Division 'Kurmark' was given the task of retaking Schönfliess village and the old positions with a counterattack and clear the breach. Our 2nd Battalion and the 2nd Company of the SS Heavy Tank Battalion 502 were assigned to this task.

I can still recall that afternoon of 16 April as our Battalion with the 'Tiger' tank company stormed the village virtually by surprise and without encountering much resistance. The Russian units were completely surprised, not having expected any resistance after apparently having attained their objectives, and were using the opportunity to have a wash, some of them fleeing in their underclothes in an easterly direction. Two T-34s that belatedly opened fire were shot up. Within a few minutes we had charged through the little village and

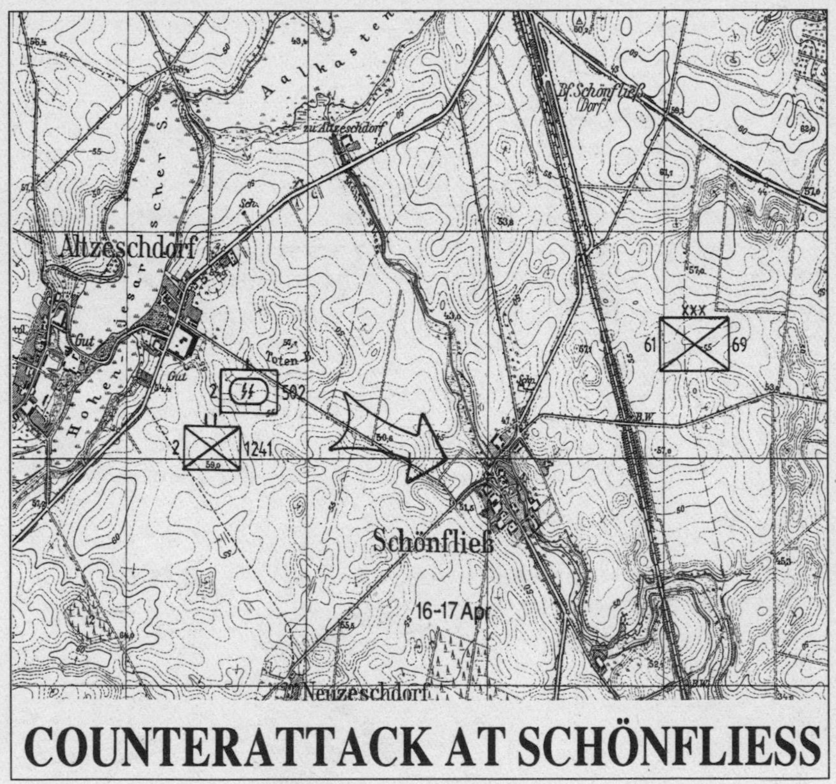

were able to roll up part of the trenches to the east of it and the communication trenches leading to the railway, and occupy the 712th Infantry Division's old defensive trench system, almost without sustaining any losses.

We soon came under intensive fire on our trenches, had to repel a counterattack and immediately suffered considerable casualties. The trenches changed hands several times during the course of the afternoon, unfortunately always with a high rate of casualties to both sides. Finally that evening our aim was reached with the railway embankment and the old front line retaken. That evening, once the fighting had quietened down, we could see that the trenches and the ground between them were full of dead and wounded. Some of the dead

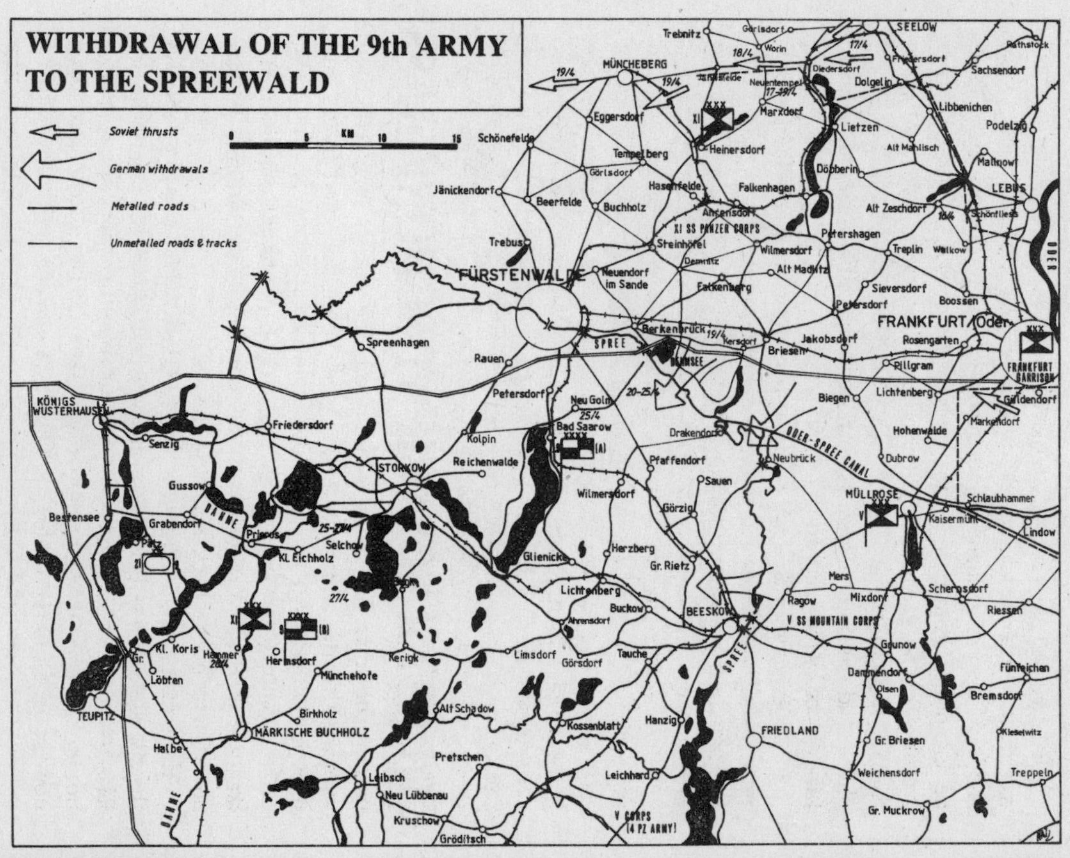
WITHDRAWAL OF THE 9th ARMY
TO THE SPREEWALD
Soviet thrusts
German withdrawals
Metalled roads
Unmetalled roads & tracks
0 5 KM 10 15
ODER
SEELOW
LEBUS
FRANKFURT/Oder
FRANKFURT GARRISON
MÜNCHEBERG
FÜRSTENWALDE
MÜLLROSE
ODER-SPREE CANAL
XI SS PANZER CORPS
V SS MOUNTAIN CORPS
V CORPS (4 PZ ARMY)
SPREE
DAHME
BEESKOW
FRIEDLAND
STORKOW
MÄRKISCHE BUCHHOLZ
TEUPITZ
KÖNIGS WUSTERHAUSEN
Trebnitz
Görlsdorf
Worin
Diedersdorf
Neuentempel
Marxdorf
Dolgelin
Sachsendorf
Rathstock
Libbenichen
Podelzig
Lietzen
Alt Mahlisch
Mallnow
Döbberin
Falkenhagen
Alt Zeschdorf
Schönfliess
Petershagen
Treplin
Wulkow
Heinersdorf
Eggersdorf
Schönefelde
Tempelberg
Görlsdorf
Hasenfelde
Ahrensdorf
Jänickendorf
Beerfelde
Buchholz
Steinhöfel
Wilmersdorf
Alt Madlitz
Trebus
Neuendorf im Sande
Falkenberg
Sieversdorf
Boossen
Petersdorf
Berkenbrück
Kersdorf
Briesen
Jakobsdorf
Rosengarten
Pillgram
Spreenhagen
Rauen
Petersdorf
Neu Golm
Bad Saarow
Biegen
Lichtenberg
Güldendorf
Markendorf
Hohenwalde
Dubrow
Drakendorf
Neubrück
Friedersdorf
Senzig
Kolpin
Reichenwalde
Pfaffendorf
Sauen
Wilmersdorf
Görzig
Schlaubhammer
Kaisermühl
Lindow
Gussow
Bestensee
Grabendorf
Prieros
Selchow
Kl. Eichholz
Pätz
Glienicke
Herzberg
Gr. Rietz
Lichtenberg
Buckow
Ahrensdorf
Mers
Ragow
Mixdorf
Schernsdorf
Riessen
Kl. Koris
Hammer
Löbten
Hermsdorf
Münchehofe
Kerigk
Limsdorf
Görsdorf
Tauche
Grunow
Dammendorf
Olsen
Fünfeichen
Bremsdorf
Kieselwitz
Birkholz
Alt Schadow
Kossenblatt
Hanzig
Gr. Briesen
Halbe
Pretschen
Leichhardt
Weichensdorf
Treppeln
Leibsch
Neu Lübbenau
Kruschow
Gröditsch
Gr. Muckrow

were from the fighting on the day before and among them were soldiers wearing German uniforms without shoulder straps, presumably Seydlitz Troops.

Once we had seen to the wounded and taken them to the rear, we received the order to take the dead from the trenches and no-man's-land and bury them in shell and bomb craters, i.e. cover them up. This had to be abandoned from time to time due to enemy activity. We were also getting tired, not having had much sleep over the last few days. As we could only do this job near the enemy by crawling and lying down, many of the dead remained unburied. Apart from mortar and rifle fire, we were left in peace by the enemy on 17 April.

In the evening of 17 April we were relieved in the Schönfliess sector and moved to defensive positions either side of Neuentempel, where Russian spear-heads had broken through and were attacking towards Müncheberg.

On 19 April elements of the Panzergrenadier Division 'Kurmark' and the starkly decimated remains of our regiment were given the task of establishing a front facing north and east along the autobahn between Berkenbrück and Kersdorf and holding it until the arrival of SS units coming from the north. Having done this, we withdrew in accordance with our orders to the Dehmsee lake, and then on 20 April occupied a sector of the Spree east of Fürstenwalde.

On 21 April there was increased enemy activity on the far bank of the Spree. Bitter house-fighting broke out in Fürstenwalde and the northern part of the town had to be abandoned. The troops engaged, then withdrew to the southern bank of the Spree occupied by us and reinforced our defence.

Then on 25 April the remains of the regiment assembled in the Golm area and marched via Storkow to Selchow, where on 27 April Russian attacks were beaten back with heavy losses.

The remains of the 'Kurmark' and Regiment 1241 then regrouped in the late afternoon of 27 April in the woods south of the Selchower-See lake, where the supply and other vehicles were tidied up and everything not strictly necessary for combat was destroyed. Our destination was now the senior forest warden's lodge at Hammer.

HELL AT HALBE

We, the remains of our regiment, now in company strength, paraded for the last time in the war near the forest warden's lodge at Hammer on 28 April. We paraded with the 9th Army's southern armoured spearhead, which consisted of fourteen 'Tiger' tanks, assault guns, APCs and motor vehicles, arranged as follows:

- The vanguard, consisting of the 2nd Company, SS Heavy Tank Battalion 502;
- The remains of Regiment 1241 as close infantry escort for the tanks;
- Part of an APC company of the 'Kurmark';
- The Reconnaissance & Pioneer Platoon of SS Heavy Tank Battalion 502;
- 1st Company, SS Heavy Tank Battalion 502, with the battalion commander and signals officers, and a mortar battery;
- The rest of SS Heavy Tank Battalion 502 with a self-propelled four-barrelled anti-aircraft gun, motorcycles, ambulance and medical officer.

This armoured spearhead had the task: 'together with the northern armoured spearhead of breaking through the Red Army's cordon around the remains of the 9th Army in the Halbe area and thrusting through in a westerly direction towards the 12th Army.'[1]

In this last issue of orders, emphasis was given to the hope in (now) Major-General Langkeit's last 'Panthers', the combat elements of Panzergrenadier Division 'Kurmark' and SS-Major Hartrampf's SS Heavy Tank Battalion 502.

This 28 April, which began so calmly as we were detailed off as tank escorts to the armoured column, and ended so tragically, will always remain in my memory. We did not know then that we were preparing for a journey into hell and for most of us it would be our death. Our platoon in the strength of one officer and fifteen grenadiers was assigned to the leading 'Tiger' tanks of the spearhead, whose platoon commander was SS-Second Lieutenant Kuhnke.

I found myself on the second tank, commanded by SS-Sergeant Major Ernst Streng, and with SS-Sergeant Ott as the driver. We fastened

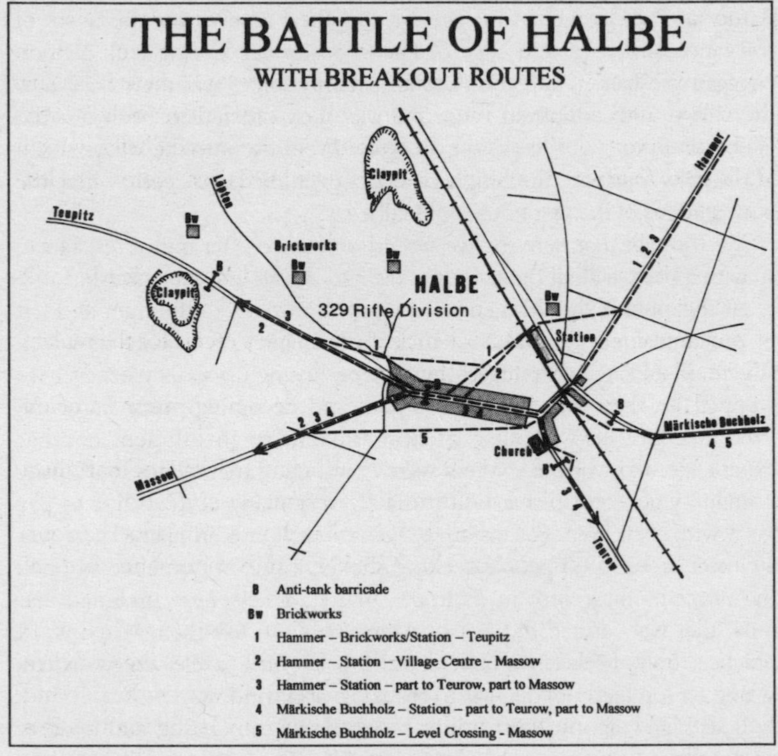

ourselves on to the tank mountings with our belts and equipment straps, so that we would have our hands free for firing our rifles and panzerfausts, and for throwing grenades.

At about 1800 hours on 28 April, the heavy weapons fired a barrage on Halbe, after which the guns were blown up. Then at about 1830 hours our armoured column moved out of the assembly area towards Märkisch Buchholz and Halbe. We thrust through Märkisch Buchholz without encountering any significant resistance, then along a woodland track towards Halbe. The northern armoured spearhead of the Panzergrenadier Division 'Kurmark' was also rolling along another woodland track towards Halbe. Short halts for observation and reconnaissance delayed our drive.

A Russian anti-tank barrier in front of Halbe caused the first big delay.

A mortar battery went into action and fired a salvo on the nests of resistance on the eastern edge of Halbe, while our leading tank platoon engaged the barrier, and the Russian security forces withdrew back into the village. Our armoured vanguard was then ordered to push on into Halbe, and our 'Tiger' tanks set off again. We drove into the village south of the railway station, reaching a straight street lined with trees, where the back gardens of the first houses of Halbe lay.

We thought that here too we would only encounter minor resistance, as with a blast, all hell broke loose. We had driven into an ambush!

At this point I should mention that in the woods to the right and left of our armoured column, if a little further back, following us was a stream of soldiers and refugees, who kept closing up to us whenever we stopped. In their fear of losing contact and becoming prisoners of the Russians, but also because of non-existent or insufficient combat experience, most of the soldiers were conducting themselves in a totally unmilitary fashion, so that unfortunately very many of them had to pay for it with their lives. For instance, behind each tank in Halbe there was a cluster of 40 to 60 people seeking shelter, and every time we stopped the numbers increased. In addition, many soldiers were unarmed and most that were armed did not or were unable to use their weapons. In practice, only the leading tank could fire forward, while we grenadiers sitting on top fired obliquely into the roofs and windows.

It was now about 2000 hours as we drove into Halbe and another anti-tank barrier appeared before us, but this time open. The leading tank had got to within about 70 metres when it fired a shot with its gun to clear the way, drove on and stopped about 30 metres from the barrier.

Suddenly the inferno began, with concentrated anti-tank gun fire from ahead, artillery and mortar fire from above and rifle fire from the roofs and windows of the houses right and left of the street. The artillery fire with explosive shrapnel and phosphorous shells and the mortar bombs caused especially frightful casualties among the uncountable, exposed and crammed-together groups of people. The street was immediately filled with dead and wounded. Panic, confusion and deadly fear could be seen in the faces of the living, as cries for help came from the wounded and dying.

Our leading tank received a direct hit and started burning. Our second tank tried to turn, got stuck and was hit by a phosphorous shell and also caught fire. The phosphorous shells burst with glowing white splashes on the tank, and there was phosphor everywhere on our steel helmets and tent-halves. Stinking smoke erupted as the tank began to burn. The crew bailed out and we also jumped off and ran to the third tank. (I later learnt that the crew managed to put the fire out and get the tank going again.)

Houses were on fire everywhere. We wanted to climb on to the third tank, but gave up and tried to establish some order behind it, which however did not fully work out. Together with other soldiers, we tended to the wounded and also persuaded the majority of the people not to seek cover behind the tanks but in and between the houses, so that the tanks could manoeuvre, but we had also to witness the dead and wounded being crushed under the tanks. The street was full of dead and wounded and every minute there were more. Meanwhile fighting had begun in the houses.

With this we got enough air and space to be able to direct our fire at the roofs and windows in the direction of the anti-tank barrier. Slowly the paralysis of the first shock began to wear off, especially among the combat-experienced soldiers, and more and more joined in, halfway restoring order out of chaos in helping the wounded and getting them off the street into the houses and gardens, and in using their weapons.

We, the soldiers on the tanks and those behind them, found, as so often during the war, that in situations like this one's ability to think becomes blocked and trained reflexes take over. It was only much later that we became fully conscious of what a suicide mission we had been committed to as cannon fodder and what enormous luck we had in coming out of this inferno alive. I still marvel that I came through Halbe hit by neither a bullet nor a splinter and only got some splashes of phosphorous on my steel helmet and tent-half.

Although during the war I had very often as an infantryman been bombarded with weapons of all kinds, especially on the Eastern Front in Russia, I had never experienced such concentrated fire on such a small area and on so many people.

Meanwhile the tanks had turned round and we sat on them with the remainder of the comrades of our platoon. Only eight men of our platoon were still alive, the others having been killed or wounded.

We were glad as our armoured column moved back slowly and we could get away from this frightful section of street. From the railway station we then went south a little and later drove westward through the woods once more.

During the manoeuvring of the 'Tigers' of the leading platoon and the change of direction of the southern armoured spearhead to a new breakthrough sector in the woods south of Halbe, even more soldiers and civilians pressed into the 9th Army's main breakout point in Halbe.

Breakout to the West

Before turning west we made a short halt to unload the wounded and redistribute the officer cadets among the tanks. The officer cadets from the two shot-up tanks were assigned to a reconnaissance APC equipped with a machine-gun, which now took over the lead. We had to reconnoitre towards the autobahn. I sat in the rear of the APC and had to cover the rear through the open door. As I was unable to see properly, I stupidly sat on the APC's rear towing hook, an error I was soon to regret. After having gone about 100 metres, we were shot at from in front and our machine-gun and sub-machine-gunners opened fire. I had not reckoned on the driver suddenly reversing at full speed. I slipped off the towing hook and fell on to the track, turning in such a way that I lay in the direction of travel and on my stomach, pressing myself close to the ground. The tracks of the APC rattled past right and left of my body. Fortunately the APC had sufficient ground clearance. Once the vehicle had gone over and past me, the driver noticed and stopped the APC. Covered by the fire of our machine-guns, I rolled aside and ran back uninjured to the back of the APC. Once more I had been lucky and I also did not have to worry about being laughed at by my comrades. Although there was nothing for me to laugh about, it could have been far worse, and I had to put a good face on it.

With all weapons firing, the APC pulled back to the armoured column, where meanwhile the tanks had turned their turrets to 2 o'clock and opened concentrated fire on an assembly of T-34s and other vehicles. Soon several T-34s were alight, making good targets of the others, which therefore withdrew.

Our 'Tigers' received the order to resume the advance towards the autobahn and those officer cadets in the APC were reallocated to the tanks. I was allocated to the tank commanded by Harlander with four other comrades. We climbed aboard and the armoured column set off once more. After a few hundred metres we came under fire again and our tank was hit in the tracks, but carried on firing.

We had again driven into a concentration of Russian troops, but under the covering fire from our 'Tiger's' crew, the armoured column was able to fight its way through towards the autobahn, and with them also went the rest of the officer cadets of our platoon. I heard nothing more of these comrades, either in the days to follow or later on.

Now it became uncomfortable for us on our immobilised tank. We came under heavy fire from panzerfausts, which fortunately were all fired too high and exploded above us in the trees, showering us with splinters and branches. From the illumination of a Very light we saw that we were in the assembly area of some heavy 'Stalin' tanks, and one of these colossi was already turning its turret in our direction as the light went out. A lightning bang and a frightful howling connected with a strong punch shook our tank, which had received a direct hit. The crew bailed out, shouting: 'Harlander is dead!'

We also jumped off and ran instinctively in the direction of the least noise of combat to the next woodland track, where we dug in. This was the time to keep our nerve. We were completely on our own, our tanks had gone over the hill, there were Russian troops in the woods, exactly where no one knew, and our tank crew had run off in another direction.

The most important questions for us were to establish whether the track was occupied by the enemy and whether it led towards the autobahn. I therefore went along the track in a westerly direction to find out. The track was free of the enemy for about 1,000 metres and led, as we luckily later discovered, to the autobahn.

I was glad to get back to my comrades and to get a little sleep before we marched on.

On the morning of 29 April, it slowly became light as we slipped along the track under cover of the wood. As this led to the west, it had to lead to the autobahn. Suddenly in front of us was the nose of an armoured vehicle. 'Take cover! One man forward to reconnoitre!'

After ten minutes came the report that it was an assault gun. Its crew, who had their dead commander aboard, were about to cross the autobahn under cover of the morning haze, but did not know if the wood opposite was occupied by the enemy or not and were also afraid that there might be flanking anti-tank gunfire along the autobahn, so they were happy to see us and for us to find out for them. A brief order: 'Under simultaneous covering fire, over the autobahn in bounds!' and we were soon on the other side. There were only empty foxholes and

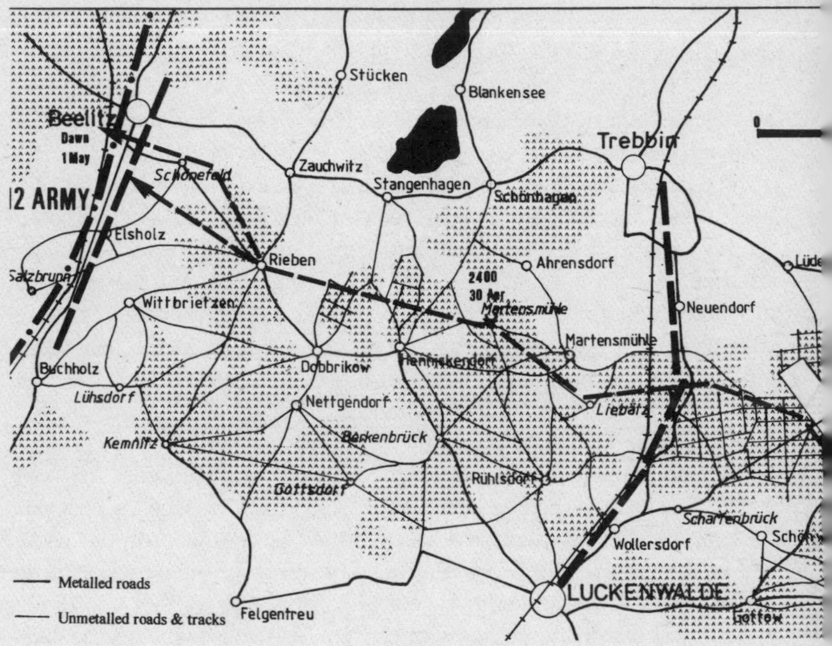

dead bodies on the other side, and for us the possibility of travelling several kilometres with the assault gun in the ordered westerly direction of the breakout to the assembly point at the forest warden's hut at Massow was welcome. We soon found ourselves on a woodland track on which soldiers were moving along in groups of all sizes.

We soon arrived at the 9th Army's assembly point, reported in and received sixteen men's worth of rations and ammunition to divide among the remaining five of us, sufficient to eat ourselves full once more, for we did not know when we would get any more.

Here the extent of the tragedy at Halbe soon became apparent. Many comrades were missing from our unit, the majority of our company of Panzergrenadiers having been killed or wounded; there was no accurate count.

We were again allocated as tank escorts for the coming march, however this time on foot with the task of screening ahead and to the flanks. Our little unit could now keep together and keep an

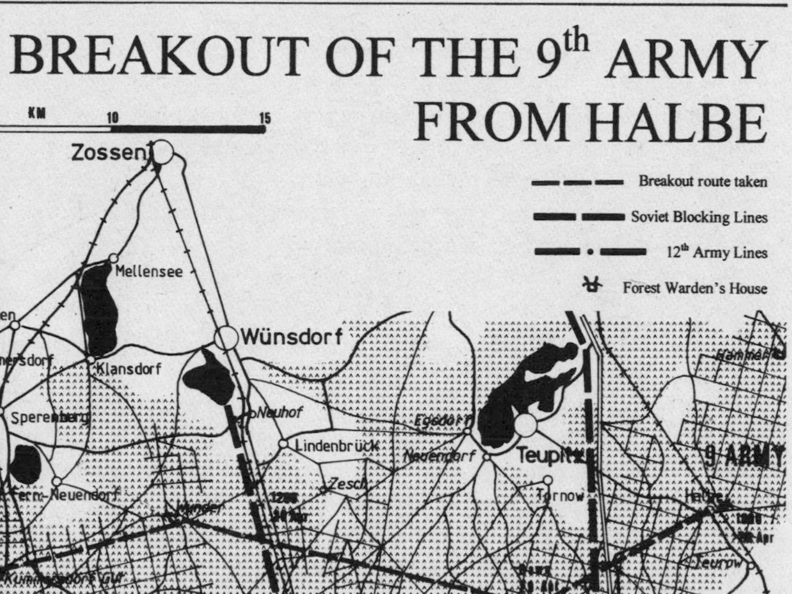

eye on each other, as we were now independent and no longer bound to the tanks.

However, we soon noticed that there was no longer a strong overall command. A leaderless mass of soldiers and refugees was wandering through the woods. Military discipline and comradeship had fallen by the wayside. The majority of soldiers of all ranks moved like sheep around and behind the tanks, trying to get aboard whenever they stopped. Just as in Halbe, hits from anti-tank, artillery and mortar fire and the many air attacks had a catastrophic impact on soldiers and civilians alike. Each impact cost ten to twenty times the number of dead and wounded as under normal combat conditions. At first the wounded were tended to and the dead laid aside in the woods but later, especially at night, this ceased. People became more and more dulled. Hunger and fatigue added to this, and only the fear of becoming prisoners of the Russians drove the soldiers on, regardless of casualties.

This stream of humanity moved not only along the woodland tracks but also left and right in the woods, so that our task of securing the tanks against enemy close-quarter engagement no longer applied, having become illusory.

Not from overwhelming bravery, but from old combat experience, our practice was to use every halt to go further ahead. We knew: 'He who does not get through the enemy cordon within five to ten minutes after it is breached and use the gap, will get the concentrated fire of the Russian weapons on the breakthrough point!'

This was the motto we kept to, and whenever the call was given: 'Infantry forward! Tanks forward!' that was how we acted, whereas, typically in such a situation, the majority of soldiers of all ranks would press back into the woods.

The advantage for us was that the way forward was free for the unfortunately few remaining soldiers and ever fewer tank crews. Each tank crew in the 9th Army's breakthrough to the west was putting its life on the line with the danger of being shot up time and time again, and each time had to face up to this and not pull back into the woods.

On the afternoon of 29 April we drew near to a Russian cordon with strong defensive positions on the line of the railway and road between Baruth and Zossen.[2]

Our little combat team worked its way forward with other soldiers under cover of the woods to the edge, where happily the equivalent of the strength of a battalion of infantry gradually accumulated. Our spearhead had been brought to a halt by tank and anti-tank gunfire from the flanks. As our tanks spread out right and left along the edge of the woods and engaged the enemy tanks and anti-tank guns with their guns, we attacked on a broad front. We crossed the railway line and road in bounds and forced our way to the other side under cover of the concentrated fire from our rifles, panzerfausts and hand grenades into the woods opposite and, once we had broken through and overcome the cordon, thrust through with our tanks to the forest warden's lodge at Wunder.

Here there were combat and front-line-experienced soldiers of all ranks, masters of the tools of war, who did the right thing without orders and still had enough of the spirit of comradeship in them not to leave the wounded behind. There were no exceptions in our little troop. Thus I can remember that an officer was wounded in the leg nearby and called out for help. We carried him out of the immediate danger zone from enemy weapons into cover, saw to his wound and transported him to the forest warden's lodge at Wunder, where we laid him down with the other wounded and had to leave him to his fate.

It was much later after the war that I first began often to think about what had happened to the many wounded and how the mass of soldiers and above all the refugees had fared when they tried to get through the enemy cordon and positions after us without the protection from our tanks and the effective use of massed weapons. There must have been some frightful tragedies, similar to those terrible hours in Halbe.

Once we had reached the forest warden's lodge at Wunder there was a halt with a forward security screen until the mass had caught up again and there was a danger of becoming a target for enemy aircraft. Then the column moved on through the dusk towards Kummersdorf.

We had to cross several open spaces during the night, each time the infantry and tanks, fighting and shooting, taking cover and making sure that we five stayed together. With this came great fatigue, hunger and thirst and the desire simply to remain lying there with the consequent danger of falling asleep. It cost us much effort to keep forcing ourselves on and remain awake. We avoided the open spaces and tried to remain in the woods, which was not always possible. I am still amazed today that in this unholy turmoil we managed to maintain contact with the leading tanks.

Everywhere there was firing, the cries of the wounded, and the dead lying around, as we overcame several enemy positions and cordons. The 12th Army's front line should be immediately behind the last Russian cordon. Would we ever reach it alive? Our leading tank drove out of the woods, was immediately engaged by the Russian anti-tank guns, and pulled back again. There was now artillery fire on our edge of the woods and we had to turn south to get away from the road. About 15 minutes later our last two remaining 'Tiger' crews attacked out of the woods to the north of us and a broad stream of soldiers and refugees poured over the open ground to the west and north west.

Unfortunately, as we later discovered, that was the most strongly manned sector of the Russian cordon between Schönefeld and Wittbrietzen. The Russians fired flat out with tanks, anti-tank guns, Stalin-organs, artillery and mortars on the defenceless people on the open ground, as bombers and ground-attack aircraft joined in. Death struck mercilessly again and reaped a rich harvest. There was no cover for the soldiers and civilians, being completely unprotected under this murderous fire. Mercilessly, the remains of the 9th Army were given their death blow only a few hundred metres from the protection of the 12th Army's front line.

Of the heavy tanks we now only had Klust's 'Königstiger' from No. 1 Company and Streng's from No. 2 Company. Streng's tank had been hit several times during this decisive breakthrough, but he was still able to engage in a tank duel and knock out three T-34s, but then his tank was hit by an anti-tank gun and burst into flames. After a dozen severe hits, this time the tank could not be saved. It was the tank that I had been on in Halbe and which had been hit by a phosphorous shell and caught fire there. A few minutes later SS-Second Lieutenant Klust's tank was also knocked out, thus writing off all fourteen 'Tiger' tanks that the 9th Army had sent to join up with the 12th Army.

For the first time I held my four comrades of Regiment 1241 back from attacking as we had done so often in the last days and weeks. We remained lying at the edge of the woods and watched the course of the uneven fight. It was not fear or cowardice, but military common sense and combat experience that led me to this decision, the correctness of this being demonstrated only a few minutes later.

An APC with Hitler Youth leaders appeared from the left flank and drove into cover near us. They had the task of warning the remains of the 9th Army about this strong enemy cordon and directing it southwest towards Wittbrietzen. These youngsters looked just like Seydlitz Troops. What an irony of fate for the many that had fallen on this open space and the soldiers and civilians that had been wounded.

While death awaited north of Wittbrietzen, the way south of it was 'an easy walk' to the 12th Army's front line. Had this APC with its certainly courageous crew only arrived two or three hours earlier, the 9th Army's spearhead could have been headed in this direction.

With unfortunately so few soldiers, we turned to the southwest, and within about 1,200 metres reached the described spot under cover of the woods, from where it was only a short distance over open ground to the woods opposite. The members of the 12th Army dug in on the edge of the woods were expecting us and directed us back behind the railway line.

We could hardly believe that we had managed to make the last section alive and without having fired a shot. It was only later that we realised how often death had stretched out a finger towards us, in the truest sense of the word our constant companion, and what enormous luck we had had to belong to the few to have survived the fighting on the Oder Front, the Hell of Halbe and the death march to the 12th Army's lines.[3]

During the course of the morning of 1 May we were taken in open goods wagons that had been awaiting us to Belzig and accommodated there in private houses. Friendly, good people looked after us, let us have a bath, we were able to change our underwear, eat and above all else sleep, sleep, sleep until the afternoon of 2 May.

We then reported to a control point and were given our marching orders to march to the Elbe via Ziesar, Genthin and Tangermünde. To avoid air attacks, we marched by night, covering some of the distance on foot and then were taken on a 12th Army truck. By the morning of 3 May we were already in Genthin, and that night reached the Elbe near Fischbeck. Now we had a chance to sound out the situation and organise fresh rations for our march. Ferry traffic had been established on the Elbe using all kinds of means to get across, and in Tangermünde engineers were working on an emergency bridge. Wounded were being sent across first. As we were not in a hurry, we looked for some food with a view to crossing the Elbe that evening.

However, it was not that easy. The pressure was great, and after an attempt to swim across at night, it was only on the morning of 6 May that we reached the other bank by ferry, as there was a big queue waiting to cross by the emergency bridge that had meanwhile been completed.

On the other side we laid down our weapons to soldiers of the 102nd US Infantry Division at an assembly point, and were searched. Despite my protests, the pay books and nametags of fallen soldiers, names and addresses were taken away and thrown into a burning barrel. Then we were formed up into a column of nameless prisoners and marched off towards Stendal.

We were then later loaded into trucks like cattle, sixty men to a truck, standing and secured with nets and ropes, and driven to Calbe-an-der-Milbe, where we were accommodated under the open sky in a prisoner-of-war camp with a capacity of 80,000 men that was secured by a barbed wire fence and sentries. Whenever a prisoner approached within ten metres of the fence, he was immediately shot. A normal US Army 4 Man/Day cold ration pack had to suffice for eighty prisoners. There was no warm food.

One week later we were transported to Magdeburg, handed over to the British and accommodated in the Bolde machine factory. A few days later we were moved to Völpke on the Magdeburg Heath, where rumours circulated that we were to be sent to work in the French mines.

As I had absolutely no desire to do this, I used a suitable opportunity to head off on my own to my home town in the Erzgebirge Mountains. After a march full of adventures, including several days in Russian captivity, I reached my goal on 12 June 1945.

In the postwar years Rudi Lindner served in the Neue Volksarmee (NVA) of the German Democratic Republic, retiring with the rank of Major-General.

NOTES

1. Three previous unsuccessful attempts had been made to break out by elements of the 9th Army, the first on 26 April to the southwest was checked near Baruth, the second on the 27th to the west near Zersch and Neuhof, and the third on the morning of the 28th to the northwest.
2. In position here were strong forces of the 3rd Guards Tank Army and further back the 69th Army, including two infantry divisions north of Baruth.
3. In the Soviet accounts they claim to have killed 60,000 German troops and captured 120,000 in the 9th Army's attempted breakout to join up with the 12th Army. However, from German accounts it is estimated that some 40,000 troops and 120,000 civilians managed to get through. The bodies of 22,000 German troops were later buried at Halbe cemetery.

RETREAT VIA HALBE

Erwin W. Bartmann

Erwin Bartmann served in the 4th Company, 1st Battalion, 1st Regiment, Leibstandarte-SS 'Adolf Hitler' from May 1941 onwards. After recovery from a lung wound sustained at the battle of Kursk, he became an instructor as an SS-Unterscharführer (Sergeant) at their training depot at Spreenhagen, east of Berlin. In April 1945 the depot was dissolved to form various units needed for the defence of the capital, and Bartmann found himself in the newly founded SS-Regiment 'Falke'.

We arrived at the Oder Front at Lichtenberg on 17 April 1945 on the country road between Pillgram and Markendorf, and on the same day were assigned to positions on the edge of a wood. I was in charge of a heavy machine-gun section, which had two machine-guns on mountings. We dug ourselves in on the edge of the woods and set up our weapons aimed as instructed.

Then I took two men and had a look around the area. We found a small distillery and searched it, finding a considerable amount of schnapps. At first we did not know what to do with it. Should we leave it to the Russians, who would then become too drunk to fight? Eventually we decided to destroy it, but took some along for our comrades. When we got back to the position we were visited by our commander, who gave us a talk about 'fighting to the last man', then left us, wishing us good luck for the future.

The night was quiet. We could hear gunfire in the distance from the direction of Frankfurt-on-the-Oder, but did not know whether they were our guns firing or the Russians'; however this did not bother us as they were too far away.

On 18 April we prepared for action and that afternoon attacked the Russians in our sector. The infantry companies went ahead and we followed them at a set distance, as we had learned in our training. Suddenly we heard the sound of Stalin-organs, just like our baptism under fire in Russia. I shouted to my section: 'Stalin-organs! Take cover!' and we survived this assault. SS-Second Lieutenant Gessner was killed in this attack.

Towards evening the orders came to return to our old location and resume our defensive positions. Unfortunately we had lost two dead in this move, as the Russians fired at us with heavy mortars and I got some small splinters in my face, but nothing serious.

The 19th passed relatively peacefully and we buried our dead in Lichtenberg cemetery. That afternoon we saw Russian troops and tanks on the Frankfurt/Oder–Müllrose road going towards Müllrose. The tanks had German women and girls, and even children, tied to their gun barrels as they drove past us, but we could not do anything about it. We did not want to shoot our own women and children. We had to watch the Russians taking up positions that would cost us dear next day.

At 0230 hours on the morning of 20 April the Russians made an all-out attack on us in which they suffered heavy casualties. Then at 0530 hours they attacked again after a heavy artillery and mortar bombardment. They advanced on a broad front in three ranks. We let them come up to within 100 metres and then opened up. We had no time to change barrels and our heavy machine-guns became so overheated with firing that we had to stop. We then moved back to the reserve position that had been prepared for us, but these positions turned out to be only a half to one metre deep.

At about 1800 hours the enemy attacked once more, using aircraft and tanks, but were unable to break through. The Russians then dug in opposite us and waited for nightfall. With evening came orders to send out a reconnaissance patrol to find out how many Russians were opposite us. I sent two men forward to find out what was in front of us, having been appointed the sector commander. The situation was really bad, as there was no longer a proper unit. We were a thrown-together crowd of *Wehrmacht*, *Volkssturm* and Hitler Youth, anyone capable of carrying a weapon. Most of the officers had vanished. Only one young second lieutenant came and gave us orders before disappearing again. My company commander was only eighteen, with no combat experience, and I did not meet him again until we crossed the Elbe.

Retreat via Halbe

On 21 April I met a senior officer cadet, my platoon commander, who told me that our regimental commander, SS-Lieutenant-Colonel Rosenbusch, had shot himself.

We were surrounded and rejoined our lines again at the village of Petersdorf, near Briesen. We were told that a train would be loading at Briesen station to take us to a location where we could be better deployed. We waited there a while for the promised train but it did not come. There were thousands of refugees waiting at the station with their luggage, as well as a large number of soldiers of all arms of the service. We eventually gave up and set off on foot towards the autobahn, where we knew where we were, withdrawing there with other units and taking up defensive positions.

The Russians attacked again at 1200 hours that day, but this time with tanks, ground-attack aircraft and so-called Seydlitz Troops. After a while and some heavy fighting, we had to abandon these positions. By this time my group had grown a little. I had acquired some Hungarian soldiers fighting on our side. They were all young and inexperienced, armed with a rifle and ten rounds of ammunition, and I wondered what one earth I could do with them. But when the opportunity came, they were at the Russians with knives, and I shot some Russians on fire with a Very pistol; they were that close. Then we had to retreat again and I lost my Hungarian friends, so our group became small once more.

I was then allocated with my men to positions close to the Berlin–Frankfurt/Oder autobahn, where there were only individual troops in position. The Russians were expected to come along the autobahn, but they did not come along the south side, but switched to the north side, heading for Fürstenwalde, and bypassed us.

We then went on from one German-held village to another, looking for something to eat, as my men only had their iron rations. People need something to eat. Without food and with hunger in one's stomach, one cannot fight. In one village we found the headquarters of a general, whose name I have forgotten. We reported to the sentry, who sent us to the orderly room, where we met the general. He asked us our circumstances and we told him, saying that we had not eaten for some time and had no food left. He looked at the group and then gave us a chit for the kitchen, where we were given food for several days. We were given as much bread and sausage as we could carry and a hot meal of pork and potatoes. We sat down in a barn and stuffed ourselves before moving on.

Near Storkow we met SS-Lieutenant-Colonel Junghans, who asked me what unit I belonged to and I told him about having been in action at Lichtenberg. He asked whether I would join him as he was looking for more men, so we went to his command post and were briefed. He asked me if I and my men would like to be his bodyguard. So I followed him everywhere. His command consisted of various units and we drove from battalion to battalion, urging the commanders to form a proper front and hold on to it. We drove over our old training grounds, which I knew well, driving through Markgrafpieske to Spreenhagen. As we came to the edge of the village we saw white sheets fastened to the windows and came under Russian mortar and rifle fire. We carried on towards Spreeau, looking for another *Waffen-SS* unit said to be there, but this unit had already redeployed to the west some time before. There we discovered that the Russians were already in occupation of Spreeau and had shot some German soldiers and in particular members of the *Waffen-SS* that had been betrayed to them by an old man who lived in a house set apart from the others there, so he was shot too.

We then drove back by detours to his command post for the latest information before driving back to visit our units. The Russians made some short attacks but we were able to hold our front, although it was only a matter of time. We were always prodding the Russians with SS-Lieutenant-Colonel Junghans, and one never knew what to expect next.

Next day, 24 April, our commander went with an armoured unit to attack a farmstead taken by the Russians the previous day. He wanted to retake this farmstead as it had strategic value, lying in a commanding position for the Russians to make an attack. Unfortunately this undertaking fell through and we lost our commander, who was wounded. As we were later told, the field hospital he was in was overrun, and he was killed.

Once more we were without a leader. We tagged on to various units, but there was always an element of mistrust whether they were ours, or Seydlitz Troops.

We came to an abandoned farmstead and thought that we might find something to eat there. A sentry was posted and my men searched the house. We found some canned sardines in oil in the cellar and started eating. After a little while I went upstairs again and found a Russian sitting there, eating our sardines. I immediately cut him down with a burst from my sub-machine-gun. As I then emerged into the yard, I saw a T-34 standing there. I shouted into the house: 'The Russians are in the yard!'

Now it was a case of out of the house, but not across the yard. We found a window out of which we climbed and came to a high wall that encompassed the yard and garden. We clambered over the wall and saw more Russians coming over an open field only 100 metres off. We ran as fast we could into a wood and reassembled.

We tagged on to other units, but it was not the same as having a properly led unit. We were on our way to Halbe, but first had to go through a wood already occupied by the Russians, where we found the forester and his family, his wife and three children, lying shot. The forester had lost his boots and been shot through the head. His house had been ransacked. Here I came across one of my old recruits, who had been wounded in the leg and was unable to move quickly. We exchanged a few words and then moved on.

Before we came to the Halbe pocket I came across a container of alcohol that we mixed with apple juice and then steadily worked our way through until it was empty. As I see it today, without this mixture on an empty stomach, we could never have got out of the pocket.

In the woods we met soldiers and refugees with the last possessions that they had been able to save. Among them were also many officers, generals and their staffs.

Our plan was to get straight through to Berlin. As a Berliner I thought that it would be better in Berlin than in the confusion of war. Now that I think about it, it was a blessing that we did not make it. Many of my former comrades failed to escape from the Halbe pocket, losing their lives on that battlefield, where they were slaughtered by the Russians.

We must have been on the edge of the pocket when we emerged from the woods and saw a country road running from left to right with a hillock on either side of the road on each of which was a Russian gun. The only way was to plough through the middle. We waited until the gun on the left fired and the one on the right was re-loading, resulting in a slight delay, which we used with some success. All my men came through, some with slight wounds, but the main thing was that we all came out of that confusion alive and well.

Once more we were without an officer and we set off again to the west. We then met a long column of soldiers and refugees trying to save their skins, and we followed them. We came to the weapon-proving ranges at Kummersdorf, where we had to fight the Russians yet again. Beyond Kummersdorf, I and a few *Waffen-SS* comrades found ourselves in an unending column of soldiers of all arms of the *Wehrmacht*, generals and senior officers with their staffs.

Again we came up against Seydlitz Troops as we went through the woods. As was later discovered, the Seydlitz Troops were under the command of Russian commissars. We were attacked in the woods by Russian infantry and Seydlitz Troops. As we went along a firebreak they moved parallel to us and then attacked us from the side. The Seydlitz Troops wore German uniforms but were armed with Russian sub-machine-guns. They kept on attacking us. Those that could not carry on and remained behind mixed in with the column. When one appeared with an armband in his pocket with the words 'Komitee Freies Deutschland', one of the officers came up shouting: 'Where are the SS? This man must be shot.' I told him to do it himself, if he wanted him shot. (I disliked these gentlemen of the senior staff intensely. At that time everyone was only thinking of saving their own skin.) We moved from place to place, from south to north, and back to the south. The long procession of human beings went from one road junction to another, meeting up with other units.

From then on we went cross-country. On 28 April I met up with my last company commander again. He was with two other officers from our old unit. We went through Beelitz, Belzig and Ziesar to Genthin, where we found a house whose inhabitants did not want to flee. We were so tired and hungry that they shared some food with us and we went to bed. That was the first time I had slept in a bed since 17 April. Next morning we went down to the Elbe, where near Jerichow there was a sunken barge containing foodstuffs. Much had already vanished, but we found sweets, chocolate and other fine things, even some bottles of schnapps. We had some pillowcases, which we stuffed full and took with us and gave some to the people with whom we had spent the night. Then we went on looking for a boat to take us over the Elbe. We found a hidden one that looked as if it could take us across to the other bank. Then we hid ourselves in some bushes so that the Americans, who were on the other side of the Elbe, could not see us.

That evening at about 1800 hours an American officer came across on a ferry and sought to take our soldiers back across with him, but demanded watches, rings, pistols, and anything of value. We remained, determined to make our own way across.

That evening a unit arrived with a general staff and everything that went with it. They wanted to confiscate our boat to save their own lives, but we

1 Werner Mihan in the uniform of a Luftwaffe Flak Auxiliary in 1943 (*Mihan*)

2 Panther (PzKpfw V) tanks being checked over. (*Author's collection*)

3 Fifteen-year-old Friedrich Grasdorf manning the flak defences outside Hanover in the autumn of 1944. (*Grasdorf*)

4 Friedrich Grasdorf with one of the guns his unit took to the Oder front. (*Grasdorf*)

5 Colonel Helmut von Lösecke, commander of Panzergrenadier Regiment 90. (*Averdieck*)

6 A Panzer IV wrecked in the terrible bombardments in the battle for the Seelow Heights. (Chronos-Film)

7 A German infantryman with an MG 42, nicknamed 'Spandau', which could fire up to 1,000 rounds a minute. (*Fleischer*)

8 A Soviet T-34/85 tank after wading a river. (*Author's collection*)

9 Rudi Lindner in 1945 wearing the uniform of a police captain. (*Lindner*)

10 Rudi Lindner (centre) as a Colonel in the East German National *Volksarmee* with his staff. (*Lindner*)

11 Rudi Lindner (right) outside the Seelow Museum commemorating the battles of the Oderbruch and the Seelow Heights of 1945. (*Lindner*)

12 One of the last four 'Tiger IIs' (PzKpfw VI) of the Panzer Regiment 'Kurmark' deliberately abandoned in a swamp after running out of fuel and ammunition before their crews joined up with the 12th Army on 1 May 1945. (*Fleischer*)

13 Erwin Bartmann in 1944 as an NCO in the Liebstandarte-SS Adolf Hitler. (*Bartmann*)

14 German soldiers as prisoners of the Americans. (*Fleischer*)

15 Erwin Bartmann at Zhukov's Command Post on the Reitwein Spur in 1992. (*Author's collection*)

16 A dead horse team in the aftermath of the Halbe breakout. (*Chronos-Film*)

17 Soviet anti-tank guns being brought into Berlin. (*Chronos-Film*)

18 Gustaf-Adolf Pourroy (1918) as second lieutenant of the 'Maikäfer' Garde Fusilier Regiment in the First World War. (*G.A. Pourroy Jnr*)

19 Pourroy's paybook as Adjutant of the 3/115 Siemensstadt *Volksturm* Battalion. (Siemens Archives)

20 View of the central cattle market that the Siemensstadt Battalion had to defend, with the footbridge used by the Soviet troops, as seen in 2002 after considerable demolition work (*Author's collection*)

21 The fountain at the junction of Friedenstrasse and Palisadenstrasse, where combatants of both sides as well as the civilian population refreshed themselves during the fighting, as seen today with the wall of the St Georg Cemetery in the background. (*Author's collection*)

22 Waltraut Lötzke, who died in Werner Mihan's arms on 4 May 1945, having been mortally wounded in their breakout attempt. (*Mihan*)

23 *Luftwaffe* Sergeant Major Walter Krause of Werner Mihan's unit, who was killed in the breakout attempt on 2 May 1945. (*Mihan*)

24 The Charlottenburg Bridge in Spandau in 1948 over which Werner Mihan's group had to fight their way on the morning of 2 May 1945. (*Mihan*)

25 Destroyed Hanomag armoured personnel carrier in the streets of Berlin. (*Author's Collection*)

26 Lieutenant Colonel Theodor von Dufving in 1945 before becoming Chief of Staff to the LVIth Panzer Corps. (*Georg von Dufving*)

27 Colonel Theodor von Dufving after ten years as a prisoner of the NKVD back in uniform with the Bundeswehr in 1962 (*Georg von Dufving*)

28 The Zoo flak tower, which formed the core of the Berlin defences, after having been stripped of its guns. (*Author's Collection*)

refused to give it up. Then the general came personally to confiscate our boat, but we came to an agreement that we would go first across the Elbe and that two men would bring the boat back to rescue the general.

We landed in an American artillery position on the other bank. There were no sentries to be seen; everyone was asleep. It must have been about midnight.

We made our way slowly through the woods. We could only move at night, as by day the Americans and British went through the woods shooting in every direction, thinking that if there were any Germans there they would quickly give themselves up. Our intention was to make for the SS Field Hospital at Königslutter, as I had two wounds in my right leg as a farewell present from the Russians. They were not deep, but needed bandaging.

We reached the field hospital at about 6 o'clock in the morning. A nursing sister let us in and took us to the senior doctor. We told him our stories and, after a short time, he made his decision. The three officers could go to a ward and were allocated beds, while I was sent to the cellar with a mattress. I was tended to, was given some food and had my leg bandaged. I had no more contact with my fellow travellers.

On 13 May a sister came and told me that I would have to obtain a pass from the mayor in order to stay at the hospital, which specialised in seriously wounded and burned cases. I made myself ready. It was a fine sunny spring day, and after breakfast I made my way to the mayor's office. The field hospital was on a road leading up a hill. I went along the street. Everything was quiet, no shooting, no thunder from the guns, all was peaceful, when suddenly there were two hands on my shoulders and I heard just the one word: 'Schutzstaffel'. I was not wearing any uniform, just leather trousers, a shirt and pullover. I had a handkerchief in my pocket and had hidden my paybook in the lining of my trousers.

As it was a Sunday, the mayor's office was not open, and I was locked in a cell in the prison. The people who had arrested me were former prisoners from Dachau concentration camp, as I was told later. I wanted to return to the field hospital to have my leg re-bandaged, but about four days later six Americans arrived with two machine-guns, two sub-machine-guns and two pistols. The door flew open and there stood these heavily armed men. I thought it was the end. One never knows what is going to happen with the Americans, those trigger-happy people. I thought they might take me back to the hospital, but we went by jeep to Helmstedt, to a building where I first experienced the American boot. Then into a room where I was interrogated with boots and a small baton. The questioning was very one-sided, as I had to accept everything that was said. After this interrogation I was taken to the town hall, where I was the first in my cell. There were already several prisoners in other cells. During the course of the afternoon my one-man cell slowly filled until by evening there were about twelve prisoners. Three days later we were loaded on trucks and then driven off into the unknown.

We were then handed over to the British Army and came to an old camp that had been occupied by Poles. When the Poles had left on liberation they took with them all the doors and windows from the buildings. Here were all soldiers with a political connection, SS and SA. We reported to the camp administration at the entrance and were then sent on to an old concentration camp at the Hermann Göring Factory near Brunswick. I was one of the first there. The British administration then looked for people to work for the British Army. I went with two SS comrades to the Northamptonshire Yeomanry.

At Christmas we were all loaded on to a train and taken through Germany to Belgium, to a camp on a hill. The way from the station was long. I had no baggage and it was easy for me. Those comrades with a lot of baggage were robbed by the Belgian people and relieved of their things. I was only there for a short time. They were looking for bakers, proper bakers, for the British Army's field kitchens covering the whole of Belgium.

In January 1946 we were loaded on to British fishing boats in Antwerp and taken to England. There I worked in various British establishments around the town and again in the big army bakery in Aldershot. Then in August 1947 we went by train to Scotland to Gosfort Camp near Edinburgh.

After three years and seven months I was discharged from the *Wehrmacht* and could work as a free worker in Britain. I could not return to Germany, as Berlin was divided between the Four Powers, and I came from the Russian Zone, where my parents lived. Therefore, in 1955 I decided to apply for British nationality, which I received on 5 November 1955.

Erwin Bartmann's rapid granting of British nationality was due to the thorough interrogation he had previously had from the British authorities seeking a man by the name of Falke, the same name as that of his last unit.

THE END OF THE 21st PANZER DIVISION

MAJOR BRAND

This translation is made from a poor copy of the original report sent me in 1993 by Werner Kortenhaus, who wrote that Major Brand had taken over command of the 21st Armoured Reconnaissance Battalion in Normandy in June 1944, and had compiled this report shortly after the war.

Colonel Hans von Luck (see below) mentions the report in his book Gefangener meiner Zeit, *published in 1991, in which he says that Major Brand had become critically ill and was no longer approachable. Colonel von Luck found the report 'disturbing' for it reveals the virtually mutinous state of the division's units' commanding officers at this stage of the war.*

After the dismissal of Lieutenant-General Feuchtinger, who was condemned to death by Hitler for ostensible treason, and was now awaiting execution in Torgau,[1] Lieutenant-General Marcks was given command of the division.

The battalion was able to fight its way back from Lower Silesia to the area south of Berlin near Königs Wusterhausen during the last days of April and was employed in a fighting and reconnaissance role. The appearance of Seydlitz Troops caused severe confusion among our own troops as, for the very first time, they were engaging in combat wearing German uniforms. Captured Seydlitz officers were usually shot by our men, and this had an adverse effect on discipline and morale. Our reconnaissance showed that Berlin had already been reached by the enemy from the east, that numerous enemy armoured units were to be found between Königs Wusterhausen and the southern outskirts of Berlin, and that a very powerful armoured thrust on Ketzin and Potsdam had the obvious aim of encircling the city of Berlin in accordance with

Russian battle plans and operational manoeuvring. Resistance was only coming from the armoured divisions, the SS and, in the beginning, units from the city. There was no longer any operational direction higher than division. Units with unpopular officers were running away. Death sentences were no longer being carried out. From the orders given, the German High Command was clearly demanding the persistent sacrifice of the army, which was why our operational tasks made no sense. Not only the leaders of reconnaissance units, but also senior staff officers were in the dark about what was going on.

The question arose whether to flee with one's troops on one's own responsibility, or stay with the parent division – a question of conscience. I sent my adjutant, Second Lieutenant Kielhorn, home to his mother in Berlin by the last remaining route, as he was an only child. One hour later the ring was closed. The artillery staff of the 'Tannenberger' commandeered my fuel and fled via Ketzin to the north–west. Through lack of fuel my own unit is reduced to 70 per cent effectiveness, so future attempts to make a motorised breakout on our own will prove unsuccessful.

The results are simply incredible chaos: hassle, no sleep, no supplies, contaminated drinking water, unbelievable casualties, the encirclement constantly closing in, ferocious enemy air attacks, and massive artillery bombardment. During this phase there is a visible sinking of morale in one's own unit. The chief of staff, Major Renner, has already fled. Unit leaders take control. The generals are no longer exercising their authority.

I am wounded twice on 26 and 27 April by shellfire.

Orders from above obviously still inevitably mean higher casualties on our side. Attempt on 27 April to persuade General Marcks to break away from the Army and break through to the west unilaterally. Marcks puts off the decision until later. Consult with von Gottberg and other commanding officers about arresting Marcks and his staff early on 28 April and leading the breakout ourselves. Marcks joins in willingly. The attempt to break out fails, with heavy casualties.

Meanwhile a big attempt to break out by von Luck, but he is captured and his regiment virtually wiped out.[2]

About two thousand leaderless officers and soldiers have tagged on to the battalion together with the same number of civilians of all ages and both sexes. Renewed breakout attempt early on 29 April. Success near Halbe at first, the Russians withdrawing with heavy losses, but at the bridge where the road crosses the autobahn west of Halbe, the whole unit falls into a Russian trap. Hundreds of dead, semi-demented civilians – frightful state of affairs. Three fatal casualties in my own command vehicle. Control is lost. Women raped to death by Russians from a nearby POW camp lying in the woods and on the roads.

Renewed contact with the Seydlitz Army. Seydlitz officers listen in to order groups and then issue false instructions, leading Russians to our units.

Second Lieutenant Böbmann killed near me; Leinhard and Hoffmann already fallen, and Marcks wounded. Order Reuche to blow up his armoured personnel carrier and climb aboard. The unprotected men come under intensive fire, jump off and are captured. Rüskes lies in the roadway without a leg and is loaded aboard. Second Lieutenant Frese suffers a severe stomach wound and is given morphine; presumably falls into Russian hands. Many civilians committing suicide.

Seriously wounded by a ground-attack aircraft. Erstermann takes over command while I am under the influence of morphine. On 30 April the rest of us reach the marshes. I give the order for the battalion to disband and the armoured vehicles to be blown up. The wounded are to be left behind with the medical officer and the remainder to try to break through to the west in small groups.

At about 0300 hours with Second Lieutenant Melzer, who is wounded like me, Stach and five of the men, we are surprised in our sleep and captured by Russian Mongolian troops. Taken to a completely destroyed village, the base of a Russian tank brigade. Russians play a game with us: they line us up against a wall with SS officers. The SS officers are shot, but not Melzer and myself. Interrogation all day long by GPU,[3] although we are well treated and our wounds attended to by a Russian doctor. Stach allowed to stay with me. First plundering. See many members of the battalion. The GPU inform me that Germany is to become a Soviet state, and that things will improve with the implementation of 'res publica'.

Raping of women at night, even seventeen-year-olds.

Then several days together with Major Flohr, Lieutenant Kuhlke and Stach as special prisoners of the brigade. Taken to a GPU prison near Luckenwalde. Much ill-treatment of German civilians seen on the way. Handling and food good. In the next cell blows and kicks.

Transport of 39 men assembled and moved from camp to camp over about ten days, but not taken on anywhere. Many deaths of *Volkssturm* in other transports seen on the way. Our escorts very humane, rations acceptable. My wounds and Flohr's worsened, unable to continue. Loaded on to small carts. More plundering on the way; even our shoes. Flohr, Stach and myself taken to the Sanftenberg field hospital. No operations, bad doctors, starvation rations, morphine against hunger, molestation by Russians.

Formed a plan of escape after external healing, although perceptibly consumptive. Acquired false papers. Fled together with a nurse on 1 June. Went past the sentries in broad daylight wearing civilian clothes taken from the dead. Stopped in the street, but let go again. Acceptance by the Germans on the way was touching. Stach left us in Oppenheim for Berlin and got through. Arrested again on account of false papers and put in prison. Escaped after three days. Rested in Wittenberg for ten days as Flohr was deadly ill.[4]

Fled to the Elbe near Dessau. Arrested for a third time while trying to cross. Much shooting, a rape, myself wounded, but good treatment.

At the end of July, by bribing a Russian officer with alcohol and a watch, I persuaded him to see to the sentries, thus making it possible for me to cross, as normally it would have been impossible with double sentries stationed every 20 metres, took a big river boat and set across. No more difficulties on the west bank. Reached home on 4 July, finding Münster totally destroyed except for a narrow area around. Own house still standing. Surprise reunion with Mother unforgettable. Collapsed with illness. Received German papers after a few days and went into my uncle's business.

It is presumed, from a superficial reckoning of both failed attempts to break out of the encirclement to the south, that about 15 per cent of the battalion's combatants lost their lives, to which must be added the severely wounded, 83 per cent ended up in Russian hands and only 2 per cent got through. Only and exceptionally, the majority of the supply company reached American captivity and were released. Of the 21st Panzer Division, apart from the extremely high and incalculable casualties it suffered, the majority, including their commanders, ended up in Russian captivity. Only the non-tactical divisional staff and the supply column had the good fortune to fall into British hands.

NOTES

1. Torgau was where the Russian and American forces met on 25 April 1945. Lieutenant-General Feuchtinger was released from prison by the Russians and survived the war.
2. Colonel Hans von Luck commanded the division's Panzergrenadier Regiment 125.
3. The GPU was the intelligence department of the Red Army.
4. Flohr survived and went on to study theology.

THE SIEMENSSTADT *VOLKSSTURM* BATTALION

DR JUR. GUSTAV-ADOLF POURROY

Dr Pourroy was born in Berlin in 1894 and served in the elite Garde-Fusilier-Regiment as a second lieutenant during the First World War, being awarded the Iron Cross First Class. He later graduated as a lawyer and in 1928 took up employment with Siemens, where in 1944 he was appointed a departmental director in the Siemens-Schuckerwerke, one of the Berlin subsidiaries.

This translation of an extract from his post-Second World War report is published with the most kind permission of his surviving family.

The idea of recording the battalion history arose as early as 1945 during Russian captivity at Landsberg/Warthe and continued in Kovno in 1946. The adjutant and Headquarters Company commander immediately agreed that the necessity of having a battalion history would inevitably arise sometime in the future. There was also the feeling that comments regarding the deeds or behaviour of individuals should be avoided, except when given from personal knowledge. All this with particular consideration for the battalion dead, whose sacrifice deserved not to be forgotten.

Reflections on the political situation, or on the war as a whole, should be omitted and the battalion history be confined to the bare facts, so the general situation is only mentioned when necessary for comprehension. This applies similarly to the more personal remarks, spread sparingly.

Life in captivity offered a good opportunity to establish the battalion history while memories were still fresh and questions could be asked to clarify points hitherto unclear.

So the first quick draft was made from the documents that the adjutant had been collecting from the beginning and which the Headquarters Company commander could enlarge on from the diary he had kept. There was further material about the Gun Company from Lieutenant von Gustedt, about the Heavy Company from Second Lieutenant Fleck, and also about the 'Siemensstadt' Reserve Battalion from Company Commander Dombrowski.

It is nigh on miraculous that it was possible to save this first draft of the battalion history despite the constant frisking (body searches) and the lack of paper, and that we were able to bring it back home.

The original draft is now in the Siemens' company archives. The transcript lay fallow for nearly two decades, being amended from time to time by the odd contribution and systematic questioning of the few still contactable members of the battalion during the course of 1966 to produce the present text.

The author is the battalion adjutant, now the sole surviving officer.

FORMATION

On 25 September 1944 the High Command issued instructions for the raising of the *Volkssturm*, which would be the mustering of the people's last resources in the defence against the overwhelming mass of Allied troops in the east and west. All men between sixteen and sixty years of age and still reasonably capable of bearing arms and marching were grouped into companies and battalions, and taught to shoot and trained in the latest combat methods, especially to have confidence in using the panzerfaust in engaging tanks.

In the general view, the raising of the *Volkssturm* came too late and without proper consideration as regards providing sufficient weapons and equipment. It soon became apparent that equipment was completely inadequate in many instances. The haste in raising the *Volkssturm* throughout Germany is exemplified by the fact that seven *Volkssturm* battalions were committed to the front in East Prussia by the end of October 1944. Some battalions were even sent into action in civilian clothes and without weapons, only to be captured immediately while detraining at their unloading points.

The *Volkssturm* were part of the *Wehrmacht* and, as such, the *Volkssturm* men soldiers, and subject to military law. The swearing in was done with a special oath, similar to that of the *Wehrmacht*, made to the leader of the Greater German Reich.

From the beginning there was a lasting conflict between the *Wehrmacht* and the Party over raising and training, as well as over who had control. Raising was the Party's concern, training that of the *Wehrmacht*. In action the *Volks-sturm* came indisputably under the *Wehrmacht*. Despite this apparently clear formulation, there were border areas, such as rationing, which caused constant difficulties. The greatest lay in the fact that the majority of men falling within the *Volkssturm* category were designated 'essential workers' in the war industry. Also the Party emphatically demanded that *Volkssturm* leaders should be 'staunch and reliable National Socialists' with front-line experience.

Finally the Party asserted that the release of formerly 'essential worker' protected forces to industry from *Volkssturm* duty would be the responsibility of the *Volkssturm* battalions themselves. This led to the 'Z-Card Action', by which, without exception, every man eligible for the *Volkssturm* had to report to his designated *Volkssturm* unit with the possibility of release to industry by the issue of a 'Z-Card'. The Party believed that with 'staunch and reliable National Socialists' in command of the battalions, releases from the *Volkssturm* would be conducted more in the interest of the *Volkssturm* than the interest of industry. For a concern like Siemens, for example, which had only part of its production devoted to the war industry, the raising of *Volkssturm* units brought the positive danger that those workers who had until then held a lesser 'essential worker' status would now be committed to military duty.

In these circumstances it was useful to have the battalion leadership drawn from Siemens, who, while legally conforming to the orders received, would also bear in mind the interests of the firm, and so lessen friction whenever possible without a clash of conscience. An example may explain this: on the Siemensstadt dynamo factory's production line were 200 of the latest submarine engines with the highest possible priority. The factory manager declared that it was absolutely impossible to release a single man from this production line, while the Party was all for a ruthless call to arms.

The proposed and accepted commander of the 'Siemensstadt' Battalion was the director and head of the personnel department of SAM (Siemens Apparate und Maschinen GmbH), Erich Krull, who had been a major in the First World War. The battalion adjutant was the director of the SSW-Abteilungen Zentralen und Bahnen, Dr G.A. Pourroy, a lieutenant and longtime regimental adjutant as well as liaison officer on the staff of a general headquarters in the First World War. The battalion's company commanders also stemmed from Siemens.

The battalion was assigned to Fortress Regiment 57 of Colonel Bärenfänger's division in the defence of Berlin.[1] The regimental commander was Major Funk and his adjutant Lieutenant von Schöenebeck. The 'Siemensstadt' Battalion was allocated the number 3/115, the '3' denoting Gau Berlin[2] and '115' the sequential number of the unit.

The battalion leadership took it upon themselves above all to equip the battalion up to combat standard in every detail. During the period leading up to mobilisation and going into action, the battalion was fully equipped with clothing, weapons light and heavy, and all necessities such as signals equipment, field kitchens and a horse-drawn supply column. The quarrels with the Gau offices in Berlin and other establishments often bordered on the dramatically grotesque. This was made more difficult by the relationship between Siemens and the Party, which had always been strained.[3] The main burden of responsibility for the 'Z-Card' allocations lay with the adjutant. Despite many difficulties, however, it proved possible to provide the various factories and departments with the necessary workforce, previously categorised as 'essential workers', so that production did not suffer anywhere. The release of personnel to Siemens went so far that eventually the battalion had to be brought up to combat strength by taking men from Charlottenburg-Nord District. With what lack of consideration the Party enlisted the *Volkssturm* in Siemensstadt with police assistance can be seen from the following anecdote.

A senior official in the SSW head office administration in Siemensstadt, Arno Bolle, was graded an 'essential worker' by the SSW in accordance with the rules. He received a summons to the *Volkssturm*, but thought himself exempt because of his 'essential worker' status. At the end of March 1945 he was arrested at his home in Siemensstadt and taken to the Army Ammunition Technical School in Treptow, where the battalion was waiting to go into action. The adjutant, hearing a particularly loud altercation coming from down the corridor, discovered that a court martial was already in process against Bolle. The death sentence was about to be passed and, as was then customary, carried out without delay. Using similar declamatory language, the adjutant was able to extricate Bolle immediately from the proceedings and have him safely escorted to the barrack gate with instructions to report back to head office. Bolle was thus able to survive.

From those reporting for *Volkssturm* service from Siemensstadt and the immediate vicinity, such as Haselhorst, Gartenfeld and so on, men and officers were selected in an extensive and arduous process, persistently disrupted by Party instructions. Having received their summons to the *Volkssturm*, they would be allocated to the battalion. This summons, as already described, was constantly being repeated through the Z-Card business. This went on for weeks until the battalion at last could provisionally muster four rifle companies, just like a *Wehrmacht* battalion. Out of these four rifle companies, a so-called Headquarters Company was formed of men with infantry training taken from all the rifle platoons for this special unit, comprising, for example, the Signals Section, the Pioneer Platoon, consisting mainly of craftsmen, and the Supply Section. Next to the Headquarters Company came the 1st, 2nd and 3rd Rifle Companies commanded by Schneehage (Haselhorst), Treutner and Dr Weinholdt, all members and some even directors of Siemens companies.

The first parade of the assembled battalion took place in the Evangelical Church in Siemensstadt, as there was no other suitable place available. Here the companies were divided into platoons and sections. The Labour Front made their offices at Schwiebertweg 25 in Siemensstadt available, with its type-writers and telephone for the battalion orderly room. At the same time as the main battalion, a reserve of the remaining men was formed.

To complete this description of the battalion, the Gun Company and Heavy Weapons Company must also be included. As has already been pointed out, the battalion leadership formed a combatant unit capable of using both infantry and heavy weapons, for, as well as its infantry weapons and heavy machine-guns, it also had mortars, rocket launchers and even a flame-thrower.

The forming of the Gun and Heavy Weapon Companies was achieved by taking specialists from among the men of the battalion, as well as some *Wehrmacht* gunners. The Gun Company was established on 26 January 1945 at the Army Ammunition Technical School in Treptow, at first under Koch's command but later taken over by Dr Mahr at the beginning of February, still without guns, and as the battalion's No. 4 Company. The company was then quartered in Biesdorf but moved on

11 February 1945 to Friedrichsfelde, where they received four 152 mm Russian howitzers with ammunition, and Lieutenant-Colonel Knopf, the Sector Artillery Commander, gave the company the name 'Blücher'.

During the course of February 1945 the battery was joined by 50 *Wehrmacht* gunners, almost all youngsters. Second Lieutenant Hahn undertook their training, but on 4 March 1945 he was transferred with 30 men to found a new battery 'Schill'. Lieutenant von Gustedt then took over the command of the Gun Company, but in the middle of March he too was transferred to another sector to set up a new battery, so Dr Mahr took over the 'Blücher' Battery with Second Lieutenant Sprung as his deputy.

The battery was then given a French 220 mm mortar, which was set up in a small square in Kaulsdorf, close to the Catholic church. Even though ammunition for the mortar was extremely limited, it substantially increased the battery's fighting strength. It should be stressed that only at the beginning was this battery with its four Russian howitzers and its mortar a fourth company of the battalion, for later, in order to increase the tactical fire-power, it came under the orders of Fortress Regiment 57 and the Sector Artillery Commander.

The Heavy Weapons Company was formed in similar fashion, but remained under the immediate command of the battalion. It was formed by order of the Regiment from equal proportions of NCOs and men taken from the 'Siemensstadt' *Volkssturm* Battalion, *Volkssturm* Battalion 'Schünke', Police Battalion 'Warnholz' and *Wehrmacht* Battalion 'Trockels'. The company was at first commanded by Lieutenant Schmidt and later by his deputy, Second Lieutenant Fleck. The establishment consisted of a platoon with two infantry guns and four heavy mortars in a second platoon. Then there were three heavy machine-guns. The mortars were meant to be replaced later by rocket launchers, but the latter failed to appear.

Training

Battalion training began immediately after the first parade on 1 November 1944 and continued until mobilisation and preparation for battle immediately before the fighting.

The whole conduct of the training, especially in Siemensstadt, was undertaken by the *Wehrmacht*. However, it must be pointed out that, in view of the time and space limitations, this could not be thorough, and could not have been achieved had the battalion not on its own initiative sought and found the means and material to complete, improve and bring it to a certain level. The underlying principle was to train the battalion up to a point where it reached true combat-worthiness. The previously mentioned fate of some *Volkssturm* units that had been thrown into battle completely unequipped and without proper training served as a warning. The battalion leadership also had to arouse and maintain a belief among the troops that the battalion had real fighting capability and was not to be offered up senselessly and without the ability to defend itself against enemy attacks. The description of the fighting will show that this aim was achieved to a certain extent. In this the leadership knew well in advance that its fighting ability was limited and that a way would have to be found between looking after the troops' interests and the dutiful fulfilment of the combat tasks expected of them.

Training for the infantry companies was particularly difficult in Siemensstadt during the final months of 1944. Training could only be conducted on workday evenings and on Sundays, as the men were still working and being employed on constructing air-raid shelters, barricades and so on, a hard enough role without adding to it. Gradually, however, the companies were able to begin their own training, if sometimes only in small numbers, in Siemensstadt itself or on the old exercise grounds in Haselhorst, or the Waldsportplatz on the Rohrdamm, the old soldiers available providing the companies with some backbone.

The SA also helped a little until the *Wehrmacht* at Ruhleben Barracks took over the patronage of the battalion's training in November 1944 as part of an overall plan. The commander of the *Wehrmacht* at Ruhleben was Major Dageförde, assisted by his training officers, Lieutenants Kräger and Schäfer. The *Wehrmacht* at Ruhleben also undertook training with the necessary weapons.

It should also be mentioned that several-day company commanders courses were run by the *Wehrmacht* in Potsdam, and the SA signals staff provided special training for the battalion's Signals Section. The latter was particularly appreciated, as the battalion depended upon secure communications in action, and the technicalities involved in the various fields of communications required specialised training for previously partly unqualified personnel. *Volkssturm* battalion commanders also received special training from the *Wehrmacht* at the Grafenwöhr training area in Bavaria, where our commanding officer attended a 14-day course.

So gradually, bit by bit, all the battalion obtained basic training. It was hoped that, once the inevitable mobilisation of the battalion had taken place and the companies gathered in, it would be possible to carry out intensive training at the assembly place under our own efforts as well as those of the *Wehrmacht*.

The training of the attached Gun Company started as soon as the guns and mortars had been delivered to the battery locations. Particular attention was given to the telephone connections between the gun and mortar positions and the forward observers located at the church in Marzahn and on the heights south of Hönow, with frequent testing to ensure that there would be no loss of communication in action.

Similarly with the training of the Heavy Weapons Company, where it was carried out in the company positions established close to the Catholic church in Kaulsdorf, and with its corresponding forward observers.

The training in both of these companies, coupled with the digging of the fire positions and ammunition stores, was the prime responsibility of the company commanders and the few officers assigned to them. In some cases the *Wehrmacht* units in Potsdam were able to provide special training personnel. There were also some old gunners among the *Volkssturm* men who were able to provide good support to these NCOs.

MOBILISATION

Towards the end of January 1945, the battalion was notified by telephone that mobilisation could be expected shortly. This meant that the battalion with its still dispersed four companies would leave the Siemensstadt area and assemble at another location for its eventual commitment to action, thus providing the first opportunity for the battalion to get together and, above all, test the necessary joint functioning of battalion headquarters, company commanders and troops. This would also provide an opportunity to train and equip up to combat standard.

From 23 January onwards the battalion orderly room in Siemensstadt was manned day and night, and telephone communications, backed up by runners, established with the commanding officer, company commanders and company sergeant-majors.

The battalion received the orders to mobilise early on 24 January, but these were cancelled and finally issued on 25 January. The commanding officer then held a conference for all commanders, after which written instructions were issued to each individual with orders to report to the drill hall at the Army Ammunition Technical School at Treptow at 1500 hours on 26 January. As always in such cases, the notice was short, but in this case convenient, as it avoided the severing from civilian life being drawn out unnecessarily.

The commanding officer and an advance party immediately undertook the allocation of accommodation to the companies at the barracks in Treptow, the first time that the battalion could be so accommodated. Training was immediately resumed in the barrack-rooms and on the square, primarily by the NCOs who had been trained at Ruhleben.

Next came the speedy issue of equipment to the battalion. Twenty-three light machine-guns (MG 42s), whose rapid rate of fire had given them the name 'Hitler's saws', arrived and special training on these was necessary before they were issued to the companies.

Four field kitchens then arrived with their horses. The field kitchens were first taken to the barracks smithy for checking and repair as necessary, and were immediately taken into use for feeding the battalion. With them also came two supply wagons with their horses.

The clothing of the battalion and the issue of such items as belts, haversacks, tent-halves, mess tins, water bottles, packs and the rest could now be carried out smoothly thanks to advance contact with the staff of the Berliner Gau. All the equipment was drawn from the Gau's large depot near Alexanderplatz in adequate quantities and then issued to the companies from an improvised quartermaster's store in the barracks. With this came the *Volkssturm* two-line armbands to be worn on the left arm:

DEUTSCHER VOLKSSTURM
WEHRMACHT

All military and Party insignia were removed from the issued clothing and *Volkssturm* badges of rank sewn on the collars, the commanding officer being given four stars, the adjutant and company commanders three, platoon commanders two and section leaders one.

So gradually the appearance of the battalion acquired uniformity. From the commanding officer down to the last *Volkssturm* man a good and comradely spirit reigned, supported by a strong feeling of unity, making it possible to consolidate the unit in a comparatively short time.

The concern at the beginning about whether it would be possible to forge the battalion into an effective unit capable of certain combat or defensive ability, bearing in mind the adverse conditions and the predominant jealousies between the *Wehrmacht* and the Party, had proved exaggerated. Now with exacting duties and the feeling of all being in it together, reliant on one another to meet whatever would come in a comradely manner, all other thoughts were precluded. In these circumstances, even a heavy daylight bombing raid, in which the barracks and surrounding area were hit, did nothing but strengthen the feeling of unity within the battalion.

Complications continued to arise during the formation and equipping of the battalion. There was a constant turnover in the company rosters from the Z-Card holders, and here the already mentioned topping-up of the battalion with *Volkssturm* men from Charlottenburg-Nord came in. Then the battalion medical officer, Dr Schreyer, was ordered to accelerate the physical examination of all the *Volkssturm* men and weed out those unfit for duty. At the same time the whole battalion was inoculated.

Then the battalion administration had to be sorted out, not only in battalion headquarters, but also at company level for the control of rosters, paybooks, clothing lists, and other formalities, none of which could be neglected.

But all these difficulties, demanding from all of us ever more work, patience and engagement, were finally mastered, so that, in the circumstances, we could be content with the results. The mass swearing-in of the battalion provided a suitable ending to this phase and the almost constant coming and going.

By 6 February our mobilisation could be said to be complete, and just in time, for on 7 February the battalion was ordered out of the Treptow barracks to its operational area at Biesdorf. In this move to the operational area the whole unit moved as one for the first time, including the field kitchens and supply wagons.

A rear party remained behind for a few days at the Army Ammunition Technical School, where on 10 February the drill hall was totally demolished in an air raid.

As all the battalion papers, as well as those of the reserve battalion in Siemensstadt, were either lost in the fighting or had to be destroyed, all the figures in this report have had to be estimated. However, these estimates can be taken as reasonably accurate.

Battalion Strength

Battalion HQ	20	CO: Krull
		Adjt: Dr Pourroy
HQ Company	200	OC: Gebhardt
No. 1 Rifle Company	150	OC: Schneehage
No. 2 Rifle Company	150	OC: Dr Weinholdt
No. 3 Rifle Company	150	OC: Treutner
Heavy Weapons Company	*	OC: 2Lt Fleck
Gun Company	100	OC: Dr Mahr
Total	770	

(* from Rifle Companies)

PREPARATION FOR ACTION

The outer defence ring of Berlin roughly followed a line around the city's outermost suburbs, including Biesdorf, Kaulsdorf and Mahlsdorf, while the inner defence roughly followed the line of the S-Bahn ring. The defence area was divided into sectors, with Defence Sector 'A' starting in the east at the three above-named places and allocated to Bärenfänger's division. The final, innermost defensive area comprised the Reichs Chancellery ('Zitadelle'), the Bendler Block (former *Reichswehr* Ministry) on the Landwehr Canal, and the flak-towers at the Zoo station.

In our new location at Biesdorf we had our first personal contact with the regiment in the form of a short visit by the regimental commander, Major Funk, and his adjutant, Lieutenant von Schoenebeck. Then on 8 February the battalion staff and company commanders inspected a sample *Volkssturm* position in Marzahn.

The issue of arms to the battalion was completed within the next few days. We received 500 French rifles with 50 rounds of ammunition apiece. In addition, we received pistols, panzerfausts, hand grenades and several sub-machine-guns. Every man in the battalion now had a weapon and ammunition.

During the period 12–14 February the battalion split up, taking quarters in private homes in Kaulsdorf and Mahlsdorf, while still retaining some accommodation in Biesdorf, including the Schloss and manor farm. (Schloss Biesdorf was a long-standing Siemens property, dating back well before the First World War, and was where Dr Otto Krell (1866–1938) had developed and built his non-rigid airship, which had its maiden flight in 1911.) The battalion then started work on constructing its defences as shown on the sketch on page 126. Battalion headquarters was established in the Catholic church at Kaulsdorf.

Two positions were planned, the first being in open land on dried-up sewage fields approximately in the middle between the north-northwest edge of Biesdorf and Kaulsdorf and the Hellersdorfer Vorwerk (farm), where this delaying position could be manned by a platoon when necessary. The second followed the northwestern edge of Biesdorf and Kaulsdorf to the edge of the sewage fields, roughly in line with Hönower Strasse.[4] To our left was a *Wehrmacht* battalion under Lieutenant Trockels sited slightly east of Biesdorf station, and on our right was the Police Battalion 'Warnholz'.

Bärenfänger's Defence Sector 'A' was thus in the forward line of defence, which, however, had still to be constructed, and was occupied by these three battalions with *Volkssturm* Battalion 3/115 'Siemensstadt' roughly east of the Wuhle stream and north of the Kaulsdorf and Mahlsdorf S-Bahn stations.

The battalion's left flank, being comparatively open and unprotected because of the sewage fields, formed a danger point, as was immediately realised, and the Pioneer Platoon was therefore sent to dam the Wuhle at the S-Bahn to make this left flank at least a bit more secure.

For the rest, it was planned, as shown on the sketch, for Nos 2 and 3 Companies to occupy the forward position, with Headquarters Company and No. 1 Company in reserve on the second position. The battalion command post was set up near the local rifle club in the at least splinter-proof dugout of a former Czech camp. The companies also prepared their own command posts either in their positions or

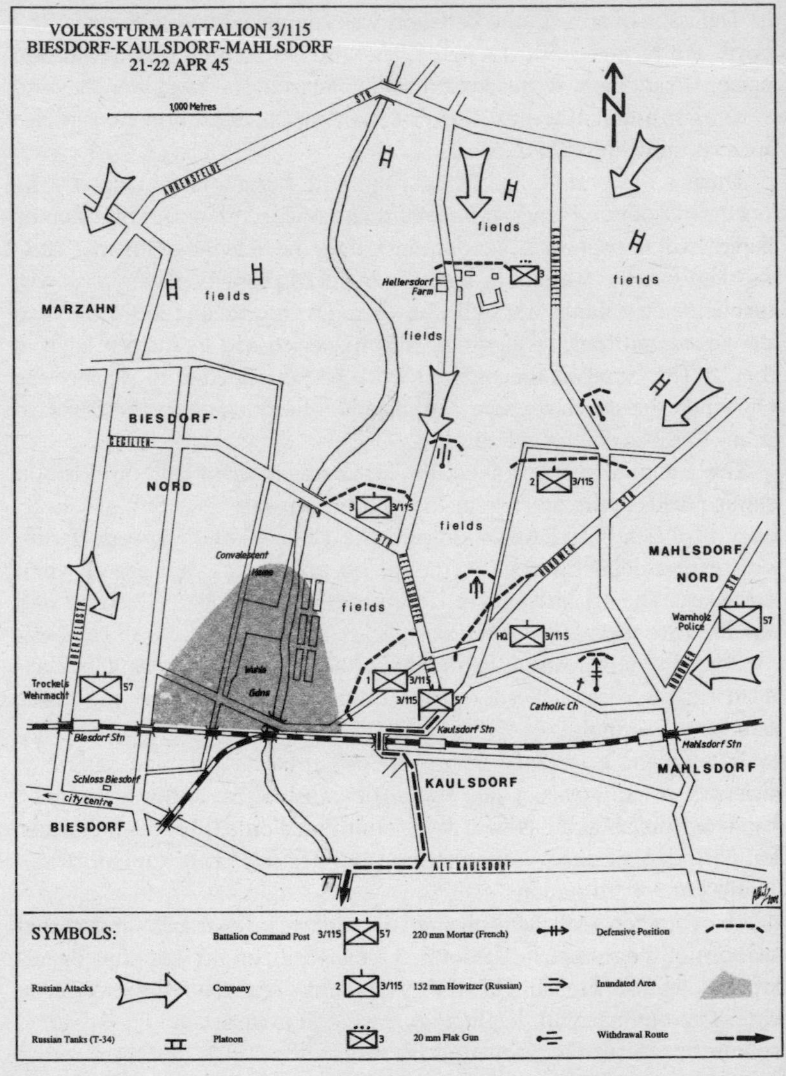
VOLKSSTURM BATTALION 3/115
BIESDORF-KAULSDORF-MAHLSDORF
21-22 APR 45
1,000 Metres
fields
MARZAHN
BIESDORF-
NORD
Hellersdorf Farm
MAHLSDORF-
NORD
Convalescent Home
Wuhle Gdns
Wamholz Police
Trockels Wehrmacht
Catholic Ch
Biesdorf Stn
Kaulsdorf Stn
Mahlsdorf Stn
MAHLSDORF
Schloss Biesdorf
city centre
BIESDORF
KAULSDORF
ALT KAULSDORF
SYMBOLS:
Battalion Command Post
220 mm Mortar (French)
Defensive Position
Russian Attacks
Company
152 mm Howitzer (Russian)
Inundated Area
Russian Tanks (T-34)
Platoon
20 mm Flak Gun
Withdrawal Route

immediately behind them. The Heavy Weapons Company deployed its heavy machine-guns and mortars partly in the defensive positions and partly outside them in all-round defence machine-gun nests.

The division had two 20 mm flak guns with their crews set up in the anti-tank role either side of Hellersdorfer Strasse level with our forward position.

During March an anti-tank ditch, for which the civilian population of Berlin had to provide workers from the various firms on specific days, was dug partly between our first and second positions, and partly between our first position and the Hellersdorfer farm. Thus by chance the Dynamowerke from Siemensstadt was engaged for several days and the battalion staff unexpectedly encountered the head of the factory, Dr Ott, and Director Besold from the Schaltwerke (both part of Siemens-Schukertwerke AG) on the site.

The Signals Section quickly laid about 16 kilometres of telephone cable connecting the command posts and the regiment, whose command post was located south of Kaulsdorf S-Bahn station on the road to Karlshorst. Should this telephone system fail, there was a back-up of cyclists and runners, who had to make themselves familiar with the area by both day and night.

Telephone communications between the various staffs was never fully interrupted right up to the last day of battle. To everyone's astonishment, the public telephone system worked without interruption even under the heaviest fire, and with patience on both sides one could always get through in the end. For instance, on the night of 1/2 May, the battalion was able to clarify details of an attack ordered by the regiment for the early hours of 2 May using the public telephone system.

The battalion dressing station was established in Schloss Biesdorf, and nearby were located the paymaster and quartermaster with his supply section for the important task of keeping the battalion supplied with food and drink. The field kitchens were deployed out to the companies, where in course of time they were dug in to provide shelter from splinters.

Next to the construction of our defences, the most important task from the middle of February to the middle of April was the constant pursuit of training both indoors and out. The major concern was that every man should know exactly what to do in an emergency and be fully competent with the weapons available, although firing practice with rifles and panzerfausts was severely restricted due to the scarcity of ammunition.

In addition there was an ever-increasing number of exercises set by the division and the regiment, as well as command exercises within the battalion. These exercises were set in the area beyond our quarters and the defences still under construction, for example in Marzahn to the north and even as far out as Ahrensfelde and Wartenberg, thus getting the troops accustomed to marching with full packs. One of these exercises almost clashed with the Russian attack of 22/23 April.

Routine plans and the construction of our defensive positions were increasingly interrupted by the almost constant day and night air attacks, Russian as well as Anglo-American. There was hardly a night that the troops were not disturbed several times by bombing attacks. In this respect, precise instructions were given for everyone to take cover in one-man holes outside their quarters, and consequently our losses from air attack were few.

In addition, and far more unpleasant for the civilian population, were the mounting losses from Russian low-level attacks on Biesdorf, Kaulsdorf and Mahlsdorf, which started on 26 March and increased in intensity until the end of April, gradually bringing all road traffic to a halt.

Similarly the S-Bahn was brought to a standstill at intervals by these air attacks, but was able to be repaired and continue service. The S-Bahn enabled relatives to visit the men in quarters and also to allow the companies to send those concerned to check on the fate of their families, and not one of these visits was abused, nor did they lead to any absences without leave.

The discipline among the troops and the strict military conduct from the beginning to the final hours can only be described as outstanding. There was not one incident, even in the worst circumstances, of lack of resolve. Discipline was applicable to all ranks, as can be shown in the following example. Some pistol ammunition was found to be missing in Dr Weinholdt's No. 2 Company, presumed stolen, so the divisional commander punished the company commander and his Sergeant-Major Käthner-Potthoff with confinement to quarters for a set period that extended beyond our going into action. The battalion rescinded the punishment on 19 April, only informing the regiment afterwards.

From all – only recently mere civilians – much was demanded in increasing quantity under primitive conditions. We had to prepare for the worst as best we could. One must also consider what an immense amount of work, both mental and physical, was demanded from the staff down to the lowest section leader and man, involving constant improvisation day and night. From a critical, and as far as possible objective, standpoint, one can see that the battalion was as fully committed to its role as it could possibly be.

During these weeks of March and April the weather remained surprisingly good, hardly ever interfering with the construction of our defences.

A curious thing should be mentioned that demonstrates what additional demands were made on us. During the first half of April orders arrived for everyone to see the newly released film *Kolberg*[5] as a means of boosting morale. The troops, however, found compliance with this order to be just another burden. The film could only be shown between 0300 and 0500 hours and at a cinema at a considerable distance from the unit lines, involving a long march there and back. The result was to tire them even more, and one can be certain that they slept through it. Even the battalion staff were not exempt, although they had the advantage of having a motorcycle combination at their disposal.

FIGHTING IN EAST BERLIN – 21–22 APRIL 1945

From 12 to 15 April the Russians reinforced their Küstrin bridgehead and on 16 April they attacked the German positions on the Seelow Heights.

The battalion was told that German units east of Berlin, including some *Volkssturm*, were fighting a delaying action as they withdrew slowly, and there was supposed to be a *Wehrmacht* screen north of the city, as well as a German Panzer army and Army Group 'Weichsel'.

It was also thought that the Russians would push through from the east to the north and south of Berlin in order to meet up with the advancing Americans west of the city, probably at the Elbe river. Consequently, we did not expect an immediate thrust from the east right into the centre of the capital.

This supposition was totally incorrect. The Russians also struck at the eastern part of Berlin, where Division Bärenfänger with our battalion at

Biesdorf, Kaulsdorf and Mahlsdorf, stood in Defence Sector 'A', advancing skilfully, feeling their way forward and avoiding big pockets of resistance, leaving them aside to take later.

This short summary of the events will serve to show how the battalion came to bear the brunt of the unending stream of Russian tanks from the east, northeast and north, instead of first being reinforced by the retreating *Wehrmacht* units coming from the east as had been expected.

The air situation remained unchanged from mid-April. There were almost continuous day and night bombing raids on the city, while the eastern suburbs were subjected to strafing from low-flying aircraft, against which there was no German flak or fighters defence.

The issue of the codeword 'Zahlmeister' in the battalion area meant that the defensive positions were to be manned, a platoon of No. 3 Company was to go out to Hellersdorf, and two reconnaissance teams to go forward to cover the approaches. At the same time the supply section was to load up ready to move and, on receipt of the codeword 'Kolberg' denoting the next stage of alert, to move back. The highest state of alert would be announced with the codeword 'Clausewitz'.

The usual duties and construction of defences continued on 19 April. Then on 20 April, Hitler's birthday, the first state of alert was ordered with the codeword 'Zahlmeister', and at midday there was a particularly severe Anglo-American bombing raid on Berlin that caused the S-Bahn to close down until evening. At noon on 21 April the state of alert was raised by the codeword 'Kolberg', and yet again at noon on 22 April with 'Clausewitz', but by this time the battalion was already in action.

The battalion staff and company commanders moved into their command posts during the night of 20/21 April, the reconnaissance teams were sent forward and the Hellersdorf platoon took up its advance position.

Then at 2200 hours on 20 April Russian infantry penetrated Hellersdorf and took our platoon by surprise without a fight. Without the support of heavy weapons, the Russians then tried to overrun our forward positions under cover of darkness, but were checked by the reconnaissance teams lying between Hellersdorf and our lines.

At dawn on 21 April several Russian tanks with strong infantry escorts were seen in Hellersdorf forming up for an attack on Kaulsdorf. At about 0900 hours the battalion received a message that four Russian tanks had passed through Hellersdorf, that our Nos 2 and 3 Companies were in action, and that their positions had already been partially breached. One of the first to fall here in a reconnaissance mission was Company Sergeant-Major Käthner-Potthoff. Simultaneously our second line and the northern and northeastern edges of Kaulsdorf and Mahlsdorf came under artillery and infantry fire for the first time, with low-flying aircraft joining in the attack. The Russian tanks overcame the anti-tank ditch without difficulty, rolling forward hesitantly out of Hellersdorf on the road to Kaulsdorf under a cloudy, rainy sky. When they came close to the two flak positions, which tried to defend themselves with their 20 mm guns, the tanks drew apart to left and right and shot up the guns, which were then taken by the escorting infantry.

The situation in our battalion sector was becoming uncomfortable. The right wing of No. 2 Company and the left wing of No. 3 Company were being forced back, despite resistance. At the same time strong artillery fire mixed with mortars and Stalin-organs was falling on Biesdorf and the Wuhl-Garten convalescent home. The situation was particularly critical, as the anti-tank barrier outside our battalion sector south of Hönow had been opened at dawn that day to enable several damaged German tanks to be towed back by tanks of other *Wehrmacht* units, and under cover of darkness several Russian tanks had also been able to slip through the barrier and had started firing on the positions of our right-hand neighbour, Police Battalion 'Warnholz', partly from the rear.

The Police Battalion immediately reported the matter to the regiment, which sent four assault guns early in the morning to our battalion with orders to support a counterattack on the foremost positions south of Hellersdorf. The counterattack with the assault guns was led in person by our commanding officer and, with the support of some of *Volkssturm* Battalion 3/121 'Wagner', which was in reserve, succeeded in regaining the positions south of Hellersdorf with comparatively few losses. The Hellersdorf farm caught fire. Our No. 1 Company, which counterattacked from the rifle club area, destroyed three Russian tanks with panzerfausts in this action.

During the battalion's speedy counterattack, marked by the outstanding spirit of the troops, who were being able to attack successfully for the first time, orders came from the regiment to withdraw to Kaulsdorf immediately. Simultaneously the battalion received messages from our right and left flanking companies that Police Battalion

'Warnholz' on our right had vacated its positions in Kaulsdorf and that the Russians could be seen advancing west of Biesdorf on our left. It was also reported that some of the assault guns had been hit and rendered unroadworthy. The *Wehrmacht* battalion on our left had also withdrawn. Neither of these battalions had communicated with us during the attack on us, nor during our counterattack. Perhaps the Russian attack had come as too much of a surprise for them. These alarming reports forced some quick decisions. The situation seemed to indicate not just a withdrawal to Kaulsdorf as already ordered by the regiment, but even further in the circumstances.

To make sure, the adjutant went forward by bicycle, escorted by a runner, Bernhardt, to make a quick reconnaissance. He confirmed that the battalion's position was now untenable. He could himself see how the Russian infantry were moving irresistibly south on and through Biesdorf, and the same applied to Kausldorf. The battalion was right in the middle of a Russian pincer movement.

Upon the adjutant's return the decision had to be made to order a withdrawal to the south immediately. Meanwhile the regiment had passed the information that an order to withdraw would follow soon, but the battalion should wait for the order to arrive. Nevertheless, the battalion ordered the withdrawal without waiting for the direct order, which arrived at 1300 hours. Preparation for withdrawal had already been made during the adjutant's reconnaissance, and following the destruction of the heavy weapons and their ammunition, the withdrawal could begin over the S-Bahn bridge at Kaulsdorf station, which was already under fire from the Russian infantry on the S-Bahn on either side. Thus the battalion got out of the trap literally at the last moment, and was able to assemble south of Kaulsdorf station on Chemnitzer Strasse and march off to Karlshorst.

Before going on to the battalion's next engagement, the actions of the Gun and Heavy Weapons Companies, as well as the Supply Section's withdrawal should be described.

Dr Mahr's Gun Company 'Blücher' had its first engagement with the enemy on 21 April, when it fired to good effect on an assembly of tanks, vehicles and infantry observed in the Hönow and Marzahn areas, as well as in Eiche, Ahrensfelde and to the north of there. When the enemy broke through at Marzahn on the evening of 22 April, Dr Mahr withdrew his forward observation post, but during the night received orders from the divisional commander to send it back. However, by then the Russians had already turned Marzahn into a strongpoint and he and his men became involved in heavy fighting in which he was killed. Second Lieutenant Sprung, the battery officer, then took over the company.

On 22 April the battery continued to provide outstanding fire support for the defence, the counterattack and the withdrawal to the next position, but eventually it was almost cut off and the enemy came so close that that evening the 'Blücher' Battery evacuated its position near Friedrichsfelde after rendering the guns useless and blowing up the last forty rounds.

The 220 mm mortar was first used against the Russian advance on 22 April, firing five shells, half its ammunition, on targets south of Hönow. That afternoon it was blown up just as the Russians were about to break into Kaulsdorf and Mahlsdorf.

Second Lieutenant Sprung then reported back with the remainder of his men to the artillery commander at the Zoo flak-tower. The battery received three new heavy howitzers with their ammunition and deployed at Schloss Bellevue,[6] with forward observation posts on the tall Karstadt building[7] and near Alexanderplatz, from where it supported the Bärenfänger Division by firing at identified targets from the map. Once the ammunition had run out, the guns were blown up and the 'Blücher' Battery became involved as infantry in the fighting in the city centre, where it survived until the end of the fighting on 2 May.

Like the 'Blücher' Battery at Friedrichsfelde and the mortar at Kaulsdorf, the Heavy Weapons Company located near the Catholic church was also involved in the fighting on 21 and 22 April with its two infantry guns and mortars, supporting the defensive action and the counterattack, and when the mass of enemy tanks and infantry units appeared on the road from Alt Landsberg at dawn on 22 April in the divisional sector, the first shots of the infantry guns roared over the battalion positions. The three machine-gun nests also played their part, firing everything they had at identified targets, and were especially helpful in the counterattack of the morning of 22 April. The gun and mortar crews fired on the Alt Landsberg/Neuenhagen road junction and other targets, quickly adjusting to the corrections and change of targets passed down from the company.

The approximately four-kilometre-long field telephone cable to the forward observation posts was soon shot through, and the emergency radio back-up failed to work as all that could be heard were Russian voices on the allocated frequencies. However, by constantly repairing the telephone cable, observed fire could be maintained successfully until the area was vacated. The last rounds were fired at point-blank range and then, for lack of transport, the guns, mortars and heavy machine-guns were blown up in accordance with orders.

Under the command of Lieutenant Schmidt, and with his company officer, Second Lieutenant Fleck, the company made its way back along the roads from Kaulsdorf at noon on 22 April, crossed the railway lines either side of Kaulsdorf S-Bahn station and rejoined the battalion marching south. The men were then shared out among the rifle companies. Lieutenant Schmidt received another assignment from the division, and Second Lieutenant Fleck became a welcome addition to the battalion's officers in the forthcoming fighting.

Meanwhile the Supply Section under Quartermaster Krüger had been made ready to move on 20 April, following receipt of the codeword 'Zahlmeister'. Warm food was distributed from the field kitchens again on 21 April, and no one would have believed that this would be the last hot meal they would get for a long time.

On the morning of 22 April, despite the already lively firing on Biesdorf and constant low-flying attacks, Krüger, brave and resourceful, collected rations for the battalion from the *Wehrmacht* supply depot in Friedrichsfelde. After many long disputes, the battalion was at last free from the Party's supply system and subject to the better-supplied *Wehrmacht*. However, the *Wehrmacht* supply depot in Friedrichsfelde was already under enemy fire, and men and horses were being wounded. Supply Section escort Nietbalk got a shell splinter in his leg that severed his main artery, but Krüger used his belt as a tourniquet and Nietbalk survived.

Then Krüger brazenly returned to the Party supply depot to see what he could get. The foreman there refused him at first, but gave in when his depot came under fire, and Krüger left with a full wagon-load.

The situation was now quite clear to him, for he could hear the ever-increasing sounds of fighting coming from the battalion sector. Having stayed overnight with the Gun Company at Friedrichsfelde, in accordance with earlier orders, he took his laden wagon along with the wounded and made his way to the assembly point at the Olympic Stadium.

As the battalion emerged from its baptism of fire and marched away south towards Karlshorst from Kaulsdorf S-Bahn station, we were unaware that the Russians had thrust past us via Hoppegarten on 20 April and that their spearheads were already in Karlshorst. In fact, General Weidling, who was later to become commander of Defence Area Berlin and whose corps headquarters had been set up in the Retirement Home in Biesdorf-Süd, had been driven out of there by Russian long-range shelling on 21 April.

The battalion's losses in the fighting of 21 and 22 April had indeed been severe. An exact figure, as for the subsequent engagements, cannot be given as all the casualty lists were lost.

The majority of the wounded could be taken with us in the march from Kaulsdorf and handed over later to dressing stations in the city, but those incapable of being moved were left behind at Kaulsdorf in the care of Medical Orderly Skroda.

During our march to the south, which was continually interrupted by low-flying aircraft, we could see that the city was still being bombed and could hear the bombs exploding.

The troops' spirits were not especially high, but we were fortunate in that we had no idea of the danger that we were marching into. We felt that we had had a measure of success, even though our fighting had been in vain. Nevertheless the battalion was holding well together, and people gave us food and especially drink as we marched along.

FRIEDRICHSFELDE-OST – 22 APRIL 1945

While still on the march, in the late afternoon of 22 April the battalion received new combat orders from regiment. Halfway between Kaulsdorf and Karlshorst the battalion swung back northwards and marched along a more westerly road towards Friedrichsfelde-Ost. The commanding officer and adjutant went on ahead to reconnoitre the new positions, and that evening the battalion was instructed on its new task at the junction of the Marzahner Chaussee with the wide Frankfurter Chaussee.

The situation was far from clear. There were no prepared positions available, so the cemetery and allotment gardens immediately south of the S-Bahn station were occupied in all haste and makeshift defensive positions established facing east, north and west, while the battalion

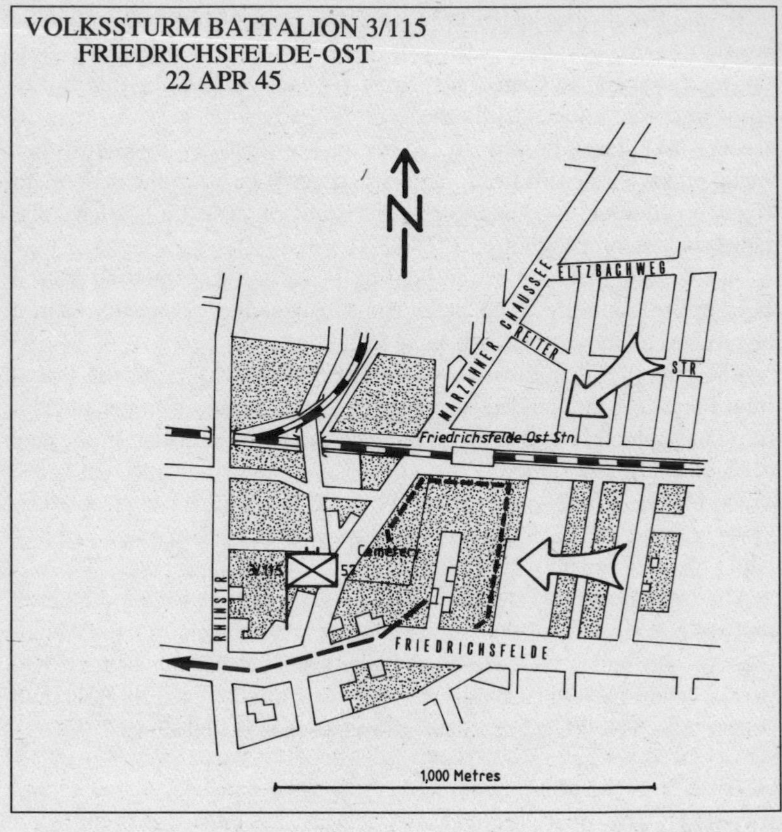

command post was set up in a building close to the junction of the main roads. On our left were elements of Parachute Officers' School No. 1 under Captain Schweikardt, with whose troops the battalion was to remain connected until the very end.

The Russians were immediately north of the S-Bahn station and in the gardens to the east of us. The whole area was under constant fire from artillery and stationary Russian tanks. Individual Russian scouts kept trying to get through our thinly manned lines, and in one case the Russians managed to get as far as the battalion command post and were only checked by firing pistols at them from the windows. In this action the battalion motorcyclist, Mogel, particularly distinguished himself.

During the night of 22/23 April it became clear that the battalion position, such as it was, was untenable in view of the obviously superior numbers of Russians. Then, at about midnight, new operational orders were received.

As it was obvious that from now on there would be no more fighting in open country, but only in Berlin's sea of buildings, and that all vehicular traffic through the rubble and glass shards lying on the streets would be absolutely impossible, except by bicycle, the cyclists were sent off with orders to get through to Siemensstadt and to report to the Reserve Battalion. Some of them actually got through, even though it took them several days and they had great difficulties. The battalion now wanted to rid itself of all those no longer fully capable of marching and fighting, for they were only ballast. The remainder of the fighting could only be undertaken by men who were tough and healthy.

THE CENTRAL CATTLE MARKET – 23–24 APRIL 1945

The new position at the Central Cattle Market, to which we were assigned, was actually inside the inner defensive ring.

The battalion, now reduced to 150 rifles as a result of the previous days' losses and having got rid of all the wounded, sick and unfit, marched away shortly after midnight along the Frankfurter Chaussee as far as Lichtenberg S-Bahn station unnoticed by the enemy. A short rest was taken in the pub below Lichtenberg town hall. This was absolutely necessary. The troops immediately fell fast asleep in the windowless, half-destroyed pub.

At about 0300 hours the commanding officer and adjutant made a reconnaissance of the new position around and in the Central Cattle Market. According to the regiment, the battle line was that of the S-Bahn, which, as it was in a cutting, appeared a good one, but in fact the Russians had already crossed over and secured themselves in the extensive area of the market, had installed several heavy tanks in the allotment gardens north of the S-Bahn and were firing with these tanks, anti-tank guns and even artillery without pause at the northern and northeastern fronts of the market buildings.

The battalion command post was established in the school on the corner of Pettenkoferstrasse and Eldenaer Strasse, where the school bordered on the market and the S-Bahn. The Russians had already flooded across the railway tracks into the market, making it impossible to occupy positions along the S-Bahn as ordered. When the troops arrived from Lichtenberg town hall at dawn, they were deployed on the north and northeastern edge of the market and further back in the market buildings in order to cover the open spaces and streets between the buildings, with Headquarters Company on the right and the other two companies, Nos 2 and 3, on the left.[8]

After daybreak the commanding officer discussed the layout in detail with the company commanders, and it was clear that it would soon be a matter of all-round defence. It was also obvious that the area was too big for the battalion, so a detachment of police troops was inserted between the battalion's two combat groups after discussion with the regimental commander. However, there was unfortunately an altercation with the police within the next few hours when the police commander asked for orders to allow him to withdraw. As the regiment could not be reached for the moment, an almighty row broke out between the commanding officer and the police commander. Even with their pistols drawn, the commanding officer and adjutant were unable to stop the police leaving. It would have meant opening fire, and the commanding officer did not want that.

The police detachment moved out soon afterwards, leaving a dangerous gap in our lines, which the Russians immediately infiltrated and started shooting in all directions. Russian infantry with light and heavy weapons were pouring into the market by the long footbridge leading across the S-Bahn, and were able to form a wedge between Headquarters Company and the other two, which was hardly surprising considering the complexity of the market with its numerous buildings, some of which had been shot to pieces and were on fire.

The companies tried with all their might to defend themselves, but the Russians quickly set up their mortars and were also firing anti-tank guns down the market streets from across the S-Bahn, and so were able to slowly push our lines back close to Eldenaer Strasse.

Here we mounted a counterattack from the command post with a handful of men who had been held back as a reserve. Led by the commanding officer and the adjutant, the counterattacking force burst out of the command post at the last moment and charged into the market complex in support of the hard-pressed companies.

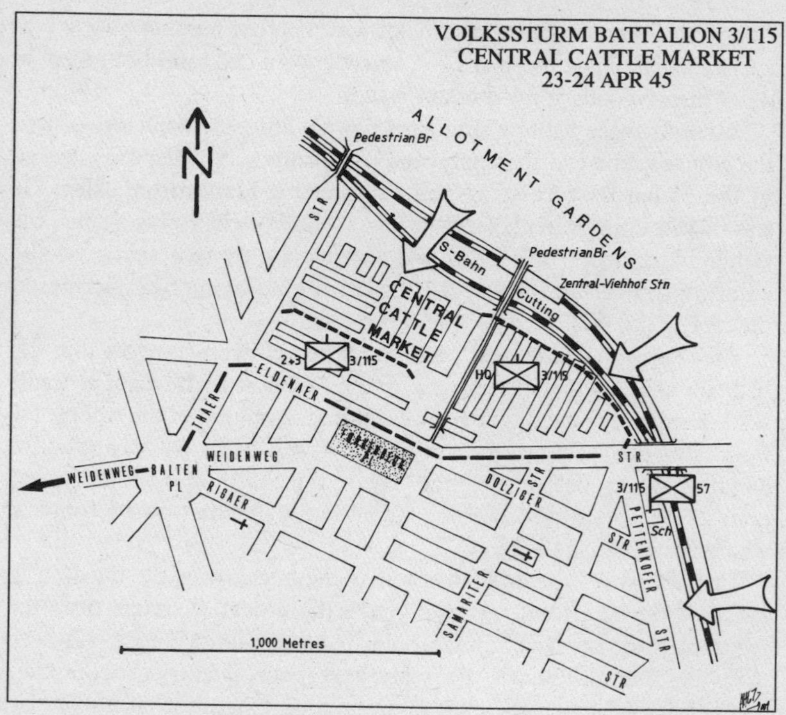

Meanwhile the Russians had been pressing forward without pause and especially hard close-quarter fighting developed, taking a dramatic form with firing from man to man in the open spaces, on the streets, between the buildings and especially in the wide halls, with ricochets whistling around everywhere, and shells bursting in a shed filled with hanging hams and sausages. Men jumped from cover to cover and shot at anything that indicated the presence of the enemy, ahead, behind and on both sides. Small pockets of resistance formed, dissolved and melded with others. This kind of fighting was particularly hard on the *Volkssturm* men, but it was simply a matter of self-defence: him or me.

The main thing the battalion lacked was heavy weapons to counter the Russian mortars and anti-tank guns, and the situation became more and more untenable. Company Commander Treutner was severely wounded and had to be carried off after an emergency dressing.

Company Commander Dr Weinholdt was reported missing but, as was later established, he too had been severely wounded, and both were to die of their wounds at the dressing station.

At noon, as the fighting simmered down a little, the adjutant received the order to report to the regimental command post, which was located in the Samariter Strasse U-Bahn station on Frankfurter Allee. He was picked up in Pettenkoferstrasse by a 'Hexer', which was a small car, rather like a jeep, but armoured and with only two seats. As the escorting officer and driver sat inside, the adjutant had to ride on the roof.

The regimental command post was in two U-Bahn carriages that still had lights. The adjutant reported on the situation at the Central Cattle Market, especially mentioning the exhausted condition of the troops, the now low level of ammunition and the lack of heavy weapons for conducting an effective defence, saying that holding on under these conditions was questionable. Major Funk listened and promised whatever help was possible.

Then, however, the adjutant came under attack over the decision to evacuate the Kaulsdorf position before the arrival of orders from the regiment to do so. The adjutant said that the warning order had been given and that the removal of the heavy weapons, infantry guns, mortars and heavy machine-guns, apart from the total exhaustion of the troops, had been impossible without transport. A sharp exchange took place, in which mention of a court martial was made. However, nothing more came of it, for at that point the Russians attacked the U-Bahn station, throwing hand grenades down the entrances. (Captivity was to preclude any chance of a court martial and, as Major Funk himself was later to admit in captivity, the removal of the heavy weapons had not been feasible.)

The adjutant returned, again by 'Hexer', through streets now under heavy fire, so it was no easy matter. In the battalion command post, after discussion with Captain Sobotta, who had been sent by the regiment to see for himself, it was agreed that the battalion should withdraw, and the relevant orders from regiment immediately followed.

Extraction from the market complex while under constant pressure from the Russians was a risky business, but the battalion managed to assemble, taking the walking wounded with it. The severely wounded had to be left behind in the school on Pettenkoferstrasse.

By this time the commanding officer, adjutant and the last remaining company commander, Gebhardt of Headquarter Company, were the only senior officers to have come out of the heavy fighting unwounded. The commanding officer had had his cap shot off his head, the adjutant had had a scratch to his shoulder, and only Gebhardt remained totally unscathed.

So that afternoon we marched across Forkenbeckplatz and along Thaer Strasse and Weidenweg to Baltenplatz (now Bersarinplatz),[9] where we stopped for a break. It was only a short break, for then the battalion received orders to go back up to Frankfurter Allee immediately.

On our way along Rigaer Strasse we came across the divisional commander with two assault guns, he himself being in the first one. He confirmed our orders to take up a new position in Samariter Strasse either side of Rigaer Strasse and facing east.

Colonel Bärenfänger then set off along Rigaer Strasse, trying to break through to Frankfurter Allee to do a reconnaissance and clear the area by fire.

Samariter Strasse – 24–25 April 1945

The battalion's new position was in the buildings on the west side of Samariter Strasse facing east with our left flank curled back on the corner with Dolziger Strasse, and the right flank on Frankfurter Allee. Attack was expected from the east with the main thrust coming along Rigaer Strasse. The battalion command post was set up in No. 32 Samariter Strasse. The troops deployed themselves in the buildings and cellar with firing position from windows and hallways.

There was some lively traffic on Frankfurter Allee moving from east to west, mainly tanks and trucks. Movement on the side streets was rendered impossible by Russian snipers in the rooftops.

No direct Russian attack occurred during the night of 24/25 April, but at dawn on 25 April heavy firing began from Frankfurter Allee down Samariter Strasse, and soon the first aimed shots were hitting the upper storeys of the command post building.

About 0800 hours new orders to withdraw arrived from the regiment. At this point the artillery and tank fire had increased to such an extent along the westward-running streets from the direction of the Frankfurter

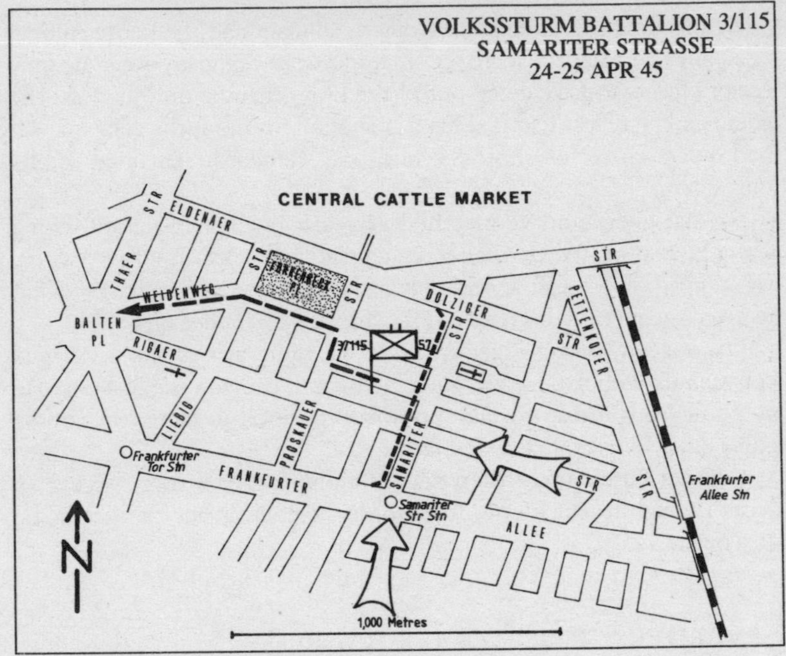

Allee S-Bahn station that it was only possible to move out using an underground route via the air raid shelters. The assembly point was Baltenplatz. It was a creepy route through the cellars, where the inhabitants were sheltering, going through one breached wall to another in the general direction of Weidenweg and Baltenplatz, while looking for a place above ground where we could reassemble. Some of our men, however, found their way above ground.

A woman from the building in which we had had our command post asked to come along with us, and was promptly taken on as a staff assistant. Carrying the scanty remains of the battalion files in one hand and a torch in the other, she led the way for us through the underground route.

In crossing Liebigstrasse, where we had to go above ground into daylight to reach Weidenweg, *Wehrmacht* Corporal Donath distinguished himself by standing in the middle of the street with a light machine-gun at his hip and firing so accurately at the Russian tank and escorting infantry shooting at us from Frankfurter Allee that they stopped firing, and we were able to dash across the street safely and reach Baltenplatz. For this act of heroism, Corporal Donath was later awarded the Iron Cross First Class.

RICHTHOFENSTRASSE – LÖWEN-BÖHMISCH BREWERY 25 APRIL – 2 MAY 1945

The battalion's next assignment had been mentioned during the adjutant's visit to the regimental command post in the Samariter Strasse U-Bahn station. After a short break at Baltenplatz with all-round defence in expectation of a Russian attack, the battalion moved towards Friedrichshain to take up its position on Richthofenstrasse (now Auerstrasse). The battalion was now down to 50 rifles and two light machine-guns, and the sub-units were all mixed up together. Stragglers from other *Volkssturm* units, members of the *Wehrmacht* and even two *Volkssturm* battalion commanders who had lost their units in the fighting, had attached themselves to us. *Volkssturm* Battalion Commander Schünke behaved so oddly that he was at first taken for a spy, until an investigation with assistance from the regiment proved him otherwise. This accumulation of people assembled on Richthofenstrasse and occupied the buildings, still full of civilians, on the northwest side of the street between Tilsiter Strasse (now Richard-Sorge-Strasse) on the left and Friedenstrasse and Pallisadenstrasse on the right, where there was a small square containing a well. The rear of these buildings backed immediately on to the St Georg cemetery. The battalion concentrated on Nos 29, 30 and 31–34, mixed with the remnants of other *Volkssturm* battalions and some small *Wehrmacht* and police units.[10]

It was relatively quiet at first, but by dawn on 25 April the Russians began attacking from the buildings opposite and from Weidenweg and Löwestrasse, which opened on to Richthofenstrasse, coupled with lively Russian air activity from the direction of Frankfurter Allee and Friedrichshain. They started shelling the buildings and laying down an almost continuous mortar bombardment on the rear of the buildings up to the edge of the cemetery. Simultaneously Russian scouts started trying to infiltrate from across Richthofenstrasse, while shells were landing on the buildings on both sides of the street, and those in

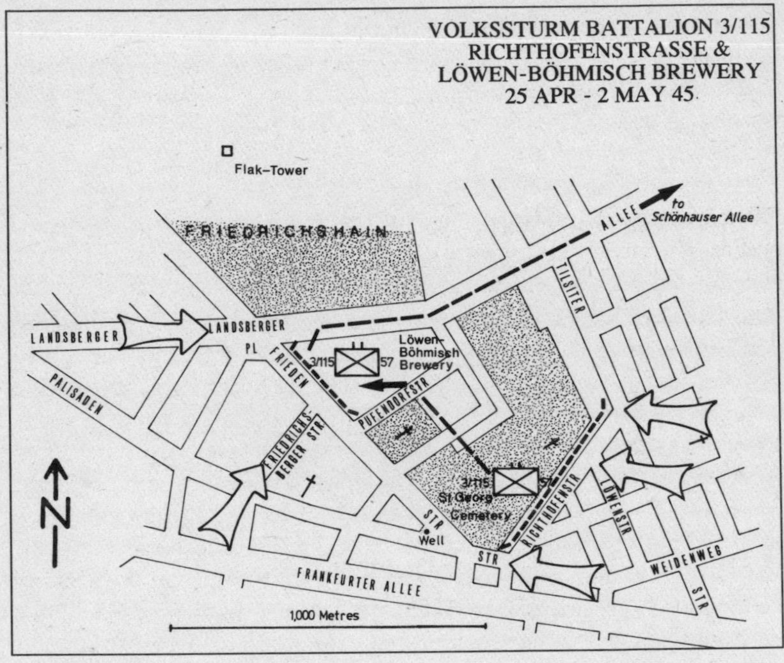

Weidenweg and Löwestrasse caught fire, giving a ghostly aspect to the night of 25/26 April.

Time and time again the buildings on Richthofenstrasse had to be cleared of the bold Russian scouts, sometimes by *Volkssturm* and other times by *Wehrmacht* or police units. It would even happen that while the anxious inhabitants sat in the cellars between the defenders, Russians would be cavorting about upstairs, and we would try to shoot them through the ceilings or up the stairwells. The main defence, however, was conducted from the upper storeys with the inhabitants wandering around, concerned about their goods and chattels. The defence of Richthofenstrasse was comparatively easy as the narrow foreground was illuminated by the burning buildings, especially in the centre opposite Löwestrasse.

From the German side only two guns fired occasionally from what seemed to be the Friedrichshain flak-tower, sending tracer towards the Russian rear.

A macabre incident occurred when a cow and its calf appeared from the brightly lit Löwestrasse in the middle of an exchange of fire from either side of the street. They trotted calmly up to the middle of Richthofenstrasse, whereupon both sides stopped firing for a few minutes, then turned round and moved off slowly back the way they had come.

It was comparatively dark at the small well on the corner of Friedenstrasse and Pallisadenstrasse, as the buildings around it were not on fire. The city's water mains had been destroyed, and here at night a ghostly hustle and bustle occurred as the local inhabitants, our own and Russian troops collected water without interfering with each other. It was dangerous, because there was always the possibility that Russians, perhaps disguised, would sneak into our defences this way, and one could never be sure that the inhabitants would not reveal too much about our positions.

Between 0800 and 0900 hours on 26 April there was an especially fierce Russian bombardment by heavy mortars, hitting the buildings above as well as the cemetery behind, and so dense that practically every metre was hit. However, no attack by Russian infantry followed.

At noon on 26 April there was another Russian break-in to No. 27. A counterattack by a team led by Captain Sobotta, who had meanwhile joined the group on Richthofenstrasse, and some men of our own battalion managed to throw the Russians back across the street. Then there was a lull for a short while before the Russians attacked again, developing into a fight in which panzerfausts and hand grenades were used.

Early in the afternoon, during a lull in the shelling and infantry fighting, a group of three figures was seen approaching Richthofenstrasse across the cemetery from the Friedrichshain. It was Lieutenant Trockels coming from the regiment with two heavily laden orderlies. As he came close, Trockels gave a friendly wave from the cemetery. He brought with him the news that at last Wenck's army's spearheads, which everyone had been talking about, had reached Potsdam on their way to the relief of Berlin, and that strong armoured units were following. (It later transpired that the spearheads amounted to a solitary lightly armoured personnel carrier that reached Potsdam long after the Russians had occupied the town in strength, only to be immediately shot up and burned out. However, we believed the lieutenant in the command post, for in such a situation one clutches at any straw.)

The food that Lieutenant Trockels had brought with him, plenty of bread and butter, as well as the highly prized cigarettes, was most welcome.

Late that afternoon came the orders from regiment for the battalion to pull out of Richthofenstrasse and move to the Löwen-Böhmisch Brewery. The battalion's withdrawal at dusk went unnoticed by the enemy. The buildings were now burning fiercely and lightened the way through the smashed cemetery, whose western boundary wall proved exceedingly difficult to cross for our exhausted men with their packs and weapons.

We reached the brewery at dawn on 27 April, only to be given counter-orders to return to Richthofenstrasse and reoccupy the buildings. These orders, however, as the regiment could see from the state of the troops, were impossible to execute.

Entering the brewery proved a tricky business. An unnatural quiet reigned, and immediately at the entrance was a long flight of cellar steps leading down. By the faint light of a pocket torch, and with drawn pistols and hand grenades at the ready, we went down the steps and suddenly saw six white oxen walking quietly towards us.[11]

We then discovered that hundreds of civilians were sitting tightly pressed together in the brewery's capacious cellars, where they had already been waiting for days for the fighting to end. There was ample food for cooking, an emergency medical service, children were being born, and a group of brewery employees under a very understanding brewmaster had set up a small brewery in a corner, which proved highly welcome to our starving troops.

In addition, the SS had a truly vast depot there, filled to the roof with wines of the best quality, French champagne and cognac. This special depot was clearly highly dangerous under the circumstances, and the brewery manager immediately asked us to provide armed guards to secure these cellars straight away.

From the remains of the battalion, now down to about 30 rifles and the two light machine-guns, three combat teams were formed to cover the front along Friedenstrasse and Pufendorfstrasse, with Schrade's on the right, Gebhardt's in the middle and Müller's on the left. They then improvised defensive positions in the cellars of the brewery buildings and adjacent ones, providing alternative firing positions for the light machine-guns.

On 27 April the Russians pressed forward on the brewery, starting from Landesberger Platz and from Friedrichsberger Strasse. Singularly, no attack came from Pufendorfstrasse. Gebhardt's team managed to knock out a Russian anti-tank gun with a panzerfaust. The Russians realised that they would be unable to take the brewery that easily, and during the following days and nights every attempt to break through was met with fire by the few men available, now well fed from the brewery cellars. On 27 April, for the first time since 21 April, there was plenty of warm food again, and with it issues of French Martell cognac.

However, everyone now realised from the general situation, whatever the news might be, that the end was in sight. The troops, with the best of intentions, were both physically and mentally spent. Thus the orders, received at 2230 hours on 1 May for a breakout at 0230 hours on 2 May, came as a relief.

So at dawn on 2 May the remains of the battalion set off from the Löwen-Böhmisch Brewery to march to Schönhauser Allee. We were by no means alone. A growing stream of elements of all kinds of units surged forward with the aim to try and either break through or breakout to the north from Berlin. In this the battalion remained relatively intact with the last officers, the commanding officer, adjutant and Company Commander Gebhardt in the lead.

On the morning of 2 May the artillery fire on the city centre was relatively quiet, and there was none on Schönhauser Allee.[12] But to the left and right the buildings were burning like torches, collapsing and flaring up again.

SIEMENSSTADT – 21–26 APRIL 1945

The Reserve Battalion in Siemensstadt had been given the number 3/132 and consisted of about 480 men with no arms or equipment, remaining under command of the local Party organisation with the following structure:

Battalion HQ	CO: Wiesthaler
	Adjt: Heydrich
No. 1 Company	OC: Dombrowski
No. 2 Company	OC: Escher (later Richter)
No. 3 Company	OC: Rolf
No. 4 Company	OC: Sodemann
	CSM: Rolf

A general military alert was declared in Berlin on 21 April, and from then on the battalion was left to its own devices, no further instructions coming from the local Party organisation, and all urgent appeals for arms and equipment being ignored. The battalion was only told that the Americans had reached the Elbe river and that the German troops on the west front were marching to the relief of Berlin in all haste (another reference to Wenck's army).

The population of Siemensstadt was set to digging trenches along the Saatwinkler Damm, parallel to the Hohenzollern Canal, and the battalion

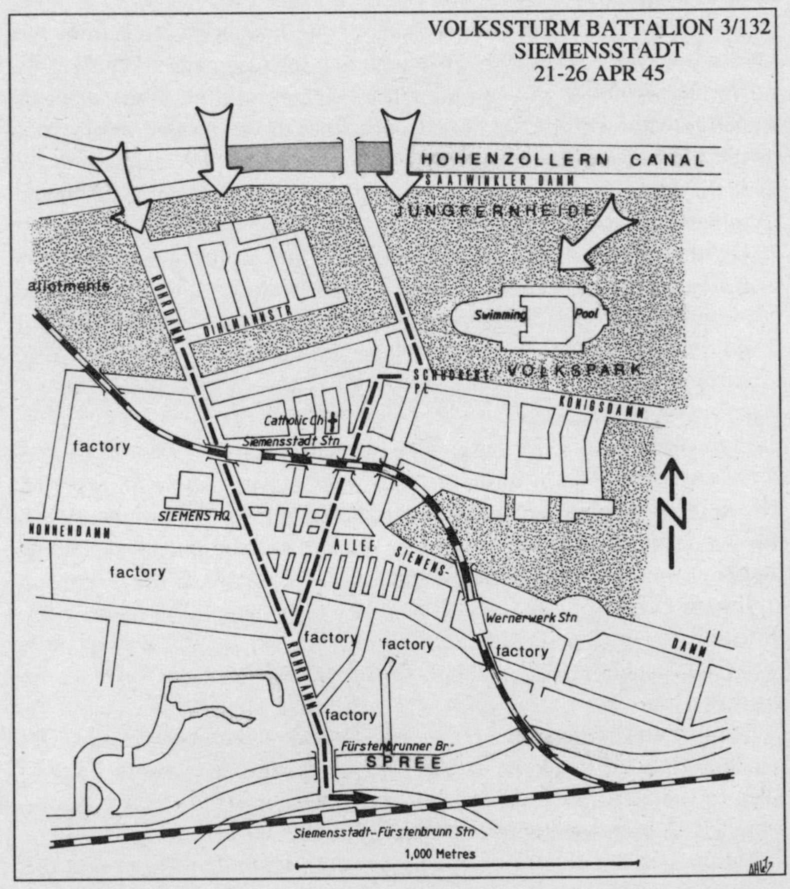

deployed itself here, still without either arms or equipment of any kind. On 24 April the Saatwinkler Damm came under infantry fire from the north and the trenches were manned. It was announced that three German armies in the vicinity were coming to Berlin's relief and that they only had to hold on for a few more days. This was a palpable lie, as the Russians had already broken through into Berlin from the north, east and south.

The blowing of the bridges over the Hohenzollern Canal was ordered, but the soldiers of the engineer unit responsible for the preparations, who had only been in the army for a short time, were so exhausted that they were incapable of doing so. The battalion willingly supported these engineers in their makeshift positions on the Saatwinkler Damm, although only equipped with a paybook and two grenades apiece.

On the evening of 24 April the Russians crossed the canal effortlessly without encountering any real resistance and installed themselves in the Jungfernheide Volkspark. The morning of 25 April was comparatively quiet in Siemensstadt. A company of SS-Panzerdivision 'Nordland' arrived in Siemensstadt and cleared the Volkspark, which had been only lightly held by the Russians. It was said that the *Wehrmacht* would soon clear the enemy from the Tegel and Siemensstadt areas. The local Party organisation still failed to issue any instructions.[13]

Then suddenly at 1400 hours on 25 April the Russians made a strong infantry attack on the Volkspark from the west and south, using machine-guns. The engineers and the tank company withdrew, even though a reconnaissance as far as the Saatwinkler Damm by Dombrowski's company found no sign of the enemy. Then the Russians started firing with mortars, and fighting broke out on the Rohrdamm on the corner with Dihlmannstrasse, as well as on Schuckertplatz, at the Catholic church and on Nonnendamm Allee.

The end came quickly. The Russians sent 16 tanks across the canal, thrusting on Gartenfeld and Siemensstadt, and causing the *Wehrmacht* to withdraw quickly in the direction of the Fürstenbrunner Bridge across the Spree river.

Dombrowski, with the rest of his company, had become the last remaining troops in Siemensstadt, and so crossed over Nonnendamm Allee to the Siemens research laboratories during the afternoon, having searched in vain for their commanding officer Wiesthaler. Part of the battalion gathered here, including, apart from Dombrowski, the

Company Commanders Richter and Sodemann, Adjutant Heydrich and Platoon Commander Schreckenbach.

After dark, in accordance with previous orders, they set off after the *Wehrmacht* infantry to reach the assembly point south of the Fürstenbrunner Bridge, where they hoped to find their commanding officer, but there was no one there.

The Supply Section

Krüger set off with his two heavily laden wagons and escort for the Olympic Stadium as ordered early on the morning of 23 April. He met up with the battalion again on its march from Friedrichsfelde to Lichtenberg that day, but was ordered on to the Olympic Stadium. However, he was able to quickly issue out some supplies before moving on.

The Supply Section then had a difficult journey under fire along Frankfurter Allee, getting as far as Alexanderplatz, from where Krüger and his men were able to find overnight accommodation in the Horst-Wessel-House. Krüger tried to contact the battalion again next day, believing that the supplies he had picked up from the Friedrichsfelde depots were needed by the troops. However, the artillery fire and constant air attacks in the area east of Alexanderplatz were such that any attempt to take the section through would have ended in its destruction. So Krüger made his way westwards via the Tiergarten and Bismarckstrasse and was able, despite shelling and other difficulties, to reach the Olympic Stadium on the night of 25/26 April, where he reported to the supply depot there. Krüger handed over his loaded wagons and immediately sought, together with the battalion's Paymaster Scharf, who had attached himself to him, to reach Siemensstadt via Fürstenbrunner Weg and report to the Reserve Battalion. As previously related, this was impossible as the fighting was already over and by 26 April there were no longer any German troops left in Siemensstadt.

The orders that Krüger and Scharf received from a command post near the Fürstenbrunner Bridge were to go to Haselhorst. This only shows the extent of confusion that reigned, with no one knowing where the front lines were, for Haselhorst had long since been occupied by the Russians. So Krüger and Scharf made their way back to the Olympic Stadium, which they found abandoned, including the supply depot.

A second attempt to reach Siemensstadt also failed. The little unit, which apart from Krüger and Scharf consisted only of the two wagon drivers, now sought to make its way through to the west and, by chance, came across the command post of the 'Wüstenhagen' *Volkssturm* Battalion, another Siemens unit, and were happy to be taken on.

On 28 April Krüger was given the task of finding rations for the battalion. However, this proved impossible even after nightfall, because the whole area was under heavy shellfire. Confusion was made even worse by the number of *Wehrmacht* and *Volkssturm* units in the process of either withdrawing or disbanding. A *Wehrmacht* officer told Krüger that 20 Russian tanks had broken through from the west and that further resistance without specific orders was pointless.

Nevertheless, Krüger reported back to the 'Wüstenhagen' battalion staff and was ordered to find rations for the battalion next day, 29 April, but again was unable to do so. He found somewhere to sleep for the night and discovered next morning that the battalion command post had been abandoned, and no one knew where it had gone.

The section remained undecided, wandering around Charlottenburg until they met up with elements of an SS division seeking to break out to the west via Spandau and Staaken. Again there was talk of Wenck's Army approaching Berlin from the west. Mixed with *Wehrmacht* and *Volkssturm*, this group reached as far as Ketzin, halfway between Spandau and Brandenburg, when Krüger was injured by a shell splinter, and was captured in an improvised dressing station at the Etzin farm. On 13 May the Russians moved the wounded from Etzin to the Reserve Field Hospital on Pappelallee in Potsdam, from where he was released on 26 June and was able to rejoin his family in Siemensstadt next day.

THE END

The leading elements of the big stream of mixed units, including the remains of *Volkssturm* Battalion 3/115, had reached about level with the elevated Schönhauser Allee S-Bahn station when the first Russian resistance was encountered. Rifle and machine-gun fire ripped into the ranks, followed by an exceptionally heavy mortar bombardment, the bombs bursting among the struts and supports of the elevated railway with increased explosive effect. The results were devastating. Within seconds some 30 to 50 dead and wounded were strewn across the street. It was a miracle that none of the remaining members of the battalion were hit.

Everyone scattered, seeking shelter in the surrounding buildings and side streets. The battalion stayed together and were taken in by a friendly tailor, who, despite his own distress, immediately sought to give everyone something to eat and something warm to drink.

It was now obvious to everyone that there was no longer any chance of breaking out to the north from Schönhauser Allee, for the Russians were sweeping the street with rifle and machine-gun fire.[14]

A group from the Parachute Officers School under Captain Schweikart tried to make their way northwards by way of the cellars and breached walls in the buildings on the right-hand side of Schönhauser Allee, but were soon forced to give up because of the strength of the Russian fire.

As it became full morning on 2 May, it became clear that this was the end. The mortar bombardment on the elevated railway was the last targeted fire the battalion experienced.

The next few hours passed in an odd way. Rumours that the capitulation of Berlin was already in effect grew stronger and stronger, especially from the local inhabitants, who were better informed from their domestic radio sets than the troops were, and more and more white cloths appeared in the windows as symbols of surrender.

The adjutant tried to get some positive information from an officer of the regimental staff on Schönhauser Allee, and came across Lieutenant von Schoenbeck, the regimental adjutant, who only knew that it seemed to be the end. So the last members of the battalion were given their discharge and sent homewards in civilian clothes and without their weapons. Everywhere one saw groups and individuals on foot and on bicycles, once even on a motorcycle, heading towards the centre of Berlin and then westwards, hoping to get out of the trap. Except when destiny and the necessary luck combined, most of these attempts failed.

As getting through to Siemensstadt was impossible, the commanding officer, adjutant and Company Commander Gebhardt decided to report to the nearest prisoner collecting point. The commanding officer and adjutant, as inseparable as ever, took the hard road alone after discarding their weapons, while Gebhardt and some of the men looked for a prisoner collecting point separately. This caution was important, as the Russians could still have opened fire on a formed-up unit.

One cannot describe how difficult it was going over to the Russians with our hands up.

During the period described, 26 members of the battalion were awarded the Iron Cross Second Class by order of the regiment, nine of whom, including the battalion commander, the author and all the company commanders, went on to be awarded the Iron Cross First Class. For Dr Pourroy, this was a repeat of his performance in the First World War.

He returned from Soviet captivity in August 1946 only to find that his wife had committed suicide in April 1945 and that he himself had been reported killed at the Reichs Chancellery. There was no room for him at Siemens, where the senior hierarchy had all changed after the war, and it was not until 1953 that a position was offered him and he resumed working for the company. He died in 1971.

Notes

1. Lieutenant-Colonel Erich Bärenfänger had achieved rapid promotion in his brief military career, winning many decorations for bravery, including the Knights' Cross of the Iron Cross, and was exactly the kind of soldier that appealed to Hitler, while also being a favourite of Goebbels, the Gauleiter of Berlin and Reichs Defence Commissar for Wehrkreis III (Berlin). On 26 April Hitler promoted Bärenfänger to Major-General, jumping the rank of Colonel, with charge of Defence Sectors A and B.
2. The Gau was the Party's political district.
3. This stemmed from Friedrich Karl Siemens's refusal to allow the concern's social-welfare and pension resources to be merged into those of Dr Robert Ley's German Labour Front (DAF) resources.
4. This area has been considerably built over since 1945, when such areas as Biesdorf, Kaulsdorf and Mahlsdorf still retained their village characteristics of pre-1920, when they were absorbed into Greater Berlin. Consequently many still have a Berliner Strasse.
5. Kolberg, a small port on the Baltic coast of Pomerania, had experienced several sieges in its history, including one in 1945, but the film in question was of the siege during the Geman War of Independence against Napoleonic domination, and was produced by Goebbels as a boost to morale towards the end of the Second World War, using a cast of thousands.
6. Schloss Bellevue is now the official Berlin residence of the President of the Federal Republic of Germany.
7. On Hermannplatz in Neukölln.
8. No explanation as to No. 1 Company is given. The Zentral-Viehhof S-Bahn station has since been renamed 'Storkower Strasse', and the site of the cattle markets is being cleared for redevelopment.

9. Colonel-General N.E. Berzarin, commander of the Soviet 5th Shock Army, was the first appointed Commandant of Berlin, and proved surprisingly popular. He was killed riding his favourite Lend-Lease Harley Davidson motorcycle later the same year, when he crashed into the unlit rear of one of his own trucks.
10. The façades of these buildings facing down Löwenstrasse had to be rebuilt after the war. The well is in fact a spring with the water bubbling out at street level in its modernised setting opposite the high brick walls of the cemetery.
11. The oxen were used for drawing the brewery drays. The brewery appears to have fallen into decay, but one of its buildings opposite Friedrichsberger Strasse is being renovated.
12. The Soviets were probably hung over from their May Day celebrations!
13. Fear of being accused of being defeatist, which carried the death penalty, was a problem that beset the various Party area offices, as a result of which many evacuations were delayed too late ahead of the Soviet advance.
14. Major-General Bärengfänger, who apparently was also taking part in this attempted breakout, committed suicide together with his young wife and brother-in-law in an adjacent side street.

THE SKORNING REPORT

COLONEL WOLFGANG SKORNING

Retired Colonel Wolfgang Skorning contacted me shortly after the publication of the first German edition of my book The Battle of Berlin 1945 *with his comments and later sent me the following report. I believe that he was, unfortunately, terminally ill at the time and so we never had a chance to meet.*

An emergency battalion of officer cadets and potential officers training as ammunition technicians was formed at the Army Ammunition Technical School (AATS) at the end of January 1945. The school, located at Gardeschützenweg 87 in Berlin-Lichterfelde, was on the site of the former Guards Infantry Barracks. It had university status and qualified students with degrees in peacetime, but only held shortened courses in wartime.

This battalion, consisting at first of four grenadier companies and an artillery battery with FH 18 field howitzers, was placed under the command of Major Lünenschloss, at that time the training detachment commander at the AATS, from whom it got its name 'Bataillon Lünenschloss'. When the Soviets reached the Oder, this battalion was deployed south of the southern part of the Berlin autobahn ring between Reichsstrasse 101 and 96 with its command post in Jühnsdorf.

On 5 February 1945, I, then a senior instructor at the AATS, was nominated by Colonel Rudolf Scholze, the last commandant of the AATS, to take over the battalion as Major Lünenschloss and his battalion staff had been moved to take over command of Fortress Regiment 60 'Berlin'. Consequently I had to bring along a new battalion staff from the AATS with me. The battalion was now renamed 'Bataillon Skorning', and

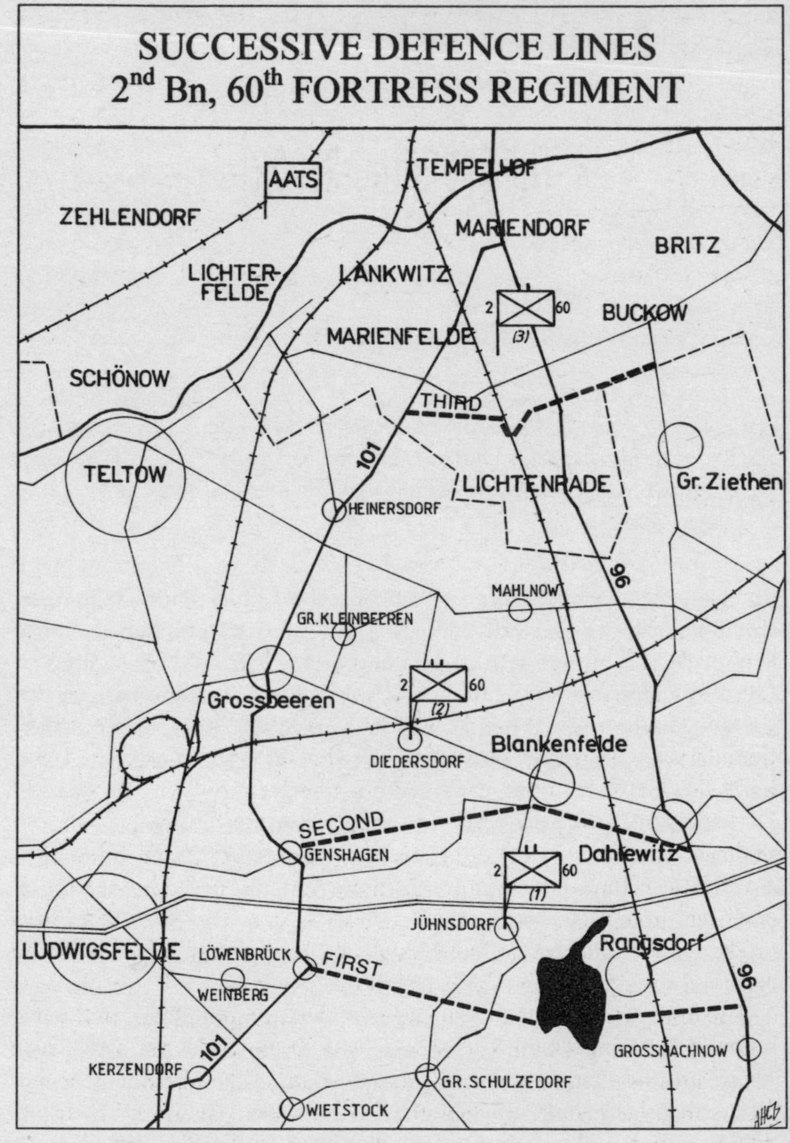
SUCCESSIVE DEFENCE LINES
2nd Bn, 60th FORTRESS REGIMENT
AATS
TEMPELHOF
ZEHLENDORF
MARIENDORF
BRITZ
LICHTER-
FELDE
LANKWITZ
BUCKOW
MARIENFELDE
SCHÖNOW
THIRD
101
TELTOW
LICHTENRADE
Gr. Ziethen
HEINERSDORF
96
MAHLNOW
GR. KLEINBEEREN
Grossbeeren
Blankenfelde
DIEDERSDORF
SECOND
GENSHAGEN
Dahlewitz
JÜHNSDORF
LUDWIGSFELDE
LÖWENBRÜCK
FIRST
Rangsdorf
WEINBERG
GROSSMACHNOW
KERZENDORF
GR. SCHULZEDORF
WIETSTOCK

then at the end of February/ beginning of March as the 2nd Battalion, Fortress Regiment 60.

Defending the autobahn ring south of Berlin necessitated the battalion being deployed south of the autobahn. The defence sector between Reichsstrasse 101 and 96 was by its very nature too large, especially as the battalion was poorly equipped with vehicles and had very little petrol. For instance, until the battalion commander was allocated a car, he had to travel in the icy cold between the widely dispersed battalion positions by a motorcycle combination, which was at first the only vehicle available.

Shortly after I took over command, the battalion was ordered back from south of the autobahn ring to the line Genshagen–Blankenfelde–Dahlewitz, the command post being in Diedersdorf. But this sector was also too large, and could not have been held by the forces available. Only a few days after taking up these new positions, which had to be prepared in makeshift fashion, came the orders for another move back to a proper defensive position.

Defence Area Berlin (corps level) now realised that a defence of Berlin on the line of the autobahn was absolutely impossible and that the defensive positions would have to be drawn back considerably closer to the city. In February 1945 Defence Sector 'Dora' (divisional level) therefore ordered the construction of a proper defensive position for the battalion in the sector Buckow-West to Mariendorf. The right-hand boundary was Mariendorfer Allee (Reichsstrasse 101) inclusive, the right-hand neighbour being an SS unit from the 'Leibstandarte' barracks in Lichterfelde-West. The left-hand boundary was the Buckower Damm in Buckow-West leading down to Gartenstadt Gross Ziethen inclusive, with a *Volkssturm* battalion as our left-hand neighbour. A lieutenant of engineers from Defence Sector 'Dora', assisted by the population, was tasked with digging an anti-tank ditch, the organisation of transport to and from the site being in the hands of the Party.

The front line consisted of an anti-tank ditch running south of the first houses of Marienfelde on Reichsstrasse 101 southwest of the Marienfelde Allee/Dorfstrasse crossroads – 150 metres south of the Marienfelde manor farm – then hard south of where the S-Bahn station 'Buckower Chaussee' now is – then jutting round the southern side of the Rheinmetall-Borsig Factory, and then following Jean-Paul-Weg, Rapstedter Weg, Fignerweg, Kettinger Strasse, Lenaustrasse and across Reichsstrasse 96 (Lichtenrader

Damm) and along Baldersheimer Weg, and thence along the city boundary as far as the Chausseestrasse leading to Gross-Ziethen. The Chausseestrasse formed the left-hand divisional, regimental and battalion boundaries, and so was of particular significance.

Despite the military contingency, Lichtenrade, which lay in front of the front line, was developed into a strongpoint on the wishes of the Party and the *Volkssturm*, and was manned by the local *Volkssturm* Company 2/311. In an emergency, this weak position, which was however under the command of an energetic second lieutenant of the Reserve, was to be reinforced by my No. 3 Company.

Gaps in the line were left on Reichsstrasse 101, 96 and Chausseestrasse with quickly closable barriers. As a diversion for when the barriers were closed, a route was prepared from Reichsstrasse 96 along Töpchiner Weg with a bridge across the anti-tank ditch capable of taking tanks and prepared for demolition. Once the barriers were closed on 21 April, all the traffic was diverted over this route, and here No. 7 Company was reinforced by the stragglers coming through, after they had been checked.

Construction of this position between the end of February and 20 April was done with the support of Party officials, who daily brought out several thousand workers from Tempelhof in trucks, buses and trams. The *Volkssturm* worked feverishly with the help of excavators, and the position was virtually complete before the enemy appeared, lacking only alternative and reserve positions.

Captain Molkow, commanding No. 1 Company, supervised the construction of positions in Buckow-West, in the central sector Cavalry Captain of the Reserve Döbrich, commanding No. 2 Company, and in Marienfelde Captain Steglitz, commanding No. 6 Company. Throughout February the battalion command post was located in a restaurant at the Tauernallee/Albulaweg crossroads, and in April in huts on the sports field at Ankogelweg.

New complications in the construction of our positions arose in March when the Master-General of the Ordnance, Lieutenant-General Danhauser, visited the battalion and ordered the students on the officer cadets' course forming Nos 5 and 6 Companies to be transferred to Landshut (Bavaria) with the AATS. Then eight days later, he ordered the other students forming Nos 1, 3 and 4 Companies to complete their courses with the AATS's rearguard. I too was ordered back to resume instructing another group. Only No. 2 Company, which was composed of former convalescents and stragglers, remained in the line.

However, Defence Sector 'Dora' headquarters laid down that the students and battalion commander should be capable of resuming their positions in the line at three hours' notice. Meanwhile Nos 5 and 6 Companies set off for Landshut and so missed further action in Berlin. A few days later they were followed by Major Lünenschloss as course commander, and he was replaced by an infantry officer, Major Friedrichs.

My command post was manned by my adjutant, Lieutenant Gottschewski, also an instructor at the AATS. The skeleton battalion and company staffs were then augmented by female auxiliaries from the searchlight positions that had been abandoned in the outer areas, being employed as waitresses and medical orderlies at battalion and company level.

This difficulty in the construction and planning of the defence was eased by my suggestion of 18 April that the regiment would in an emergency operate without my battalion as such, which instead would be deployed as counter-attack reserves within the regimental area, completely removed from my tactical command.

Meanwhile the *Wehrmacht* command in Berlin had formed 'Bataillon Krause' under Infantry Major of the Reserve Krause from convalescent soldiers mainly drawn from garrison workshops. (Whether this battalion was meant to be the 1st Battalion, Fortress Regiment 60, I cannot say.) This battalion of one and a half companies took over the right-hand third of my sector between Reichsstrasse 101 and the S-Bahn line to Lichtenrade at the beginning of April. Their command post was in the 'Zur grünen Linde' pub on the sports field on Dorfstrasse in Marienfelde.

In order to render No. 2 Company under Cavalry Captain of the Reserve Erich Döbrich and his deputy Second Lieutenant Werner more effectively combatant, a No. 7 Company was formed to which all the battalion's lame and uncertain elements, as well as stragglers from the flood of refugees, could be allocated. No. 2 Company had its command post in the bakery on the Marienfelder Chaussee, No. 7 Company on the Mariendorf sports field on Breitunger Weg.

I was awakened at dawn on 21 April. I immediately alerted my Nos 1, 3 and 4 Companies at the AATS. My adjutant, Lieutenant Gottschewski, had sent an official car for me and simultaneously alerted Nos 2 and 7

Companies, the 'Scharnhorst' Battery and the *Volkssturm*. It was said that Soviet tanks had already reached Zossen from Baruth.

During 21 April the anti-tank barriers were closed. Nos 1 and 4 Companies were allocated in support of the regiment as a counterattack force and the 2nd Battalion, 60th Fortress Regiment became 'Combat Group Skorning'.

In the combat group's sector were deployed:

a. *Bukow-West Sector*
   Lieutenant Gottschewski as strongpoint commander with a platoon from the battalion, the local *Volkssturm* Company 4/309 and the 'Scharnhorst' Battery forward observer at the Buckow-West School.[1]
b. *Töpchiner Weg Sector*
   Volkssturm Company 2/311 under an infantry captain of the Reserve, whose name I have forgotten.
c. *Crossroads Sector* (Lichtenrader Damm/Buckower Chaussee)
   No. 2 Company under Cavalry Captain of the Reserve Döbrich.
d. *Rheinmetall-Borsig Sector*
   No. 3 Company under Captain Zwicker, who was later badly wounded and died in Reserve Field Hospital 122, and the forward observer of the 'Scharnhorst' Battery, Second Lieutenant Schwärzler, in the Rheinmetall-Borsig-Werk.
e. *Forward Strongpoint Lichtenrade*
   Volkssturm Company 2/311, under an energetic infantry second lieutenant of the Reserve, supported by a section from No. 3 Company. (This forward strongpoint was evacuated without a fight during the night of 21/22 April on instructions from the Regiment. *Volkssturm* Company 2/311 was then placed under command of No. 2 Company and deployed in its sector, and the section from No. 3 Company returned to its unit.)

THE FIRST ENEMY ACTIVITY IN THE BATTALION SECTOR

After the supply units and refugees passing along Töpchiner Weg had had a very demoralising effect on the troops, the first Soviet scouts penetrated the Buckow-West sector on Reichsstrasse 96, which was

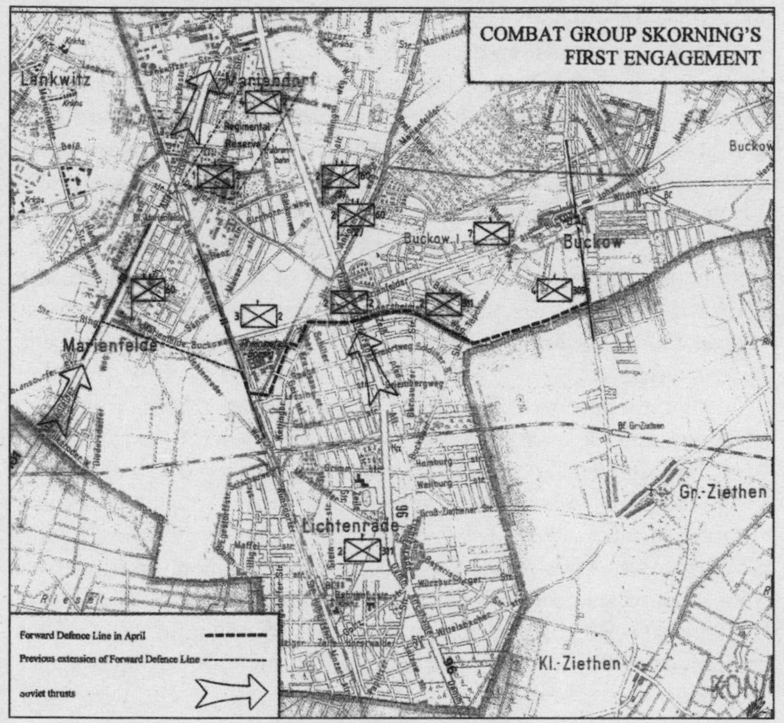

mined in front of the anti-tank barriers, and we suffered our first casualties from Soviet mortar fire. The Soviets were driven back and this raised the fighting morale of the battalion considerably.

On the other hand the Soviets were able to get through the anti-tank barrier in our right neighbour's sector, that of the Krause Battalion, at their first attempt, as the barriers had not been closed, despite the orders to do so! Some tanks that had broken through were eventually destroyed in the Alt Mariendorf street by regimental troops, apparently by my No. 4 Company under Captain Ehrhardt.

All attempts by the neighbouring battalion to redress the situation failed. On the night of 22/23 April, I led the Rheinmetall-Borsig-Werk's guard unit of about fifteen men to the breach point and made a diversionary attack on the Marienfelde manor farm early on the morning of the 23rd with my battalion's assault platoon, during which Second Lieutenant Schreier was severely wounded.

My 'Scharnhorst' Battery supported this attack. By chance, in preparing this attack I was able with the battery commander and the help of my No. 3 Company, which appeared at the last minute in the form of an assault group under Captain Zwicker, to attack a Soviet assault group of about twelve to fourteen men armed with machine-guns and wearing steel helmets (something I had never seen before in all my experience in Russia!) and captured some of them. After the fight a wounded Russian lying on the ground tried to shoot me with his revolver, but a sergeant from Captain Zwicker's Company jumped in and prevented this.

On the afternoon of 23 April, I was in Buckow-West, where the Soviets were trying once more to break through, when I received orders to ring my regimental commander urgently. I discovered that on the left of my battalion's sector the Russians had broken through a *Volkssturm* battalion and had already reached the Teltow Canal in Britz via Rudow and Bukow-Ost. I was ordered to withdraw the battalion during the rest of the day over the Stubenrauch Bridge to the Ullstein printing works on the Teltow Canal position. Extracting the individual companies was naturally very difficult. The battalion's first assembly point was the Francke Park on Albrechtstrasse.

The night before the 60th Fortress Regiment's order to withdraw, part of a Luftwaffe interpreter company consisting mainly of senior NCOs of the Reserve went over to the enemy with their company commander where S-Bahnhof 'Buckower Chaussee' now stands. They had only been attached to me that day!

Retreat to the Teltow Canal

Despite serious difficulties, such as the unavailability of vehicles, the bulk of the battalion was able to reassemble in the park on Albrechtstrasse. Nevertheless, the *Volkssturm* companies were greatly reduced in numbers.

My regimental commander had told me when he gave me the order to withdraw on 23 April that I would have the time and opportunity to put the battalion in order after the retreat. When I reported to him at about

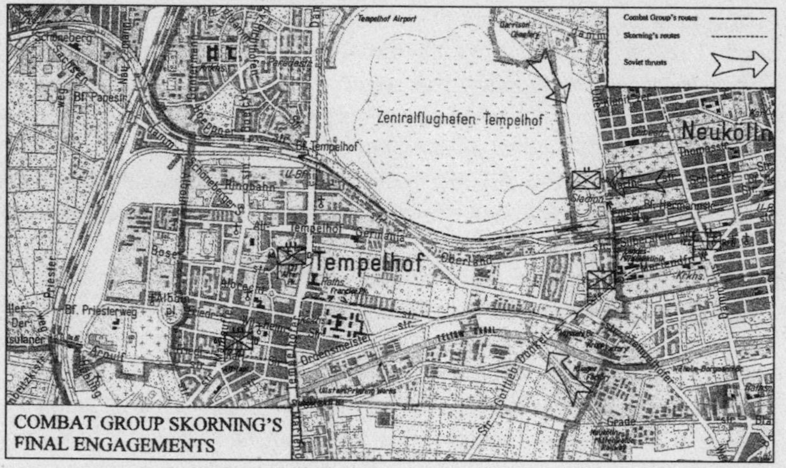

COMBAT GROUP SKORNING'S FINAL ENGAGEMENTS

1900 hours on the 23rd in the tall bunker on Attilaplatz he threatened me with court martial (on the 22nd he had congratulated me on my Iron Cross Second Class!) unless I immediately went into action on the Teltow Canal sector between the railway bridge of the Neukölln–Mittenwalde Railway and the Wilhelm-Borgmann Bridge.[2] I immediately drove to the Mussehl Bridge,[3] where I found great uproar. The engineer sergeant responsible for blowing the bridge was drunk and had shot himself in the foot while playing about with a panzerfaust and had to be carried off. One Soviet tank had already taken up position behind the Klinger Factory and was firing at the Mussehl Bridge, although to little effect because of the flat trajectory of its gun and the poor aim of the Russians. Certainly it was not out to destroy the bridge, but its fire was demoralising.

With a few men of my battalion quickly brought forward, I formed a bridgehead, which was reinforced by soldiers, *Reicharbeitsdienst* Flak gunners and *Volkssturm* streaming back, who had to be forced at gunpoint to stay. As these stragglers were known neither by name nor personally, the bridgehead garrison dwindled during the night.

The battalion command post was set up in a restaurant on the Gottlieb-Dunkel-Strasse/Germaniastrasse crossroads. No. 2 Company – reinforced by *Volkssturm* found on the Teltow Canal mainly in positions at the cemetery north of the Mussehl Bridge – took over the sector between the railway bridge and the beginning of the Krupp-

Druckenmüller Factory, where Second Lieutenant Werner's platoon were sited. This continued on the left with No. 3 Company, reinforced by *Volkssturm* Company 3/311. I discovered that during the retreat to the Teltow Canal, Captain Zwicker commanding No. 3 Company had been severely wounded. He died after having a leg amputated and was buried in the Heidefriedhof, Alt Mariendorf. To my knowledge Second Lieutenant Werner took over this company, as Lieutenant J. Schulz had been reported taken prisoner.

The Russians pressed forward during the night under heavy fire, the Soviet tank in the end standing directly south of the Mussehl Bridge and the little bridgehead garrison north of the bridge. I had the bridge blown shortly after midnight, which was only done with difficulty on account of the drunken engineer sergeant. The railway bridge refused to blow despite the demolition charges that had been laid, and the noise of battle abated. An attempt by the Russians at dawn to cross over to the Krupp-Drukenmüller factory by inflatable boats failed. The single-track railway bridge, which was kept under machine-gun fire, was avoided by the Russians because its narrow approach and structure rendered it impassable.

On 25 April the Russians tried to soften the defence with mortar fire. But apart from several assault troops' attempts at dawn that we were able to repel, the rest of the day was quieter. I was wounded in an artillery barrage on the afternoon of the 25th (shrapnel in the right hand and neck) and was taken to the previously mentioned Reserve Field Hospital 122 (today the Wenckebach-Krankenhaus). Cavalry Captain Döbrich took over command of the remains of the battalion – one could no longer talk of a combat group. During the afternoon the Russians fired constantly on the hospital, where an end-of-the-world atmosphere reigned, and I left on foot to rejoin my battalion. I found my deputy very upset, the Russians having managed to cross the Teltow Canal, and he wanted to commit suicide. He had an artificial leg and by now was completely exhausted. I had the remains of the battalion, as much as could be contacted by runner, assemble at the Landes-Frauenklinik on Mariendorfer Weg, a conspicuous place, but then had a frightful argument with the doctor, who understandably forbade soldiers to come onto his territory. I had the wounded taken off by official car, together with the completely exhausted Captain Döbrich. They were supposed to drive across a bridge over the S-Bahn to the Oderstrasse Stadium, but fell into the hands of the Russians, who, according to the same source, immediately shot them, including an NCO of my battalion who had the Knight's Cross.

DEFENCE OF THE SOUTHEASTERN CORNER OF TEMPELHOF AIRFIELD

I reached the Neukölln Sportpark with the remains of my battalion via the Oderstrasse Bridge over the S-Bahn, which had been completely wrecked by a direct hit. The defence of the southeast corner of this park I entrusted to the previously mentioned Second Lieutenant Werner, who had prevented the Russians from crossing over to the Krupp-Druckenmüller factory in inflatable boats.

We found the 88 mm flak positions on the edge of the airfield intact but unmanned. Only a 20 mm flak gun north of the battery position was manned, and its crew, completely without reason and apparently only to give themselves courage, was firing at the buildings on Oderstrasse. I ordered these soldiers to hold their fire, got hold of the telephone in the 88 mm flak battery command post and reported to the Flak Division at the Zoo bunker. I told the Flak Division's Chief of Staff, a *Luftwaffe* staff colonel, that I as a battalion commander was standing in his flak position, where no personnel were to be found although the guns were completely intact, which caused me to wonder what had happened. During the night a flak lieutenant reported to me with 20 men but next day they were gone again.

This same night of 25/26 April, Lieutenant Gottschewski (later to become a lieutenant-colonel in the *Bundeswehr*) reported back, having had been wounded and come on foot across the airfield via Defence Sector 'Dora'. I telephoned the Chief of Staff, Major Thoma, and asked for a medical officer to be sent us, as our own had not returned from the Teltow Canal position. Apart from this we were able to re-establish telephone communication with the regiment via Defence Sector 'Dora'. The regimental command post was in the air-raid shelter in the Alter Park opposite Tempelhof town hall. Both headquarters assured me that I only had to hold on for another 24 hours, as then parachutists would be landing on the airfield, which, however, did not occur.

The Russians approached under cover of the buildings to my positions on the Oderstrasse and cleared them out. The remains of my battalion were now confined to the Neukölln Sportpark. During the morning a tank attack from the north from the Hasenheide Garrison Cemetery was beaten back inasmuch as the tanks turned away when the first panzerfaust was fired at them, although prematurely and without inflicting damage. This was followed towards noon by artillery and mortar fire that decided me to evacuate the Sportpark that afternoon. We were able to reach the S-Bahn ring by sections under cover of the northern side of the railway embankment. Then we were suddenly fired on by an anti-tank gun from the almost destroyed Oderstrasse Bridge and so changed over to the southern side of the embankment after passing the bend. There we encountered some Soviet soldiers established in the factory area, and the often-mentioned Second Lieutenant Werner was seriously wounded. I do not know what became of him.

The Russians kept following us so that we were gradually forced back on to Tempelhof S-Bahn station. On this stretch of the railway a group of Hitler Youth messengers led by a Nazi Party Block Leader reached us from the west bringing two 88 mm shell boxes full of rifle ammunition from the regiment. At Tempelhof station I suddenly came across Major Krause, my neighbouring battalion commander in the original defensive position at the beginning of the battle. He was alone, physically and mentally at the end – he was fifty–sixty years old – standing in front of me. His battalion had run away! I handed over the remains of my battalion to an engineer lieutenant who had appeared previously and went off with Major Krause to the regimental command post in the air-raid shelter in the Alter Park. Despite heavy fire we came through unscathed and found the regimental staff, only to discover that no communication with Division (Defence Sector 'Dora') existed any longer and that they wanted to surrender. When I got back I found that the remains of my battalion, ten or twelve men, had vanished with the engineer lieutenant.

I was able to make my way back to the city centre via Schöneberg S-Bahn station behind the S-Bahn ring still occupied by *Volkssturm*.

I know that Captain Ehrhardt of No. 4 Company fought with the rest of his men in the OKH building on Fehrbelliner Platz until the beginning of May, for I met him in Berlin by chance after the collapse when he was making his way on foot to western Germany.

Skorning was a professional soldier, serving with the Reichswehr *from 1931 to 1936, the* Wehrmacht *from 1936 to 1945 and then the* Bundeswehr *from 1956 to 1970. He eventually retired to Aachen, my last contact with him being in February 1992.*

NOTES

1. Today Leonardo-da-Vinci Gymnasium.
2. Tempelhofer Weg.
3. Gottlieb-Dunkel-Strasse.

SEARCHLIGHT IN SPANDAU

WERNER MIHAN

While he was on convalescent leave in Potsdam, a wound sustained on the middle finger of Mihan's left hand during an air attack on the way home from Stuttgart deteriorated to such an extent that an operation became necessary. He thus became entitled to an extension of his convalescent leave.

23 APRIL 1945

Cap cocked at an angle, haversack on my back, trousers hanging in breach of regulations over my boots, my girlfriend's red scarf round my neck and my arm in a sling, was how I returned to my old battery, where the 'hero collectors' were already at work mustering stragglers from all possible parts of the armed services into combat teams but, with my sick leave discharge chit from the field hospital, I felt immune to this for the moment.

I had a look around. Most of the old battery seemed to have gone, but then I saw a familiar face.

'Mihan, what are you doing here?'

'Ah, Sergeant Rödiger! You still here? Where are the others?'

Sergeant Rödiger grinned: 'We're now stationed in Spandau, doing bridge and ground target illumination.'

'OK! I'll join you!'

Lieutenant Engelhardt appeared. 'Mihan, what are you doing here? How are you?'

'I was operated on three days ago, sir.'

'Yes,' he said, 'but this is not the right time to say "good-bye". We are all getting ready to leave.'

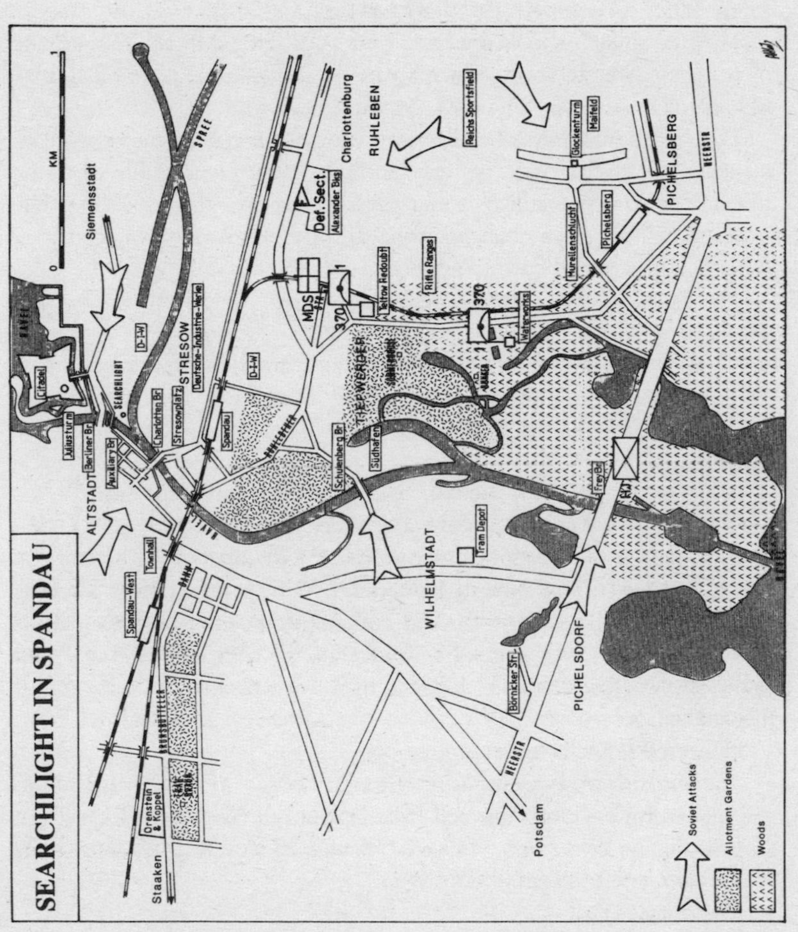
SEARCHLIGHT IN SPANDAU
Siemensstadt
KM
0
1
SPREE
HAVEL
Charlottenburg
RUHLEBEN
Def. Sect.
Alexander Bks
Reichs Sportsfield
Glockenturm
Maifeld
PICHELSBERG
HEERSTR
Pichelsberg
Murellenschlucht
Rifle Ranges
Teltow Redoubt
MDS
370
1
Waterworks
TIEFWERDER
Südhafen
Schulenberg Br
Frey Br
Tram Depot
WILHELMSTADT
PICHELSDORF
Börnicker Str.
Potsdam
Citadel
Juliusturm
Berliner Br
Auxiliary Br
ALTSTADT
SEARCHLIGHT
Charlotten Br
Stresowplatz
STRESOW
Deutsche-Industrie-Werke
D-I-W
Spandau
Townhall
Spandau-West
Orenstein & Koppel
Staaken
Soviet Attacks
Allotment Gardens
Woods

'I haven't come to say "good-bye", sir; on the contrary!'

'What?'

'Please, sir, I would like to be taken on by the battery again and go along with it. I have convalescent leave until the 29th, and the way back to my battery in southern Germany has been cut.'

Then he smiled, shook my hand and said: 'Fine, Mihan, you are one of us again. We are short of a man in the Juliusturm[1] position. Lipke, Mihan will go with you to Tiefwerder on the wagon.'

The wagon was only a horse-drawn cart, but I was happy to be taken on again by my old battery, even though I was not capable of doing much. The pain was still considerable and my arm was in a sling. The dressing had not been changed since the operation. How would it look underneath? It would have to get better somehow.

The Russians were already in Schönwalde.[2] One hour later and I would not have got through. I had been lucky!

We rattled our way along to Spandau and carried on to the Tiefwerder Waterworks, where our battery office was located. I had hardly entered the grounds when it began: 'Hi, Christl, how are you? Still the tailor?'

'Oh, I'm still OK. Who are you visiting in these turbulent times?'

'Visiting? I am a member of the 1st/370th again!'

He looked at me in astonishment. 'What, a member of the battery?'

This is how I was greeted in general. Old acquaintances such as Steidle and Bretthauer from the old Finkenkrug position, Kretzer, Schulz and Frömmert from battery headquarters, all were happy that I had found my way back 'home', looking back with pleasure to our time as flak auxiliaries.

I reported to the battery commander.

'So, Mihan, here is a chit as a temporary pass. Go with Tschernitz to the Juliusturm position. You still have leave until the 29th, so I will not stop you going if you want. You are not obliged to stay, but I would like you in there when it starts.'

'Of course, sir.'

'Lipke, come with me to the rations store!'

My ears heard music with the magic word 'rations'. The chief gave me a whole loaf, with some butter and sausage. A proper meal once more!

Once everything was sorted, I walked with Corporal Tschernitz, whom I knew from Falkensee days, to the Juliusturm position. With one arm in a sling and carrying a panzerfaust, I must have looked odd, and someone gave each of us a cigarette on the way. 'Thank you!'

So I came, somewhat tired, to the Juliusturm position. It lay on the peninsula formed by the junction of the Spree with the Havel river, not far from the bridge where the road from Siemensstadt crossed. On the far side of the road was the old Spandau Citadel with its Juliusturm. Our role was to illuminate the bridge in the event of a night attack by tanks – a suicidal task!

I also knew the position commander, Sergeant Kaiser, from before. 'So, Sergeant Kaiser, how goes it? I am here to reinforce you, but have leave until the 29th. I think we will soon be in action!'

Kaiser gave me a warm welcome. Our accommodation was in a building beside the road, where I ate my first decent supper in a while.

'Have you heard about Garbe?' asked Kaiser.

'No. I have only just arrived. What about him?'

'Sergeants Garbe, Börner, Gruber and two others that you don't know, have decamped. Simply gone!'

'What? This is happening in the 1st too?'

I was not especially surprised about Sergeant Garbe, he was always a yes-man. At least the battery had not lost much with Garbe, I thought. It was only later, after the war, that I realised that they had been more far-sighted than ourselves.

Night brought its surprise. Russian biplanes put-putted to and fro, each dropping two bombs, all night long. As I had become accustomed to the pace of war in the West, I was quite happy with this at first. The 'Sewing-Machines' droned by and then switched off their engines and glided quietly along and then the two bombs would explode with a crash.[3]

Some claimed that the pilot had to switch the engine off so that he could kick the bombs out with his feet, but the accuracy of the bombing soon commanded respect, and they also sprayed around with their machine-guns.

24 April 1945

When next morning broke I was fast asleep and did not wake up until 9 o'clock. I then went back to the battery office, where I had my papers put in order and met some other old acquaintances, Sergeant Sodt and Sergeant Major Gahlke. As an 'old soldier' I naturally cultivated the friendship of the cook, earning myself a hearty breakfast. The cookhouse was always a favourite port of call. Apart from Kretzer I also met Henke and Herzfeld in the office. What a welcome! 'What Hermann, you here too? Have you finished your auxiliary service then? So, old chum, that'll cost you a pint!'

Hermann Müller, my acquaintance from flak auxiliary days, was also very surprised to see me there.

Then I sauntered back to the Juliusturm position. Round the corner came someone fast on a bicycle whistling a well-known tune.

'Hello!'

Astonished, Staff Sergeant Krause looked round wondering who could have addressed him so familiarly. 'Ah, Mihan, back home, and with your arm in a sling? Are you wanting to visit us? It is hardly the right time for it!'

'Visit, no, Staff, I am back with the battery.'

'What? You missed us as much as that? Nevertheless, I am pleased!' And he smiled, flashing his teeth.

Eventually I reached the Juliusturm position, where a special ration issue awaited me: three bars of chocolate, five small packets of tobacco and four packets of cigarettes. What was up? Why were we being treated so lavishly?

25 April 1945

After a night disturbed by bombing, we woke to a sunny day. During the morning I set off to visit Helga Zunder, whom I had met during my *Luftwaffe* auxiliary time at the Falkensee High School. She was what one might call beautiful, with a lovely, well-proportioned face, long black hair falling almost to her waist in waves, and a flawless figure. We had met several times in Berlin during the last Christmas holidays. She had no idea that I was in Berlin, as our postal services had collapsed during the last stormy weeks.

I had only gone halfway when I saw her by chance on the far side of the street. I went across. 'Excuse me, miss, would you allow me to escort you?'

Her face lit up with delight. 'Werner! What are you doing here?'

'I want to play at war in familiar surroundings!'

'I am so pleased to see you. When the post stopped coming, I thought that something must have happened to you. But I thought that you were in the West.'

I told her what had happened during the past few weeks.

'An idea,' I said. 'Would you like to visit me at our position on the Berliner Bridge this afternoon?' I told her how to get there.

'Gladly,' she replied. 'I'll come. When would be the best time? I have to see to some things for my parents right now.'

'Shall we say 5 o'clock?'

'Good. I'll look forward to it!'

Back at the position I was asked – note this: asked – due to the shortage of manpower, if I wouldn't mind taking over the guard duty on the apparatus that afternoon. I didn't mind, as I would be waiting for Helga.

There was a constant noise from the *Volkssturm* and Spandau Hitler Youth practising with sub-machine-guns and pistols. I got up, climbed carefully on to the searchlight mounting and started enjoying the sunshine, dreaming that Helga would soon be joining me, and had a quiet smoke.

Suddenly there was a whistling past my ears. What was that? Those damned Russians! They had occupied the industrial area in front of us, our position being on the factory waste ground.

I peeped round the corner of the wall surrounding the apparatus, but could see no one. I jumped up and ran over the open ground that was being raked with sub-machine-gun fire to our billets unscathed. I hoped to goodness that Helga would not arrive in the middle of this mess.

I grapped my ready pack, took a hand grenade, the only one I had, and got everything ready. Then I hammered the sleeping Sergeant Kaiser awake. 'Come on, Fritz, get up! The shit is flying, Ivan is here! Where's Tschernitz?'

'He's sleeping in the back cellar.'

I rushed in. 'Tschernitz! Get up! It's started!'

As we were about to leave the building, a figure in a brown coat and cap and with a carbine at the ready went past on the other side of a wooden fence, only three metres away. 'Damn! Russians!' I whispered, and took cover. Tschernitz went back down into the cellar. The brown figure turned round and went back. I went quietly to my pack, took the hand grenade, removed the safety cap and was about to pull the pin, when: 'Stop! Let the poor devil live!' a voice said quietly next to me. Then I saw that it was a *Volkssturm* man who had passed by in his brown uniform. A 35-year-old was standing beside me with a drawn pistol. 'We nearly had him!'

Somewhat later we met up with the man in brown and advised him to change his uniform as soon as possible. He went quite pale when we told him why.

RUMMS-BUMM!

'Panzerfaust!' said Alfons, who had introduced himself to me in the meantime. 'Behind the house, on the road!'

'Damn, I have to get my coat. There are 360 marks and my cigarettes in it!'

'You have a problem there,' grinned Alfons.

Back into the building and to my coat. RUMM-BUMM!

A tank had been knocked out almost in front of the building!

I prepared to leave, but Alfons suggested going back and crossing over the bridge to the other side of the Havel. 'First let us see what is happening, and then we can get some more panzerfausts.'

'OK. I'll come too – though I won't be able to hold anyone up with only one hand grenade!'

But we were unable to cross the Havel over the broad Berliner Bridge, which lay under heavy fire, so we used the half-completed emergency wooden bridge alongside it, jumping from beam to beam with the water visible beneath us, and reached the other bank despite heavy fire.

'Damn!' said Alfons. 'I dropped my 7.65 pistol under the bridge on the other side. I only have one left!'

'Alfons, can you let me have it if we go back and you can find it again? I have no weapon.'

'Yes, if you can find it, you can have it!'

We stood behind the corner of a building and lit cigarettes for each other. The sounds of fighting came from the other bank – bursts of sub-machine-gun fire, panzerfausts, explosions. Once we had sized up the situation, we set off for the town hall, and just in time!

A tank on the other bank fired a direct hit at the corner we had come from, sending bits of chalk, dust and timber flying about our ears. Immediately afterwards the street came under heavy fire. Alfons grinned:

'One has to have a nose for these things!'

At a command post near the Charlotten Bridge we were told that the Heerstrasse to the south was still free of the enemy. With other soldiers, we picked up panzerfausts and ammunition, and set off back to our peninsula in a boat. Fighting was still going on, but already dying down.

I found Sergeant Kaiser and Corporal Tschernitz in the searchlight bunker. I told Sergeant Kaiser that I was going forward again. Then I looked for and found the 7.65 pistol in the sand under the bridge. I cleaned it and Alfons found a holster and some ammunition for me.

The Russians had been driven back under heavy pressure about 500 metres with the loss of three or more tanks. Peace and quiet had returned. I went back to the searchlight.

'Now, Fritz,' I grinned, 'you can come out. The firing has stopped.' Like me they were defenceless.

'Are we not supposed to blow up the searchlight? I would love to blow it up with a hand grenade.' He considered the matter. 'Well, come on! We are not going to be here much longer!'

He still hesitated.

'Come on, Fritz, think about it! We cannot illuminate the bridge in an attack. The Russians have already come from the other side, on the road from Siemensstadt, so the searchlight is no use any more, but you should know what you are supposed to do. I'm not the one in charge.'

'The telephone cable has gone, otherwise I would have called the battery commander.'

'Well I can go to him,' I suggested, 'now that things have quietened down.'

'A good idea. Do it, if you want to.'

Kaiser and Tschernitz were much older than myself, quieter and more level-headed. They knew what was involved and had already long since sized up our hopeless position. Survival was all that mattered. I set off.

On the corner of the Teltower Chaussee and Ruhlebener Strasse I called out to a passing motorcyclist. In the meantime it had become dark. 'Can you take me to . . . Sergeant Rödiger! I hadn't recognised you in the dark!'

'Come on, climb aboard!'

We raced along the Teltower Chaussee at a hair-raising speed and stopped in front of the battery commander. I reported the situation to him and was given two packets of explosives with fuses and then was taken back to the Charlotten Bridge by Sergeant Rödiger. After that I went along the 400 metres to the Berliner Bridge and back to Sergeant Kaiser, who was naturally very pleased.

I went out of the door on to the road, where a shot-up Sherman tank[4] lay almost in front of the building. The dead tank commander, who had managed to climb out of the turret, lay in front of it, his bloodstained body horribly burnt.

'It's still smoking,' remarked one of those standing by unemotionally. I climbed into the tank, rummaged around and found a pound of sugar in two packets. There was a knocked-out T-34 behind and several other burnt-out vehicles.

I walked through the industrial area, now our front line, where soldiers were standing or lying around. The quiet was unnatural.

The peninsula was to be evacuated at 1.30 that night in complete silence. No demolitions were allowed, but we smashed our searchlight, taking everything of importance with us, before going back over the Berliner Bridge, apparently the last to leave.

26 April 1945

We were covered in dirt, with sweat running down our faces. Sergeant Kaiser whispered: 'Tschernitz has done a bunk. He almost shit himself with fear. If you find him, kill him!' He could hardly contain his anger.

We did not find Tschernitz.

'We will have to reinforce our Südhafen position now,' said Sergeant Kaiser, 'our other position.'

'Where is the Südhafen?' I should not have asked.

'I don't know myself!'

'So we'll have to look for it!'

At about 5 o'clock that morning we sat frozen through and hungry on the railway bridge as an infantry company marched past. In front of them was someone carrying a packet. 'Who's that up in front?' We wanted to know. He came up to us, opened the packet and gave us each a carton of cigarettes before marching on, leaving us with our mouths open. 'Is this a new kind of sales service?'

My finger, whose dressing had not been changed since the 20th, was giving me real pain, and was cold and without feeling.

We didn't find the position.

'Fritz, I can't take any more of this. The bandage has to come off. I can't untie it!'

I had tried to, but without success. A woman in a house lent me some scissors and I cut off one small bit of the bandage after another until the finger was exposed. Finger? The upper half could not be seen for pus, and it stank. Then came a cleansing bathe in lukewarm water and a new bandage.

We found the position we were looking for at about 7 o'clock. Sergeant Fritsch appeared. 'So you've been thrown out of your position, have you? Buzz off!' was the way he greeted us.

'Calm down,' I replied. 'Take care that you too don't have to make a run for it!' He grinned. We knew each other from my *Luftwaffe* auxiliary days.

'Listen,' I said, 'I have still one more visit to make. I am going to disappear again.'

'Where are you going then?'

'Up there, to the Heerstrasse.'

'What do you want there?'

'Have you got to know everything?' Then I played my trump card. 'I am still on leave. Do you want to see my leave pass?'

He read it in astonishment; leave until 29 April.

'Well, I'm darned,' he said. 'I haven't seen such a thing for a long time! I must let you go then!' He grinned at me.

On the way to Börnicker Strasse, where Helga lived, a girl came towards me carrying three bottles. My thirsty throat asserted itself. 'Hello, miss! Isn't that too heavy for you? You are surely not going to go past me with those bottles?' They seemed to contain red wine. 'Can you spare some for a thirsty throat?'

To my astonishment, she willingly handed over one of the three bottles. 'Why not? Please take one.'

'Oh, thank you very much indeed!'

So out with the cork and in with the red wine.

'Hey, what's this?' The bottles contained cold coffee!

Helga was at home. Her parents, whom she had told about me, also welcomed me. Her father brought up the general situation. 'Yesterday the Russians and the Americans met at Torgau on the Elbe. The war can only go on for a few more days. An army under General Wenck is supposed to be on its way to Berlin from the southwest, but what can it achieve? The ring around Berlin is closed.'

We had also heard about Wenck's army, and it was our hope. We did not want to become prisoners of the Russians. If we had to become prisoners, then better with the Americans. Years of propaganda had borne fruit.

Herr Zunder had been in the First World War. 'Blind obedience to death at all costs!' he said.

'Not with us,' I said. 'I always have the last word.'

'Impossible!' he exclaimed.

'No,' I went on, 'whenever an officer says something to me, I reply: "Yes, sir!" So, don't I have the last word?'

He laughed: 'You still have your sense of humour!'

After half an hour's conversation, I had to leave. I found it difficult; Helga was such a beauty!

'Have you really to go back? It seems to have become so senseless!'

'You are right,' I said. 'That is the problem. I have sworn an oath. There are so many in my battery that think just like your father and are not running away. And it is not so easy to run away. In any case, I would be ashamed of myself.'

'Will we see each other again?'

'Don't you know what my slogan is, Helga? Weeds never die!'

Parting was difficult for us.

Sergeant Kaiser and I were to report to the battery office. We set off cheerfully. 'Who knows what they want with us now,' said Kaiser.

Meanwhile it had become quite warm. I had my wretched pack on my back with a blanket tied round it as we set off for the Tiefwerder Waterworks via the Schulenburg Bridge and the Teltower Chaussee. Suddenly I burst out laughing.

'What's the matter?' asked Kaiser in concern.

'Nothing,' I went on laughing, 'but just look at that sign!' It read:

WARNING
LIVE FIRING
100 METRES

'Look out,' I said. 'Live firing!'

He grinned. But 'nomen est omen', as we had learnt at school, and we were hardly ten metres from the sign when the howling started. On the S-Bahn embankment on our left I saw several positions being blown into the air and the explosions coming closer. 'Take cover!'

I pressed myself to the ground, in the gutter, my head down and clutched myself tight. Don't jump up, I had learnt, or you are a dead man. And it thundered down around me like a drumroll. Then the fire shifted from the barracks behind us on to the roadway where we were lying up as far as the waterworks. I was sweating. Damned Stalin-organs! This was the frightful weapon that we had heard about. Without cover, how could we survive? There was burning everywhere, even the tarmac on the road, with the trees splintering and branches falling.

We got up, checking carefully to see if everything still functioned.

'What shall we do now, Fritz?'

We wanted to get away from this fast.

Again there was a howling in the air. 'Take cover!'

Again we lay pressed down in the gutter, waiting for the next barrage.

Dirt, splinters and stones flew past our ears. Six seconds seemed like hours! Forty-eight rockets around us in six seconds! The second barrage covered the length of the street around us. When a rocket detonated two or three metres behind me, my fortunately unfastened helmet was sent rolling several metres off as splinters struck the tree-trunk. As we later heard, there were several dead on the road who had jumped up from their cover.

We could not take this any longer. Away from this hell, away from the iron-filled air, no third time!

Despite my left hand, I vaulted over garden fences and we raced across meadows and through bushes back to the Südhafen.

'Children,' gasped Sergeant Fritsch, 'your faces are as white as sheets!'

That evening the Südhafen was evacuated. Fritsch remained behind alone and we never saw him again.

The battery assembled ready for a breakout.

'You have come just in time,' said Lieutenant Engelhardt in greeting. Rations, ammunition and packs, everything was being loaded on to our cart, weighing it down, and another smaller cart was hitched on to it.

'You get the place of honour,' the chief said to me, 'up on the wagon!' He did not have to tell me twice. We set off towards Pichelsdorf S-Bahn station, stopping at the Murellenschlucht road junction.

'Unload the weapons! The quartermaster and his men stay with the wagon, all the rest fall in! Cock weapons!'

I jumped off the wagon.

'Mihan, you stay with the quartermaster!'

Then, to my surprise I saw four Labour Service girls among the forty or so-strong group.

'Hey, Hermann,' I said to Müller, 'what are they doing here?'

'They were discharged too late. The older one was the leader, the one next to her is her sister, who had just come to join her from another unit. The little blonde led the 3rd Platoon, and the one over there the 4th Platoon.'

'And they want to come with us?'

'Want to? They have to! Their discharge papers arrived too late, so what can they do?'

All those carrying weapons stayed behind while the wagon went on up the Murellenschlucht and then left, across the S-Bahn bridge up to the Reichs Sportsfield with the four girls, the chief, Sergeant-Major Gahlke, Sergeant Sodt, Hofmann, Müller, Lipke, the cook Feldner and myself. An eighteen-year-old grenadier, Paul Bohle, whom the chief had taken on as a straggler like myself, pushed the chief's motorcycle.

The night was quite light. Muffled explosions in the woods, as well as light machine-gun bursts, showed that there was still a war on. We soon reached the Glockenturm, pushed our wagon under the right-hand entrance and sat down on the steps. In the circumstances, it was quite a pleasant evening. A bottle of cognac did the rounds between Lipke, Müller and myself. Hermann tried to sing a song, but could not remember the words properly.

We fell asleep. I could hear the salvoes of a Stalin-organ sweeping the square in front of us, drumming away and the splinters striking, but I fell asleep.

27 April 1945

I woke again at 4.30. When I looked around me I discovered a 5 cm long splinter of a Stalin-organ on the step above my head. That was close!

Then I was surprised that I could have slept so deeply. I climbed up the steps to the top of the stands. Ivan was starting to wake up, as the artillery and machine-gun fire showed. I assessed the situation.

'Sir, they are attacking towards us from the other side of the Reichs Sportsfield! There is still a Fieseler "Storch" there, but nothing else in sight!'

It was about 5.30, the usual attack time, then at about 6.45 the first soldiers started running back from the positions the Stalin-organs had struck. The noise of battle grew louder and seemed to be nearer. Then the retreat turned into flight. Loud 'Hurrahs!' could be heard coming from the Sportsfield. Lieutenant Engelhardt had gone off to assess the situation.

Artillery shells hit the tower above us, causing plaster and stones to fall. The chief did not come back. Soon shells were landing on the square in front of us, and still the chief did not return. The situation was critical. There were fewer and fewer soldiers to be seen. Should we stay there, and be taken prisoner?

At last Lieutenant Engelhardt arrived: 'Hitch up the horses immediately!'

The horses were hitched to the wagon. Still Lieutenant Engelhardt hesitated, until finally the last trucks drove off and he gave the order to move out.

The wagon rolled off with the girls on board, the horses racing off as if the devil were driving them, so that we more flew than ran. We left the square and swept down the street, and two or three minutes later the Russians took the Glockenturm.

As our new goal, Lieutenant Engelhardt gave the Teltow Redoubt where the Stalin-organs had caught us the day before, an unappealing location!

We reached it in the early morning. I was walking about three metres behind the wagon when I heard bullets whistle past between me and the wagon, and I quickly hit the ground. Shortly afterwards I saw a major lying dead in the entrance yard, shot through the head.

We spent the morning in the Teltow Redoubt, where shooting and mortars prevented life from becoming boring. And there was another salvo from the Stalin-organs, the last rockets exploding right in front of our bunker and causing some severe casualties.

The chief called me over: 'Mihan, you can't do much with your arm, so go with the four girls back to the waterworks and find a bunker!' Then he called after me: 'I'll send Lipke later!'

An army sergeant who had come sick from Ruhleben asked if he could come with us. 'Alfred Kreutzberg, Sergeant!' he reported.

'Well, look at me!' I laughed. 'Werner Mihan, Officer-Cadet!'

'Well, look at me!' he grinned, and a friendship was formed.

The four girls came up: 'Are you the former *Luftwaffe* auxiliary that came back to the battery?'

'Yes. That's me. Why?'

'Lieutenant Engelhardt has been telling us about you.'

'About me?'

'Yes, about you. He must have been really pleased that you came back to the battery. You should have gone to the hospital in Neustadt/Dosse.'

'Well, you seem to know more about me than I do!'

'The Chief has certainly spoken enough about you.'

Then they introduced themselves. Lydia Lötzke was their leader, with her sister Waltraut, Ingeborg Borm and Ute Lange.

I found Alfred Kreutzberg and we then all went back to the Tiefwerder Waterworks as soon as there was a pause in the firing. Lydia showed me two bunkers, one of which was within the waterworks and the other further on in the woods. 'Which do you think is the best?'

'The one in the woods. I reckon the waterworks will soon be under fire again, so the one in the woods will be safer.'

'I think so too.'

The bunker was already occupied by some policemen, so we chased them out. Then we sorted out the bunker, which had two double bunks and a single bed.

'Lipke is here with the rations!' called Ute.

'Who will come with me to collect the rations?' I asked.

Ingeborg volunteered. Lipke and Feldner, the cook, were with the wagon in the waterworks 150 metres away, and we collected bread, margarine, sausage, canned meat and sugar from them, everything to please one's heart.

I drew Lipke aside. 'Listen, haven't you got something special there, since you will soon be sold out?'

He caught on quickly. 'Sure, you can have it. Ten bottles of apple juice for the girls, and you can have a bottle of white wine with it. We have run out of cognac, but wait a minute, we still have a small barrel of rum.'

Ingeborg and I wrapped everything up in a blanket and carefully carried it back to the bunker.

'Well, that was a good deal!'

'Are we safe here?' she asked.

'You know, I don't believe in "Peace". I reckon that the Russians will soon be here, so, just as we ran here today, who's going to stick his neck out?'

'Do you think . . .'

Pitsch!

'What was that?'

'Drop the blanket and take cover!'

Dropping the blanket, I grabbed Ingeborg's hand and dived instinctively under the bushes on the side of the path and straight into some stinging nettles!

Another bullet into the grass, and then another.

Astonished, suddenly Ute was looking down at us from the side of the path. 'What's going on here? I was coming to help you.'

The firing had stopped. But even today, I am sure that there were enemy riflemen somewhere close, as this happened more than once.

We made our bunker comfortable. We had plenty of food, I had some cigarettes and we also had something to drink. What more could we want?

Alfred and I got on well together. We spent the whole afternoon chatting with the girls, who were now also involved in the war. Apart from Lydia, who was twenty-seven, the others were all twenty-one–twenty-two years old. They did not once complain about having been landed in this mess. Alfred told me that his cousin was the famous dancer Harald Kreutzberg. 'He dances and I have to sit here in the shit!' was his comment on their relationship.

It soon started to become dark. 'Time for supper!' said Alfred.

'Oh,' I said, 'we don't have to worry about that! The Chief gave me the girls to see to that. They'll take care of everything!'

'And we'll do it,' laughed Ute, and stuffed the first sandwich into my mouth, thickly spread. I sat there astonished with the sandwich stuck in my mouth.

'Tell me, is this a children's home, or a nursing home perhaps? I thought we were at war!'

'Shut up and eat,' said Lydia, 'or you can make your own sandwiches in future!'

With this threat in mind, I kept quiet and ate. To finish I took a strong slug of rum as reinforcement. Somehow we all found a place to sleep in the narrow earthen bunker, above, next to and side by side each other, and fell asleep.

28 April 1945

When I awoke next morning out of a deep sleep in spite of the still continuing pain in my arm and shoulder, I was given another surprise. I hardly had my eyes open when Ute stuffed a thick liverpaste sandwich into my mouth. Breakfast in bed! Something I had only dreamed about in the army, but here my wish had become true!

'How does that taste?' asked Ute, as she bit into the next one that she was holding in her hand. 'The jam's not bad,' she said. 'It tastes good. Here, Lydia, this is for you!' handing her the bitten slice. She grinned and waited.

The next tasted slice went to Waltraut.

'Will my next one be bitten too?' I laughed, 'What are you testing next? Or do you intend keeping yours for a rainy day?'

'That is what one might call her cut for making the effort,' Alfred said, which earned him a slap over the head with a cloth.

'And that's for your cheek! From now on you can make your own!'

At noon I collected our lunch from the waterworks kitchen, where Feldner had cooked it, and brought it back to the bunker. Even the washing up was done for us. After the meal we sat down together. Alfred and I dozed, Waltraut slept, Lydia chatted with Ute and Ingeborg prepared some more food.

Then Alfred suddenly called out: 'The Chief!'

Paul Bohle brought him in and we laid him down on the single bed. The war had come back to us. Bohle remained in the bunker.

'What happened?'

'Where was he wounded?'

Paul reported: 'Our Chief and Sergeant Major Gahlke wanted to knock out a tank, but it got them first. Sergeant Rödiger immediately established that the Chief had been shot through the lower arm and one in the shoulder. He was lucky!'

Lieutenant Engelhardt was asleep, groaning on his bed in a feverish dream.

'Hopefully he won't get tetanus,' said Alfred. 'I have some training as a medic, so I'll go and get a tetanus injection from the auxiliary field hospital.'

'Wait, Alfred, I'll come with you!'

Helmet on, pistol belt on, and off to Ruhlebener Strasse, but we got nothing.

29 April 1945

First thing in the morning Alfred and I set off again. We found the main dressing station in a building on Teltower Strasse. My hand was cleaned of pus again and rebandaged. The Russians were only firing occasionally. We were standing in the hall of the dressing station looking through the glass in the door, when a tree on the other side of the street suddenly fell as if sawn through.

'What was that?'

Alfred opened the door and we looked outside. Something exploded on the roadway right in front of us, presumably a mortar bomb, and cries came from behind us.

I still cannot understand it. Nothing had happened to either Alfred or myself, but the man standing behind me had three splinters in his leg, and the lower part of the door looked like a sieve. Alfred, who was not wearing a helmet, was hit on the head by a brick, which had no effect on him, he said. We dashed down into the cellar, where we had a chance to take things in. The wounded were being bandaged, poor devils, and the Russians were drumming, drumming away, one explosion after another.

During a gap in the firing, Alfred and I went to see a girl he knew, Fräulein Hildebrand, where we waited for the firing to stop. It became quieter towards midday, and we dashed off. There were some dead on the S-Bahn tracks.

We ran so fast that Alfred, who had a weak heart, nearly collapsed.

Gradually the remains of our battery gathered at the waterworks: Sergeants Rödiger, Sodt and Rohde, and Kretzer. Lunch was laid out in the waterworks kitchen, where we sat down in a friendly group and were talking when the door opened: 'Steidle! How did you get here?'

'Only just made it! Herzfeld is here too.'

'We were fighting in Siemensstadt and . . .'

KLIRR – PITSCH!

'Now the brothers are shooting into the kitchen!'

But no one was hurt. The pleasure of seeing those who returned was great, but many did not come back!

Lieutenant Engelhart woke out of a deep, long sleep.

'How are you?'

'Not so good, my dear. Could be better!'

'Still in pain?'

'A little. Bearable. Now Mihan, are people generally satisfied with you?'

'I'll say!' said Alfred in my place. 'You'd be surprised! Here we even get breakfast in bed, real hotel service!'

'Even you healthy ones?'

'It has its drawbacks, sir,' I said. 'Ute only serves sandwiches that she has taken a bite out of!' which earned me a cuff on the ear.

'So you seem to be getting on well here. How is your hand doing?'

'It's slowly getting better, sir.'

'I'm glad. Well girls, has he looked after you as he should?'

I was given a good report.

'You're lucky, Mihan!' he said, 'otherwise I would have sent you back home!' He had not lost his sense of humour.

'Lipke!'

'Sir?'

'Bring the box!'

'Yes, sir!' The box was brought in.

'What's inside it, sir?' I could not contain my curiosity.

'Ammunition.'

'Ammunition, sir?'

'Yes, you can see for yourself!'

I unwrapped the paper. The ammunition was so light . . . Oh-ho, 1,200 cigarettes! That really was ammunition!

'To celebrate the day, we need a tot of rum!'

Ingeborg said concernedly: 'But, Werner, you shouldn't drink so much, or smoke so much!'

Liquor and cognac were also available for once. This was the life! Eating, drinking, smoking, sleeping . . . But the pain in my hand was still uncomfortable. The doctor who had operated on me in Potsdam had been quite right when he said that I would have pain for a long time.

The Chief often received visits from officers, which meant that Feldner had to prepare potato pancakes for them. We seemed to be the only ones in the Spandau encirclement that had sufficient rations, as a result of Lieutenant Engelhardt's provisioning. Even the combat group commander, Lieutenant Colonel von Gnaden, paid a call.

'Mihan,' Lieutenant Engelhardt said to me, 'please tell Feldner . . . you know what!'

So I went across to the kitchen and announced: 'The Chief has some high-ranking visitors.'

'I know. That means potato pancakes!'

While they were frying, I downed a few so that my healthy appetite would not be so noticeable upon my return to the bunker. The pile of pancakes grew higher and higher. Then, with a plateful in either hand, I headed back, but had gone only a short distance when the fireworks started up again, seemingly destined for the waterworks. Mortars! With my head tucked in and the plates in my hands, I rushed across the open ground as the splinters struck against the buildings, but I got through safely with all the pancakes!

Lieutenant Colonel von Gnaden had gone.

'You know, sir,' Alfred said to Lieutenant Engelhardt, 'I have good grounds for suspecting that the visitors are not for you, but for the pancakes!'

Alfred returned that evening from Spandau panting and sweating.

'What's the matter, Sergeant Kreutzberg?' asked the Chief.

'Oh, my head!' panted Alfred, 'I could've done without that.' He wheezed. 'I was going so peacefully across the rifle ranges when the brothers dropped four mortar bombs on me . . . then I ran for it!'

Everyone laughed.

'Was a brick involved?' I asked sympathetically.

'No.' he wheezed. 'I had my tin hat on, but they were out to get me!'

'And now your pulse is up to 180, isn't it?'

Then something whistled over our bunker in confirmation and exploded.

'Werner, come outside!' called Paul Bohle, and pointed to the waterworks' tall chimneystack. There was a hole right through the middle of it.

These little shooting incidents within the encircled area in which we sat could be discomforting. On one occasion I had gone some distance from our bunker into the little wood to do something that one has to do during the course of the day, and no sooner had I lowered my trousers than a machine-gun sent bullets whistling through the branches above my head. What a target I must have offered as I dived for cover! The brothers from the other side were no longer holding back!

I said nothing about this incident in the bunker, as I did not want them ribbing me.

30 April 1945

'There was certainly enough firing during the night,' said Ute.

'It really was a sleepless night!' groaned Waltraut.

'Firing?' I asked. 'I didn't hear anything.'

'We were all kept awake practically the whole night long,' said Ingeborg, 'and you heard nothing?'

'No, nothing at all.'

'I wish that I could sleep like you,' declared Ute enviously. 'Just look!'

The waterworks had been completely inundated, with shellholes everywhere.

Outside, I said to Bohle: 'I'm going to try to use the toilet in the waterworks. I have to go. Will you wait here?'

'OK. You should be safer there than in the woods.'

I had hardly sat down when there was an explosion. I was deafened and the plaster started trickling down. Outside Paul pointed to the wall behind which the toilet was located on the first floor of the building. 'Look at the shellholes! I think I'll go back to using the woods! Can they see us through the walls?'

Lieutenant Engelhardt was soon back on his feet. He was a tough fellow and set us an example.

We reinforced our bunker with iron rails to make it splinterproof. They could keep on firing, but only a direct hit would get us.

Staff Sergeant Krause appeared wearing a bandage on his head.

'Staff! You here? What happened?'

'I was unlucky, sir. A bullet grazed my head.'

'Where did that happen?'

'We were engaged in streetfighting in Wilhelmstadt near the tram depot, sir.[5] I had just spotted a machine-gun nest when a sniper got me in his sights. Just as he was pressing the trigger, a civilian came between us. He was shot in the head and I got scratched.'

'So now you have two partings, eh?'

'Yes, sir!' he laughed, 'now I will have to develop a centre parting in my old age!'

Ute produced some sandwiches.

'Wow,' said Staff Sergeant Krause, as he licked one with his tongue. 'This is good! Is it always like this here?'

'I can tell you,' I said, 'but can I see your sandwich?' He showed it to me in astonishment.

'No, it's not always like this,' I said to his bewilderment. 'Your sandwich hasn't been bitten first!'

'You nasty thing, you!' and Ute clouted me over the ear.

'But Ute, who's complaining?'

'Just you wait! I'll show you!'

1 May 1945

Staff Sergeant Krause woke us up at 4 in the morning. 'Come on, citizens, let's greet the First of May!'

'And celebrate it too!' I interjected.

'Who knows what we will be doing in four weeks' time,' said Alfred.

'Why, stone-breaking, of course!' said Lieutenant Engelhardt.

'With separate roles,' continued Krause. 'Mihan breaks them, I sort them, and you carry them away. Quite easy!'

'Now I have a future to think about!' laughed Lydia. (Little could she have known, that very autumn I would be breaking stones in Brest-Litovsk!)

Alfred cleared his throat: 'Two men meet. One says to the other, "And what are you going to do after the war?" The other one replies, "I'll take a bicycle tour around Germany." The first one continues: "And what will you do in the afternoon?"'

'That's a fine outlook!'

'But we all have it! Why should we deceive ourselves?' said Lieutenant Engelhardt. 'The situation's hopeless! Or do you still believe in final victory, Staff?'

'No! At most that I will be able to sleep again soon.'

The cork popped from the sekt bottle.

That afternoon the girls and I decided to go back to the gardenhouse where they had previously been accommodated, and where they had left some clothing and other things. It was situated in the meadows and marshland west of the waterworks. Ute, Waltraut, Bohle and I set off and reached it without incident. The whole area had been transformed into a wasteland of craters, and the little house . . .

'Oh, look at this!' cried Waltraut, 'everything's been ransacked or stolen!'

Ute was more practically inclined: 'Let's see if anything is still usable!'

Waltraut was the baby among the girls. With a fine, quiet nature, modest and withdrawn, she depended a great deal on her older sister. Perhaps too much. I liked her a lot.

I found the Chief's camouflage trousers, and the girls some of their things.

Later I tried out my 7.65 pistol, putting some tin cans on a fence and firing at them, but most remained undamaged. Suddenly a man appeared from behind the fence. 'Can't you try that out somewhere else, instead of firing at me through the summerhouse?'

PSST! There was a spurt in the sand in front of me, and I quickly made off. Did the fire come from within our lines, as we had experienced so often already? Where was it coming from? It was quite frightening!

That evening the rumour came that Spandau was to be evacuated. A breakout to the west, to Wenck's army, which was reported to be advancing to our relief?

'Mihan and Bohle, go to the battalion command post in the Teltow Redoubt and ask what is happening!'

We were back within an hour. 'They're already packing up, sir. There's to be a powerful breakout towards the west in the morning!'

'That should do it then! It's bound to go wrong!' The comments were far from optimistic.

I took my blanket and nothing else, sticking some food and cigarettes into my trouser pockets, the absolute minimum. The girls were packing heavy rucksacks. I warned them: 'You will throw them away once you get going. Only pack things you really need!'

'Why throw anything away?'

'Listen! When you have to run for it, when you have to be quick, then you will gladly throw everything away. I have seen it happen in the West.'

'Well, we're going to take everything with us!'

'Well then, the best of luck!'

'Sergeant Rödiger!' said Lieutenant Engelhardt, 'Get them together here and follow on. We'll meet in the battalion command post at the Teltow Redoubt.'

'Yes, sir!'

'No, not at the redoubt, the command post is now at 14 Ruhlebener Strasse. Do you know where that is?'

Rödiger did, and so we went back into the town, the four girls, the Chief, Staff Sergeant Krause, Alfred, Bohle and myself. What would tomorrow bring?

2 MAY 1945

Getting on for midnight, we assembled in the command post in the Ruhlebener Strasse. Lieutenant Engelhardt came up to me and said: 'Lieutenant Colonel von Gnaden is sending his vehicle back to the waterworks. Go along and see if you can bring back some provisions.'

We were soon on our way. Big groups of troops were coming towards us. After some hard fighting that afternoon, they had managed to break through to us, even using the U-Bahn tunnels on the Ruhleben line. Civilians were mixed up with these units, women, children and old people. We could only proceed at walking pace, while I sat on the wing directing the driver. At last we found our way back to Ruhlebener Strasse.

I stood watch outside the building with Paul.

'Do you think we'll find our people again in all this turmoil and darkness?'

'I doubt it!'

After an hour still none of our people had appeared.

Two civilians stopped in front of us. 'The war is now surely over!' 'It's nonsense starting it off again here!'

'Where've you come from?'

'Charlottenburg.'

'You want to break through to the West, do you?'

'Yes. That will make a fine business this morning!'

'If we do get across . . .' There was a brief whistling and an explosion. One of the civilians cried out, a splinter in his arm. An anti-tank gun shell went right through a window near us, and we dashed round the corner.

Paul said: 'There must be one of their observers around here somewhere. How else could they have spotted us?'

'Remember, we were all smoking.'

'OK, but that came from the meadows. An enemy anti-tank gun inside our lines?'

We did not discuss it further, but sought out our quarters and tried to get some sleep. The others still did not turn up.

The morning dawned and we were woken up: 'Get ready! The first combat teams are already across the Charlotten Bridge,' explained the Chief, 'and the town hall has been cleared of the enemy, but contact with them has already been severed.'

The battle was on outside with dull explosions, the whistling of bullets, the fast rattle of MG-42s, and sub-machine-gun bursts: the sounds of hell!

We marched off, surrounded by the sounds of fighting.

'The Russian lines along the railway embankment have been breached. Fighting is now going on at the bridge!'

The morning was still quite cold and we were shivering. We got as far as the air-raid shelter at the far end of Ruhlebener Strasse, where we came across the first dead. The bullets here were whistling more loudly, striking the walls of the buildings. Explosive bullets!

We stopped for a moment in front of the railway underpass. Suddenly Ute cried out: 'There're the others!'

'Hey, Sergeant Sodt, Lipke! Over here!'

With them came Hofmann, Steidle, Kretzer, Feldner and three others that I did not know.

'A fine racket!' grinned Steidle. How could he be so happy?

'Are we all together now?'

'Hullo, Feldner. Where're the potato pancakes?'

'Shall I get some?'

Everyone laughed. Spirits were rising.

'We can't stop here for ever,' said Lieutenant Engelhardt. 'Let's get on!'

Each of us had been given a carbine at the command post. Mine was absolutely useless – a French model that our ammunition did not fit. That was how low we had sunk!

There were more dead at the underpass, including civilians. We paused there, eating our breakfast within sight of the corpses. The noise of battle did not diminish. Sub-machine-guns were firing uninterruptedly, and in between came the dull sound of explosions, then again the slow tacking of the Russian machine-guns, and the roaring of low-flying aircraft skimming over the town hall to attack the bridge.

Now from where we were we could see the Charlotten Bridge that we would have to cross. Heavy fighting was going on, and a burning ammunition truck was blocking the bridge with its exploding ammunition. Masses of people were crowded on the square some 150 metres from the bridge waiting as the battle raged and the aircraft roared overhead.

'We'll go into the ruined buildings on the square, where we'll have some cover from the firing!'

'Will we get through?' asked Ute anxiously.

'Of course! It won't last much longer. The waiting is the worst.'

'I just hope that the Russians don't attack us from the rear!' I muttered.

'There're still plenty of our troops there,' said the Chief. 'They're covering us. But up in front, that's costing some casualties!'

'But look at all the people in front of us,' said Waltraut. 'What if the aircraft shoot into them!'

An armoured assault gun rattled forward, followed by a self-propelled 2 cm quadruple anti-aircraft gun. 'Fire!' shouted the commander, and the gun swung round and opened up at the enemy planes attacking the bridge.

'Keep firing!' shouted someone. 'At least keep them from our throats!'

There was a reckless spate of fire coming from several roofs and windows opposite, and explosions thundered on the bridge. The assault gun smashed the hindering anti-tank barrier and the ammunition truck apart. The firing continued.

'2 cm gun forward!'

The gun rolled slowly up to the bridge.

'At the roofs and windows opposite, fire!'

One magazine after another was emptied, and the firing from across the river diminished a little.[6]

'Charge! To the bridge!'

Thick smoke covered the bridge, where the ammunition was still exploding.

'Charge!'

The mass of humanity started to move and at last we too were moving forward.

'The other side of the street!' shouted Lieutenant Engelhardt. 'Stay together!'

We pushed across and stood in a dead corner, the high walls offering us cover as far as the steps leading up to the bridge. There were all kinds of people, soldiers from all arms of the services, and civilians mixed up with them.

The first ones dared to dash up the steps. Immediately heavy infantry fire was directed on the bridge in a hail of shots mixed with shells, and aircraft crossed over, attacking. The leaders wavered, leaving dead and screaming wounded. We advanced slowly as far as the steps, Paul and I pushed back behind the others. Those in front of us flooded back.

A young second lieutenant wearing the Knight's Cross jumped up on the parapet and stood erect shouting: 'Come on, comrades! We have to go forward! Behind us lies captivity! Forward to a new life!'

He collapsed in a hail of bullets, but his example had its effect, and the move forward continued. I reached the top of the steps at last with Paul alongside me. We were met by a hail of bullets. There were many, many dead on the bridge, and wounded were tottering back, while others were being bandaged. Thick smoke covered us at times. I lay down, pressed to the ground, and slowly worked my way forward. Another dense mob came forward and I jumped up and joined them, but again we were met by a hail of bullets. At that moment I saw Lipke and Ingeborg coming across, so I got up again. Those in front were caught in machine-gun bursts, and those standing up were falling. Again everyone flooded back.

'It's now or never!' I thought, and jumped up alone. In four or five bounds I found cover behind a car. A few brave ones followed me, the mass remaining behind. Just as I was about to jump up again, an explosive bullet went off right in front of me, the tiny splinters burning into my face, but lacking penetrating power. I staggered, temporarily blinded, felt my way forward over a dead man and fell into a shell hole on the bridge. Finished? No, not yet!

Somebody shouted near me; 'Go faster!' and I saw him kick the man in front of him, so that the bicycle he was pushing fell down a hole and him with it, into the Havel!

Ammunition again exploded in front of me from the burning truck, and the bullets were flying round me like a swarm of bees.

Up and onwards! I went past that damned ammunition truck in long strides and down the steps into cover. I was gasping for breath, but I had made it!

Below stood Paul. 'Did you see how many dead there were?'

'And how! There must have been at least a hundred!'

'And we are only some of the first to have got across the bridge!'

'Let's get on quickly now and find the others.'

We hurried on but did not see any of the others. We went past the town hall, which had received hundreds of hits.

'Paul,' I said, 'there's something going on in the underpass. Be careful!'

Other people in front of us were jumping up, lying down and taking cover. We kept pressed to the wall of the railway embankment as we hurried forward. Then a machine-gun opened up.

'Take cover!' The machine-gun salvo smashed into the wall above our heads. 'That was lucky!'

'Come on!'

We went through the underpass, where fire was pouring in from both ends. A dash of 150 metres brought us into Brunsbütteler Damm and temporary safety, for there were only the odd shots here. Five minutes later we saw some familiar headscarves.

'Hullo, girls! Wait for us!'

They looked across at us. 'You made it too?'

'We're so glad you made it!'

They immediately crowded round us.

'This is nice!' cried Ingeborg.

'What's nice?'

'Why, that you managed to get through. We thought that you must have stayed on the bridge.'

'Stay there and let ourselves be shot? No, girls, you are forgetting my motto: weeds never die!'

'Just us and no more here?' said Paul with a smile. He gave a forced laugh.

'Where are the Chief, Lydia and Ute?' I asked.

Waltraut came up to me. 'They are up in front. There's my sister.'

Shortly afterwards the sad remains of the battery gathered together; the four girls, Lieutenant Engelhardt, Hofmann, Paul and myself.

Then, 'Hallo!' I shouted. 'Alfred, over here!'

Sergeant Kreutzberg came up. 'What, you're still alive?'

'Where've you been hiding yourself for so long?'

'Not on that damned bridge for sure!' he grinned. 'I got that over with as fast as I could.'

A white head-bandage appeared. 'Staff Sergeant Krause! Over here!'

He looked at us in astonishment. 'So you are all here! We made it at last! Who's missing then?'

'Kretzer, Steidle, Sergeant Sodt, Feldner and others.'

'The horror of it all is still in my bones!'

'So many dead!'

'So many that they were lying on top of each other, and squashed by the tanks. I will never forget that scene!'

I offered Staff Sergeant Krause a cigarette, and he said: 'You can be sure that from now on I will celebrate today as my second birthday. By God, that was a close shave!'

Of the twenty that we had numbered at the bridge, only eleven remained.

We carried on along Brunsbütteler Damm. Quietly and discreetly, I disposed of my useless French carbine behind a fence. Perhaps someone over there would like it. The odd bullets flying about did not disturb us; we had grown used to them. We gathered together again roughly across from the Orenstein & Koppel factory, where we rested and smoked in the air-raid trenches.

'We were so pleased that you found us again,' Waltraut said to me.

'We were already separated at the bridge steps,' I recalled, 'and after that we were in a bit of a hurry!'

'Hopefully, it will go on like this!'

My ears pricked up. 'They seem to have found us!'

The firing increased. A 'Tiger' and two assault guns rolled past and stopped 150 metres from us hard on the right-hand side of the street. 'Let's go!'

We went on and got as far as the 'Tiger'. When I turned round, the others were still some distance behind me. Machine-gun salvoes were whipping down the street from up ahead. In a few strides I was across the street and standing on some open ground a few metres off it. The others came forward in a dense bunch. I moved slowly towards them. Then in a fraction of a second there came a whistling and a sharp explosion, and splinters flew off the front of the 'Tiger'. I threw myself down. People were screaming or lying still, waving their arms in the air, falling, stumbling bloodily around, and collapsing here and there. The rest fled away from the street, where the next shells were already exploding. Immediately afterwards there were two explosions in the gardens from tank or anti-tank gunfire. It was horrifying!

The battery survivors gathered together. Lieutenant Engelhardt had his chest bandaged. Ingeborg had splinters in her upper arm and face, Ute in her leg and face. Lipke and Paul had also been wounded.

Snipers were firing from somewhere in the meadows, and shells were exploding. I became scared for the first time, really frightened! Those who have never been frightened have never had to undergo such an experience!

I lay down under cover for a few minutes and then went back to the others. They were looking for a shelter in the gardens close by. But wasn't somebody missing? They must be back on the street. I went back to the roadside, where bullets were still whistling and shells exploding. Suddenly I heard a low voice: 'Werner!'

I turned to my right from where the call had come and saw a girl wrapped in a blanket lying there looking at me. 'Waltraut! What's happened?'

I knelt down beside her. She lay there with a bloodless face and pale lips. She had a tiny wound in her right cheek, but there must be something else. 'Waltraut, what's wrong? Is it very bad?'

'Here, in my right shoulder. It's sitting there!' she whispered. There was a small pea-sized hole between her breast and shoulder. I wanted to find a medical orderly. 'Werner, stay with me! Don't leave me alone!'

'I'll stay here, Waltraut. I only want to get some help.'

'Never mind, just stay with me!'

Hofmann came past.

'See if you can find a medic!' He promised to.

The bullets were whistling past, even where we were lying, as the mass of humanity streamed past, heading west. Some frightful individual fates were being met, but the majority moved on westward, despite their losses, onward to the west!

Two medical orderlies came past. I called them over and they bandaged Waltraut's shoulder, which had become blue and was bleeding profusely.

'Werner, I'll die here. Go with the others!'

'But, Waltraut, you're not going to die. The wound is not as bad as that.'

'I can't move my arm any more.'

'It'll soon get better. You've no need to be afraid.'

'Where are the others?'

'Safe in the gardens.'

'Where's my sister? Why doesn't she come and look after me?'

Now I realised who was still missing, and I would have to lie. 'She's with the Chief, Waltraut. She's been wounded too.'

'Badly?'

'No, only lightly.' She calmed down.

After an hour, during which we were under constant sniper fire, I was at last able to call over three civilians and together we moved Waltraut into a summerhouse. The people living there took good care of us, bringing steaming soup, something to drink and everything necessary. A woman wearing a Red Cross armband appeared. 'Frau Braun,' she announced herself. 'This garden house belongs to me.'

'Mihan,' I bowed. 'Thank you very much indeed for allowing us to stay, and for the food.'

'But of course!'

What should I do? Rejoin the others, leaving Waltraut on her own? A difficult decision. But here lay Waltraut, who wanted to live and needed me. I decided to stay.

Toward evening another woman arrived bringing greetings from Lieutenant Engelhardt with instructions for me to stay and look after Waltraut. But what about him? 'The lieutenant and the others went off in a truck towards Staaken.'

'Were the girls with him?'

'Two.'

'An older one?'

'No, two young ones.'

I realised that Lydia must be dead. What should I do? As a soldier, I should really carry on. My orders from Lieutenant Engelhardt were not in writing. I thought it over a long time before finally deciding to stay.

All night long I kept watch from a deck chair, chatting with Waltraut whenever she was conscious. There were explosions, the night was cold and the hours very, very long.

3 May 1945

The dawn came at last. Waltraut talked of her parents and her sisters, whom she loved. They had lived in East Prussia, from where her parents had been evacuated to Sonneberg in Thüringia. She herself had become a flak auxiliary in Essen and had come to visit her sister in Berlin. And her visit had to end like this!

Waltraut thought for a bit. 'Werner.'

'Yes.'

'Have you ever kissed a girl?'

'Yes, I have. Why?'

'Werner,' she said hesitantly, 'I've never kissed a man. If I'm going to die here, please kiss me!'

I shall never forget that kiss in all my life.

'Thank you, Werner. I . . . I'm so ashamed!'

'Don't worry about it, Waltraut. I like you very much.'

She fell asleep with a smile on her lips.

Frau Braun returned, bringing breakfast and clothing. 'How is she?'

'She's fallen asleep again.'

'Good. Here's some of my husband's civilian clothing for you. He's at the front somewhere or other. Put them on. There are hardly any of our troops around at the moment. The Russians will soon be here.'

Then she went out again.

I was left to my thoughts once more, with yet another difficult decision to make. Change clothes? Desertion or captivity? A thousand thoughts filled my head. Good. I'll change clothes. They fitted. I put my paybook in the stove and dug a deep hole in the garden and buried my uniform in it. I held my 7.65 pistol in my hand for a while. What would the future hold? Nazi propaganda was firmly embedded in us. Shoot myself? No, I wanted to live! After five minutes the pistol went into the hole with my uniform and I shovelled earth on top. My decision was final: to live!

I was still painfully uncomfortable whenever Waltraut mentioned her sister. I had to know for certain. I found it hard to lie, but I found it impossible to tell her what I thought was the truth. I had found both their rucksacks.

It was a strange sensation seeing the first Russian tanks and soldiers on the street. The tanks were heading towards Staaken, where some heavy fighting was taking place. Artillery, mortars, tanks and aircraft were all being set on our troops. A bloody ending! Fighting was going on as far off as Paaren and Döberitz.[7]

The dead were being buried alongside the street. I dared to venture out to where they were lying in rows. Lydia was not among them. There were also many dead in the allotments around. Then I went to look along the edge of the road where the catastrophe had occurred, and there I found Lydia where she had fallen. She must have been killed instantly. She was full of splinters. I removed some papers and other items belonging to her, then she was carried over to the others.

A woman was writing down names and field post office numbers. By coincidence, I read my own: 1./370! Who could that be? I looked at the dead and was astonished to see Staff Sergeant Krause. So he too was dead, he who wanted to celebrate 2 May as a second birthday with me.

Deeply moved, I watched the burial of the 30 dead in a long grave. How could I tell Waltraut? Another difficult decision.

That afternoon the first Russian infantry started combing through the gardens and summerhouses. An elderly soldier entered carrying a sub-machine-gun. In mixed German and Russian he asked me whether I was a soldier, which I denied, and then for my documents, which I did not have. Eventually I convinced him that I was too young to have been a soldier and he went off. We remained undisturbed after that.

That evening the fighting flared up in the distance. Night returned; the third that I had been unable to sleep. I kept watch. Waltraut had difficulty with her breathing, and often asked me to hold her up to enable her to breathe more easily.

4 May 1945

But she did not complain. The morphine injected the previous afternoon had deadened the pain. The night dragged on and at about 6.30 in the morning she asked me to lift her up again. I held her as she leant against my breast.

'Is that any better, Waltraut?'

'Yes, it's better.'

Then suddenly she cried out: 'Werner! Werner! I'm choking! I am not getting any air any more!'

After some frantic gasping for breath, she became unconscious, her body writhing with pain. It all happened quickly. Her heart beat became steadily weaker and weaker until it finally stopped. Waltraut was no more.

And I had been unable to do anything other than watch idly and helplessly as her life came to an end. The arduous circumstances of the past three days and nights, the lack of sleep, the whole experience had reached its climax and I was totally exhausted.

With the help of Frau Braun's son, Horst, I dug a grave close to the big one, and we buried Waltraut at about 11 o'clock. A last glimpse of her dead, peaceful face, some flowers in the grave, and then we shovelled it full, forming a mound over it.

I got my things together and set off for home in my borrowed suit of Manchester cloth. A last look at her grave and I was on my way, taking my thoughts with me those 22 kilometres back to Potsdam. I had decided to put an end to the war for myself. Had not others, cleverer and with more foresight than myself, done the same?

New thoughts kept arising, the road introducing them with the dead lying on the verges, abandoned equipment and shot-up tanks. Peace reigned on the roads. There were no more sounds of fighting, no more aircraft, no air attacks. Peace!

What kind of life was facing me? What would the future bring? Thoughts after thoughts all the way to Potsdam.

On 5 May 1945 I reported to the Russian Kommandatura in Potsdam and was discharged as a civilian. How good that sounds!

It was my eighteenth birthday.

In May 1945 Werner Mihan returned to his old school in Potsdam to take the examinations he had been unable to complete two years earlier. Then towards the end of June 1945 he was summoned to the town hall and, along with about 400 other former soldiers, was arrested and eventually transported off to labour camps in Russia, presumably as a security precaution prior to the Potsdam Conference. He sustained a severe back injury while logging and was repatriated in August 1946.

Upon his return from the Soviet Union, Werner Mihan enquired with the Red Cross about the fate of his battery comrades, all of whom had been reported missing, apart from Steidle, who was still a prisoner of war.

Werner Mihan later qualified as a school teacher for hearing impaired children, while retaining a keen interest in photography and local history, writing various articles for local newspapers. In 1997 he published his study of the bombing of Potsdam under the title Die Nacht von Potsdam, *proving that much of the damage within the city centre attributed to the RAF by the East German regime had in fact been caused by Soviet shelling.*

NOTES

1. The 30 metre high Juliusturm is located within the sixteenth-century Spandau Citadel, which it pre-dates, and was used as a storehouse for the reparation money extracted from the French after the Franco-Prussian War. The searchlight position was a good 300 metres south of the tower.
2. Immediately north of Falkensee, from where the battery had come.
3. The Po-2 Soviet biplane was armoured against infantry fire and used mainly for night bombing attacks on communications areas.
4. The Soviet 2nd Guards Tank Army, attacking from Siemensstadt, was primarily equipped with American Lend-Lease material. This thrust towards the Berliner Bridge served to bring them up to the boundary with the 47th Army attacking Spandau from the other side of the Havel, and as a diversion from the main attack from Siemensstadt into Charlottenburg. It was also presumably intended to take Spandau Citadel but, the tank attack having been repulsed, this did not surrender until 1 May 1945.
5. It was outside this tram depot that Major-General Lewis Lyne, commanding the 7th Armoured Division 'The Desert Rats', took the salute as British troops drove into Berlin on 4 July 1945.
6. The exploding ammunition truck and the use of the quadruple anti-aircraft gun were also witnessed by Helmuth Altner. See my translation of his book, *Berlin Dance of Death*.
7. The German infantry training area due west of Berlin.

SURRENDER NEGOTIATIONS

COLONEL THEODOR VON DUFVING (1907–2001)

I first saw Colonel von Dufving on video in an interview he gave for Chronos-Film in Berlin in 1993, as a result of which I went to visit him at his home in West Germany and we remained in correspondence until his death. He even lent me his historically valuable archives to study at leisure, for which I remain extremely grateful.

Colonel von Dufving was a regular officer in the Wehrmacht*, promoted to captain on 1 January 1939, qualified as a major in the General Staff on 1 April 1941 and was promoted to lieutenant-colonel on 1 January 1943. In April 1945 he was assigned as Chief of Staff to the newly reactivated Headquarters LVI Panzer Corps, which was switched from the Harz Mountains to take over several divisions of the 9th Army on the Oder front astride Seelow on the night of 12/13 April 1945. His final promotion to colonel was on 1 April 1945, but he was not informed of this until a month later.*

My notes on the surrender negotiations were taken from me on 9 May 1945 in the Butyrka Prison in Moscow, by which time I had read them through and learnt them by heart. During my long captivity of ten years and seven months, and especially during my solitary confinement of thirteen months, I systematically reviewed the events in my mind. It is possible that I made some mistakes and that some aspects were revised subjectively, but I did try to portray things as objectively as possible. However, absolute objectivity is impossible to achieve, our views and descriptions are always tied to ourselves and our attitude towards life and death.

After my return from captivity in 1956, I took pains to study the relevant literature on the final fighting in Berlin and I am still not finished. My manuscript about the surrender negotiations has still to be supplemented and completed by me, and several points have to be corrected.

The confusion on Monday, 30 April 1945 was so great that I can only amend my text from those of General Weidling[1] and Colonel Refior.[2]

At about 1000 hours there was a commanders' conference in the Information Room of the Bendler Block[3] about the intended breakout at 2200 hours by the Berlin defence. It was intended to offer the opportunity to do so to all those positions still holding out in the combat area. It was no longer possible to assemble the troops at any one point to form a driving wedge, as all our forces were tied down on all fronts.

At about 1300 hours a messenger from the Reichs Chancellery arrived at the Bendler Block bringing a written message from Hitler to Weidling, the contents of which read something like:

> In the event that there should be a shortage of ammunition or supplies in the Reichs capital, I hereby give my permission for our troops to attempt a breakout. This operation should be organised in combat teams as small as possible. Every effort should be made to link up with German units still carrying on the fight outside the city of Berlin. If such cannot be located, then the Berlin forces must take to the woods and continue resistance from there.

Apparently General Krebs[4] had obtained this order from Hitler, but I accept that General Weidling's very pressing proposals to alleviate the useless suffering of the population had contributed to Hitler allowing the breakout.

We worked on the preparations for the breakout from 1200 to 1800 hours.

Then at about 1800 hours the same SS messenger brought a new letter from the Reichs Chancellery:

> General Weidling is to report to General Krebs in the Reichs Chancellery immediately. All preparations for the breakout planned for 30 April are to cease.

General Weidling complied with this order and at about 2000 hours he sent for me. I set off immediately. Major Siegfried Knappe[5] (Ia LVI Panzer Corps), a clerk and one or two runners came with me in an armoured personnel carrier. The route was very hard to follow, with smoke and dust hampering visibility. Attics were on fire and there was rubble and shot-up, burnt-out vehicles littering the streets. The shelling was so fierce that, despite the short distance, we were hit by shell splinters and a runner was injured. During the journey there was a sudden bang and a violent jolt as we drove into a burnt-out vehicle.

The Reichs Chancellery offered a glimpse of Armageddon, but I would rather not comment further.

In a tiny side room, General Weidling told me personally, in strict confidence, that Hitler had committed suicide. Later Weidling told me of the in-comprehensible marriage of Hitler to Eva Braun, which was the first time I had heard of her, and that General Krebs had been tasked, although he did not say by whom, to conduct surrender negotiations. I was to escort him, for the Chief of Staff no longer had any senior officers on his staff. This was how I was requisitioned as General Krebs's escort. General Weidling was unable to brief me on the proposed negotiations, saying only that Krebs would give me my instructions. This was between 2200 and 2400 hours. Shortly before midnight, Krebs called for me: 'We're off, von Dufving. Have you got a pass?'

'A special pass for negotiations? No!'

A pass was quickly prepared for me by Bormann[6] and his secretary. SS-Brigadier Wilhelm Mohnke[7] then led us from the Reichs Chancellery to the 'Zitadelle' command post,[8] which was located in the Air Ministry building. Krebs was wearing a leather overcoat. He had some fresh scars on his face, where he had been wounded from glass splinters in March. I had no overcoat, so an SS officer lent me his.

We ran across the street during a pause in the firing and climbed down a shaft and then along by U-Bahn tunnel to the 'Zitadelle' command post, where Lieutenant-Colonel Seifert reported to General Krebs that the 'crossing point' for the parliamentarians, about 100 metres wide and 250 metres long, had been arranged with the Soviet troops. A ceasefire was in existence here for the troops on both sides.

We set off. Lieutenant-Colonel Seifert led us through a shell-damaged garden. It was very dark. An interpreter and two soldiers accompanied us. The interpreter wore Luftwaffe uniform with the insignia of a specialist of officer rank, but was in fact SS-Lieutenant-Colonel Nielandis, the commander of the 15th (Latvian) SS Fusilier Battalion, who had once worked in Russia as an engineer.

We came to the remains of a destroyed building. Several words in Russian were called out to us and our interpreter replied. I climbed over a wall and was suddenly surrounded by Russians, who shone a torch on me, clapped me in friendly fashion on the shoulder and addressed me as if we were old friends. I had difficulty keeping close to General Krebs. We then found ourselves in an overcrowded cellar, which was the command post of the 102nd Guards Rifle Regiment.

A Russian officer exchanged a few words with our interpreter. Lieutenant- Colonel Seifert went back. Our passes and the handing over of our pistols were demanded, but Krebs said: 'A brave enemy allows one one's weapons during negotiations,' and we kept our pistols.

We were taken in a kind of convoy to another command post, that of the 35th Guards Rifle Division of Colonel Smolin. Also present were Colonel Lebed, Chief of Staff of the 4th Guards Rifle Corps and Lieutenant-General Gladsky. Then we drove on farther through the rubble of Berlin. I lost my sense of direction in the dark and it was only later that I discovered that we had been taken to No. 2 Schulenburgring in Tempelhof. Up until then I had had no opportunity of asking General Krebs what the object of our negotiations was and what I was supposed to do.

At No. 2 Schulenburgring, General Krebs told the Soviet officers who received us through our interpreter that he wanted a private conversation with the Soviet officer authorised to conduct the negotiations. This request was refused, but Krebs did not give up and repeated his request very forcibly. (He was speaking in German and had the interpreter translate for him.)

We waited a while and then were led into a room, where a big table stood in the centre with some ten to fifteen senior Soviet officers in various kinds of uniform standing around it, some with their hats on. Among them were Colonel-General Chuikov, Commander-in-Chief 8th Guards Army, Lieutenant-General Dukhanov, Pozhersky, a doctor, General Pronin, Colonels Tolkopyk, Gladsky and Mutosov, the interpreter Captain Kleber and the writers Vishnevsky, Dolmatovsky and Blanter. On the table, a dining table, stood two field telephones in brand-new leather cases. One Soviet officer stood out, being dressed in naval uniform, and I later knew him to be the poet Dolmatovsky. The Soviet officers conducted themselves in an observant but distant manner.

General Krebs tried once more to obtain a private interview, and the reply of the head of the Soviet delegation was translated into German by the interpreter of the opposite party. (I had previously told Krebs that I knew no Russian, and he had said to me: 'I'll be using an interpreter. Take notes!')

Yet again General Krebs said that he had been tasked with obtaining a personal interview with the commander of the Red Army. Colonel-General Chuikov's reply was: 'Inform the general that this is only my War Council and that he can speak!'

Chuikov remained quiet during the negotiations, telephoning occasionally, and I remember his 'Tak, tak' sounding like an 'OK, yes'.

All General Krebs's repeated attempts to obtain a private interview with the Soviet negotiator came up against a brick wall. His requests were simply ignored and were turned to the authorisation of himself and his escort. Our passes were examined and questions asked, such as: 'Who is Bormann? What rank has the German interpreter?' Krebs gave our interpreter's rank as equivalent to that of a major. (It was reported that General Krebs was escorted by a colonel and a major. I was wearing the rank insignia of a lieutenant-colonel at this time, as I only heard of my promotion to colonel on 1 April 1945 on the evening of 1 May.)

After about half an hour, General Krebs eventually said: 'I have been repeatedly and pointedly asking for a private interview because I have been tasked with something that is especially important and of an especially confidential nature.'

General Krebs was requested by Colonel-General Chuikov to present his case, as he, General Chuikov, was authorised to conduct the negotiations and all those present were entitled to listen in as members of his War Council.

Following this awkward beginning, General Krebs was able to commence the first part of his task. It was to divulge the information that:

1. The Führer of the German Reich, Adolf Hitler, was dead, and
2. This information had not been divulged to anyone until then.

The Soviets remained unconcerned and acted as if they had known it for some time. To General Krebs's astonished query 'How?' the reply came that Hitler's death had been announced in a foreign newspaper several days ago. General Krebs then said that Hitler had ended his life at 1530 hours on 30 April, only a few hours previously. There had been no announcement on the German side and he, General Krebs, had been authorised to divulge it to his Soviet negotiating partner in confidence.

General Chuikov then asked who had authorised him, and if he, General Krebs, was authorised to offer surrender. General Krebs produced a letter authorising him to conduct these negotiations and held another piece of paper in his hand on which were written the names of the new government.

The negotiations continued.

At this point, General Krebs appeared to have reached the point of asking for an immediate ceasefire to enable the so-called legal government to assemble.

As the individual members, apart from Goebbels and Bormann, were outside Berlin, only a ceasefire in Berlin could be offered as the first step. The second step would be the meeting of the so-called legal government in Berlin or somewhere else.

The third step could then be the new government offering the surrender of the whole of Germany to the Soviet Union.

The negotiations became even more difficult, the reason lying in the Soviets' negotiating tactics and the difficulties of translation. It was only much later that I realised that we were dealing here with the typical slow-moving negotiating tactics of the Soviets: repeating the same thing in other words so as to wear down the opponent.

General Krebs was using our interpreter and speaking only in German, although he knew Russian well, having been the military attaché in Moscow until the war began in 1941. When the opposition spoke in Russian, their interpreter translated into German. Speech and counterspeech exchanged quickly, and I was hardly able to keep up with my note-taking. It even happened that both interpreters spoke simultaneously. The German interpreter was visibly tiring, when General Chuikov suddenly engaged the wishes and arguments of General Krebs, speaking in Russian.

What he said was not translated, so I do not know what it was. Anyhow, turning to our German interpreter, General Krebs said: 'You may only interpret what I say, and not interject things on your own initiative.'

It was then agreed that only one interpreter would interpret for both sides. The Soviet interpreter was nominated and, although he was not qualified for political negotiations, he did well.

Once the negotiations were interrupted when another general entered the room, and everyone stood up. General Chuikov appeared to be reporting to the newcomer and briefing him on the course of the negotiations so far. The Russian interpreter quietly gave me the name of the newcomer, which I understood to be 'General of the Army Sokolovski, Member of the Supreme Soviet'.[9]

General Chuikov then pursued strongly the answers to the following questions:

1. Why was the surrender being offered to the Soviets first?
2. Was the German side (Goebbels, Bormann) aware that negotiations were being conducted with the Allies elsewhere, and, if so, through whom?

In the middle of this General Chuikov made a telephone call. I assume it was to Marshal Zhukov. Then Chuikov stressed the fidelity of the Soviet Union to their Allies.

General Krebs sought to overcome the stubborn attitude of the Soviets and to evoke some sympathy for his proposals. He even went so far as to ask for Soviet support for the meeting of the so-called legal government, suggesting that the Soviets promote the German–Soviet negotiations by radio and other means of communication and forestall the negotiations of others, such as Himmler.[10] He even went so far as to say: 'According to Goebbels, Himmler is a traitor.' (Goebbels against Himmler? What was that about? I wondered.)

General Krebs went on trying to achieve a part surrender or a ceasefire for Berlin, but made no progress. I was therefore pleased when at last the following agreement was reached:

1. The Soviet side would ask Moscow how to proceed;
2. General Krebs' escort, i.e. myself, should go to Goebbels, give an interim report and ask for further instructions for General Krebs;
3. A direct telephone line should be established with Goebbels, so that General Krebs could communicate with Goebbels in the Reichs Chancellery from General Chuikov's command post.

Details of this 'Three Point Agreement' were then discussed with the usual Soviet stickiness. During a brief pause for breath, I asked General Krebs for instructions on my interim report to Goebbels, and handed him my notebook with the request that he jot down his further intentions. General Krebs wrote in my notebook something on the lines of: 'My intention is to achieve an immediate ceasefire for Berlin and then to discuss the meeting of the new government.'

It must have been about 0830 or 0900 hours, or even a little later, when I was taken by jeep to our crossing point of the previous night, escorted by a Russian lieutenant-colonel and our German interpreter Nielandis. I tried to get my bearings as we drove along, but the street signs had either been removed or were obscured, so that I could get only a rough idea of where we were. I saw the concentration of Russian forces, seeing many Russian guns and well-equipped tanks. Perhaps it was intentionally done, but perhaps not, for they were massed everywhere.

As we reached the crossing point, we turned into a gateway. The lieutenant- colonel ordered a major, who I believe was the local battalion commander, to go on ahead with the German interpreter. This sequence did not seem correct to me and I tried to make myself understood, but our interpreter, the Russian major and a Russian signaller had already gone ahead, and I hurried after them. It was now between 0900 and 1000 hours and the weather was fine. We were all walking upright when suddenly shots came from the German side. This was impossible! Firing at us from the German side? The Russian lieutenant-colonel grabbed me by the arm and pulled me behind a wall. The others ahead of us threw themselves down and came back one at a time, using every available bit of cover. The Russian major had been wounded and the German interpreter had had a shot through his ripped overcoat. A Russian soldier had also been wounded. I could hardly believe it. Through my head went the thoughts: 'What now? How can I complete my task?'

As soon as I exposed myself the firing started up again. I tried to go ahead alone, using a large sheet as a parliamentarian flag, taking the telephone cable with me and moving up to the German lines. However, firing immediately broke out from the German side and I was no longer able to make my way forward jumping from cover to cover in the manner learnt long ago. I discovered that the Russians had been busy digging during the night and had advanced their positions within the crossing point. This was incorrect, as I now realised.

I had gone about halfway, 125 metres, when the firing stopped and I was able to walk upright. Unfortunately my telephone cable was not long enough, being short by about 50 metres. I saw a German officer, half under cover, watching me through binoculars. I called out to the officer, whom I thought was SS: 'Take me to the sector commander, Lieutenant-Colonel Seifert, immediately!' After some hesitation, he agreed to my energetic, repeated demands and led me to the 'Zitadelle' command post. On the way he said that he had to arrest me! Two SS soldiers blocked my way. I said: 'Arrested or not, does not matter, now take me immediately to the telephone. I must speak to either Minister Goebbels or Party Leader Bormann.'

After some more hesitation, he took me to Lieutenant-Colonel Seifert's command post. I recognised the room again and hurried to the telephone, but the SS officer wanted to stop me using it. 'Where is Lieutenant-Colonel Seifert?' I asked.

'He has been replaced. SS-Brigadier Krukenberg[11] is in command here now, but he is not here at this moment.'

I showed him my parliamentary pass and explained the urgency of my request. It took some time for me to get through. I called the Reichs Chancellery and Bormann came on the line. I explained my orders to him briefly and asked him to give the order for me to be taken to Goebbels immediately. Bormann gave the order to my escort, but his reply to Bormann was: 'Only SS orders apply here.'

SS Brigadier Mohnke had to be called to the phone to substantiate Bormann's order. At last we had come so far that my escort switched on and led me through the rubble. I called out to him: 'Faster, we have no time to lose! Take the shortest route and run as fast as you can! I'm right behind you!'

And the youngster ran well. We jumped over the rubble, raced across open spaces, and were in the Reichs Chancellery within ten minutes. When I told him that Hitler was dead, he burst into tears.

Inside the Reichs Chancellery, I was led to Goebbels. We were in a small room with benches lining the walls. In due course Bormann and Mohnke appeared. Goebbels was calm, speaking clearly and politely. Only some red flecks on his face indicated his agitation to me. In contrast to Bormann and others that I saw in the Reichs Chancellery, this man did not seem to me to be afraid, but with Bormann I had the feeling that he was trembling for his life.

I wanted, as usual, to present my report in brief military fashion, only saying the most important things, but Goebbels took his time. I had to report in detail, and describe my own impressions. At the end, Goebbels asked some questions. I remember especially those about the establishment of a field telephone connection between Chuikov's command post and the Reichs Chancellery, and the assessment of our defence capability. Goebbels asked how much longer we could hold out.

'At the most two days, then there will only be individual groups of resistance,' was my reply.

Mohnke was called in and asked how much longer the Reichs Chancellery could hold out. Mohnke also said: 'Two days at most.'

Then Goebbels asked me whether I thought that General Krebs's negotiations could still succeed.

'I don't think so,' was my reply. 'While I was there, the Soviets were demanding an immediate surrender.'

Goebbels cried out: 'That I will never do, never!'

I asked Goebbels not to make a decision based upon my report alone, as the responsible leader of the delegation was General Krebs. He should report back first before the last word could be spoken on the subject. I added that I had left General Krebs at about 0700 hours, and that it was now 1100 hours, so the answer should have been received from Moscow.

'Good, bring Krebs back. I will hear what he has to say,' was Goebbels's reply.

So I hurried back to the 'Zitadelle' command post. The telephone cable to the Soviet side had been laid, but no communication had been established. The cable had been shot through again, as the crossing point and the area around it were under constant fire. When I arrived at the Russian command post, I met our interpreter there and, with his help, tried to reach General Krebs by telephone. I succeeded and General Krebs told me that they were still waiting for an answer from Moscow, and that he wanted to wait for it. Meanwhile I should try to establish a direct line to Goebbels.

So the cable had to be repaired. Both sides ceased firing. The Russian battalion placed a signaller at my disposal and I was able to repair the cable with his help. It was not much use. No sooner had we got through to the Reichs Chancellery than the firing resumed and the cable was shot through again, the rupture being within the crossing point, so I had to cross over to the Russian side yet again. As I entered, a call arrived from General Krebs. I went to the telephone and received the following order: 'The reply from Moscow is here. Wait for me at the crossing point and we will go to the Reichs Chancellery together.'

I told General Krebs that the firing had increased and that shells were falling on the safe passage so that it was almost impossible to get to the Reichs Chancellery. General Krebs arrived at the Russian battalion's command post at about 1200 hours. We hurried across to the German side and from there to the Reichs Chancellery.

The shelling was so heavily concentrated on the Reichs Chancellery that it took us nearly an hour to cover the short distance. Krebs said: 'This firing could be deliberate!'

Once we arrived at the Reichs Chancellery I asked General Krebs what I should do. He only said briefly to me: 'I have no further jobs for you. We will be giving our answer to the Soviets in writing. Report back to General Weidling.'

I waited for General Weidling, and while I was waiting observed what was going on around me. There was a coming and going, a helplessness, as panic gradually spread.

General Burgdorf came, sat down and had me report. One of the secretaries sitting there saw my torn trousers and helpfully produced a needle and thread and repaired them. Frau Goebbels came past several times, then I saw one of her children. Was it Frau Goebbels or someone else taking the child to the toilet? I cannot remember. I can only recall someone whispering to me: 'Now they will get their injections!'

'Who?' I asked quietly.

'The Goebbels children,' came the reply.

General Burgdorf and Krebs discussed the possibility of an eventual breakout together and asked me my opinion and what I had seen of weaponry on the Russian side. I reported and presented my views as follows: 'There is hardly any chance of a combined breakout, but individual small groups or individuals familiar with the area could break their way out. But that would only make sense if they could reach the Elbe. It is too late for a breakout by units.'

I seem to recall that General Burgdorf said: 'As the Führer's Chief Adjutant and Head of the Personnel Office, I have only one possibility: to shoot myself!'

Weidling, who had come in the meantime, said nothing at first. Krebs stood up, shook our hands and said to me: 'There are only desperate men, but no desperate situations.'[12]

Weidling and I decided to hurry back to our command post in the Bendler Block where we belonged. Together with the Berliners, the remainder of our Panzer Corps were engaged in a desperate battle and could not be left fighting leaderless any longer. Because of the heavy shelling, it took us half an hour to make our way back to the Bendler Block from the Reichs Chancellery on foot.

At about 2030 hours, General Weidling, Major Knappe and I entered the signals bunker at the Bendler Block, where Colonel Refior was eagerly awaiting us. A short discussion between General Weidling and his two chiefs of staff produced the following result:

- Prolonging the fighting in Berlin was seen as pointless. It was only causing the civilian population casualties and further hardships.
- A breakout by units was seen as impossible. The experience of many breakouts from encirclement had taught us that very small groups had the best chance of breaking out and getting through. However, among other prerequisites, some troops had to fight on and form a 'front' from which one could break out. These conditions no longer existed on 1/2 May, so one had to allow everyone the chance to break out under the motto: 'Break out whoever can! Try to get through to the Americans!'

It was clear to us that surrender meant neither a solution to this situation, nor a way out of this catastrophe.

Before the question of surrender was finally decided, General Weidling wanted to address the responsible commanders still contactable as well as representatives of all ranks, so it was decided to summon another conference for about 2300 hours.

In discussion with me, General Weidling declared: 'If it is to be surrender, I cannot escape captivity by either committing suicide or flight. I must go wherever the German soldier has to go.'

No one can relate today exactly what was said during the conference at 2300 hours. No notes made during or immediately after the conference any longer exist. The result was a unanimous vote for surrender, and General Weidling gave me the task of leading the surrender negotiations.[13]

The text of the radio message to the Red Army went something like this: 'Hello! Hello! This is the German LVI Panzer Corps. Please cease fire. A German parliamentary will be at the Bendlerstrasse Bridge at 0500 hours. Identification: a white flag. Please reply!'

This message was transmitted several times until the reply was received by the German station: 'Message understood!'

The individual points of negotiation that I dictated concerned the following items, of which, naturally, I can only give the gist:

1. *Authority*
   General Weidling's for surrender.
2. *Grounds for Surrender*
   General Weidling requests surrender in order to avoid further bloodshed.
3. *Details*
   The cessation of fighting and the laying down of arms on the German side will be ordered by General Weidling for the troops under his command providing the Red Army agrees:

– that the Red Army will also cease fighting;
– that the Red Army will will assume the protection of the defenceless and prevent terrorism;
– that the surrender will be under honourable conditions.

There were a few other points and, although I no longer can recall how they went, they concerned the following:

– recognition of the Red Cross, care of the wounded, civilians, women and children,
– support for General Weidling in making the surrender known, as there were no longer communications to all the surrounded strongpoints and units,
– the request for German units and formations to remain together in captivity.

Escorted by an interpreter, an officer and two soldiers to carry the white flag, we went along Bendlerstrasse (today Stauffenbergstrasse). As it was dark, we signalled with our torches. I can no longer remember if there was heavy firing going on at this point or not; however, I do remember shouting out in the dark street: 'Hold your fire! We are parliamentarians acting on behalf of the military commander!'

But from some building or other on the German side came calls like: 'A German never surrenders!' or 'You are traitors!'

Without being shot at by the Russian side we approached the former bridge that had extended across the Landwehr Canal from Bendlerstrasse. The Soviets had already established themselves on the near bank of the canal (the north bank) even though the bridge had been destroyed, and built a kind of barricade of cobbles, stones and rubble. As we clambered over it, hand grenades thrown from the German side burst and flashed all around us!

I saw some dark shapes in front of me ducking down. I jumped over the barricade and found myself standing in a group of Soviet soldiers. A hullabaloo broke out on the Russian side with everyone shouting and crowding in on us. One bleeding, small Red Army soldier wanted to knock me down with the butt of his sub-machine-gun, but I was able to defend myself against him and several others until the Russian major in charge intervened on the prompting of our interpreter.

This Russian major re-established order with a lot of shouting, which proved effective. Meanwhile I saw several Red Army soldiers armed with panzerfausts go over the barricade and try to cross the street into the neighbouring buildings, and firing flared up again on both sides.

Gradually our interpreter managed to explain to the major that we had come as fully authorised parliamentarians. The major then asked of me, and I of him, that there should be a complete ceasefire at the crossing point. I therefore had to tell him that his men had to remain behind the barricade and not try to gain ground, as was happening at the moment.

After a few minutes of discussion it was agreed that there would be, firstly, a total ceasefire from both sides at the crossing point. In order to achieve this, I would return to the German side and he would recall his men.

I went back and summoned the company and battalion commanders in charge to explain to them what was going on. Although they already knew, they had not passed it on to all the combatants and auxiliaries under their command during the night as they should have done. One or two of these officers knew me, so it was easier for me to explain to them that I was no turncoat or traitor. Then I had to go back again to our signals centre, about five or ten minutes away. I spoke briefly with General Weidling and Colonel Refior and stated again: 'All Germans, especially on the Tirpitzufer, should be aware that I am a parliamentarian and that a ceasefire should be in force at the crossing point for the duration of the negotiations.'

Then I set off once more. An officer reported to me in the Bendlerstrasse: 'Everything is in order, all Germans have been briefed.'

It really was quiet. I met our interpreter at the barricade again. He informed me that meanwhile a Soviet reception party was now waiting for me with a vehicle on the other side of the canal, having apparently first gone to the Potsdamer Strasse Bridge by mistake.

I was taken to a command post, apparently that of a regiment, and from there on to the command post of a guards rifle division. In the presence of several Soviet officers, I was informed by a guards colonel that he was authorised to hear me.

I showed him my pass. Then I slowly enunciated my negotiation points in German. The German interpreter, who knew the text by heart, translated slowly, sentence by sentence.

My negotiating partner nodded his head. Then he made a telephone call and said to me that:

1 The Soviet High Command had authorised him to accept the surrender of General Weidling. The German side was assured of:
– An honourable surrender and
– honourable conditions. Officers could retain their small sidearms.
2 Everyone could take as much as he could carry in his personal pack into captivity. Every prisoner's personal pack would be regarded as his private property.
3 The Soviet High Command would undertake the protection of the civilian population and the care of the wounded.

I did not quite understand the sentence about small sidearms, so it was explained to me: daggers, bayonets, or similar objects, but no firearms to be included. I got the impression that the Soviets wanted to show themselves as being generous victors.

The next point for negotiation was the time for the laying down of arms. The Soviets were very pressing, and I had to make them understand that I would have first to return to inform our troops. This required time as nearly all radio communications had been destroyed and we would have to send out liaison officers and messengers. I told them that we needed at least three to four hours. We also had to reckon with Goebbels's orders. (I did not know then that Goebbels was already dead.)

I think that the time of 0600 hours was agreed. Sunrise was about 0500 hours, so it would be daylight by 0300 hours. There were numerous misunderstandings about timings, as the Russians' watches gave a different time to ours.

My way back to General Weidling went without any special incident. It was about 0300 hours when I returned to the Bendler Block, where they were waiting anxiously for me, as after the preliminary incidents they feared the worst and that the negotiations had fallen through. However, I was able to report to Weidling that the authorised negotiator on the other side had agreed to all the points in my proposed requirements as set out in writing for the cessation of the fighting.

As I had been on my feet for 36 hours now without a break, and with nothing to eat, my exhausted state must have made an impression, for General Weidling ordered that something be brought for me to eat.

Informing the troops that the fighting was to cease and that we were going into captivity with our own provisions and packs, as much as we could carry, did not proceed without difficulty, as our communications with the troops were catastrophic. We were entirely reliant upon messengers, most of whom were officers. Refior, Knappe, Wolff[14] and others of the staff did all that was possible.

When I looked at my rucksack and saw that it was lacking its straps and several other things, the faithful Buksch appeared and helped me to organise things a little. We prepared ourselves for the way into captivity. I recall Weidling saying to me: 'So we will be taking the final step into captivity too!' and then 'Make sure that the corps staff go into captivity in an orderly and soldierly manner.'

This must have been about the time when someone called out to us: 'Two Russian officers are already at the Bendler Block asking for General Weidling!' A little later I realised that the Russians were not operating on Berlin time and had come to collect General Weidling almost an hour early.

I knew that the way into captivity would be very, very difficult for us all. It was made even worse by the circumstances, the rubble and calls in the night of: 'A German never surrenders! Traitor!'

But in this desperate situation we also heard the cries for help: 'Pack it in, we can't take any more. Fighting is pointless, give some thought to the civilian population!'

But there was also: 'We are not going to surrender. We will fight to the end and to the death!'

I still remember the words of some officers, especially some that had been at the Bendler Block on 20 July 1944, SS and Hitler Youth officers. They told us: 'The Führer is dead, you have already lied to us, and we don't believe you!'

My Way into Captivity

Outside – it was now between 0530 and 0630 hours – the corps staff and defenders of the Bendler Block sector paraded on Bendlerstrasse. A large mass of people assembled, including flak auxiliaries and *Volkssturm* in uniform or just wearing an armband, covering about 200 metres of the street. Where did they all come from?

The first groups crossed the canal. The Russians had prepared some wooden rafts, which, however, were some distance away from the destroyed bridge, which was easier to cross in daylight as several hand lines had been stretched across.[15]

They were waiting for me on the other side. Refior, Knappe, Wolff and I were driven to a Russian divisional command post, where we were greeted in Russian style with bread and salt, as well as meat and vodka served in tumblers. The Russian colonel downed his whole glass in one go, but I just sipped mine. We wondered about this friendly reception, and later I learnt that it was an old Russian custom to offer bread and salt.

Then we were taken quickly to the Schulenburgring in Tempelhof. I recognised the building, for it was the place where General Krebs and I had been taken for the negotiations 25 hours earlier. We were ushered into the anteroom, and I could hear General Weidling's voice nearby. He appeared and beckoned us in. Refior, Knappe and the others complied, but I did not go with them, perhaps because I was somewhat switched off and thought that it was the others' turn to do something.

There was a civilian in the anteroom with me. I recall that he was walking up and down and was wearing top boots, dark trousers and a civilian jacket. Realising that he was a German, I asked him what he was doing there. He replied: 'To conduct the surrender negotiations.'

I said: 'You should have come earlier.'

Later I discovered that he came from one of the ministries and that his name was Heinersdorf, a senior civil servant and adjutant of Goebbels, who had been sent by the head of radio, Hans Fritsche.

Meanwhile Weidling had prepared his appeal with the help of Refior and Knappe in the room next door. The door to the negotiating room was opened and it was announced that German officers would take the appeal, which the Russians had turned into an order, informing the troops of the cessation of the fighting.

Weidling, the other generals,[16] Refior, myself and some other staff officers were led into another room, where the table was laid and eating had already begun. We were amazed at this hospitality, which was extended to other German officers, even members of the SS, at this time, being astonished at our victors' reconciliatory behaviour.

We were then taken to another building in which camp beds and mattresses had been set out. I lay down and slept and slept. Later I was told by Refior and Weidling that several attempts had been made to waken me without success. It seems that I was completely exhausted, which was not surprising, for I had been in action for 16 days without a break. I had not stopped and the last days had been physically the most demanding. Weidling later said something to me reproachfully: 'Since we couldn't wake you up, they kept coming for me!'

On the evening of 2 May 1945 – it was already dark – we were transported on further under a strong guard. We stopped at some building, where we were given an opulent meal, served by smartly dressed girls in silk blouses. For a breakfast, it was a very rich meal. To finish off we were given pies, cakes and alcohol. Refior commented: 'They must have stolen it from us!'

We had hardly finished eating when we were taken on under heavy guard with an armoured car in front and behind. We sat in the back of a truck closed with tarpaulins and could not orientate ourselves. We disembarked at night in a small provisional prisoner-of-war camp that was fenced in with barbed wire. There was little room and provisions were scarce, consisting only of soup and bread. Apart from ourselves, there were 20–30 other staff officers. We could move about the yard and a small garden, and when we were not continually being disturbed, we had a few minutes during the following days to adjust ourselves to the situation.

I recall that on one occasion Refior and I were summoned, and very forcibly. However, I was already engaged in washing my underwear, and it was high time too! Three weeks of always wearing the same things in dust and sweat had made washing urgently needed. I was not dressed, having only underpants on, and that turned out to be a good thing, for the others, Wiedling, Refior, etc., were driven to the Reichs Chancellery to identify the dead in the Führerbunker. That was what they were told, but it was only a pretext. They were led rapidly through the bunker exit and filmed as they emerged. This was most probably on 6 May 1945. The result was then shown under the title: 'And this how we drove the Nazi rats out of their hiding place and took them prisoner in Berlin!'

We were not left alone during the period 5 to 8 May. Principally they wanted to know from me how, where and with what forces we had held out against the concentrated Russian breakthrough attack on the Oder front, especially in and around Seelow. I was also asked questions about the fighting in and around Berlin. For example: 'What is your opinion of Hitler's order: "Berlin is to be defended to the last!"? or "What was the effect of the fighting upon the civilian population?"'

In my first interrogation I had said: 'The military forces for the defence of Berlin were totally inadequate. When Hitler demanded that the city be defended, it was a crime against the civilian population.'

I had to repeat this statement, which I was prepared to do. But when I realised that microphones had been set up, I came to realise that the 'crime' also implicated Weidling and myself and gave the Russians material against us, for we had indeed defended Berlin for a week. I then chose my words more carefully and informed them that Weidling had first been condemned to death, then appointed Defence Commandant of Berlin, and had then wanted to break out of Berlin in order to shorten the fighting. And then, after General Krebs's negotiations had collapsed, it was General Weidling who discontinued the fighting and called upon our troops to lay down their arms. The expression 'Crimes against the civilian population' did not apply to him. They were not so happy with this statement, and I have never heard or read of it again.

Between 3 and 8 April I met Weidling several times in the little garden. He told me that it was both correct and important to record how the final battle in Berlin had been conducted as seen from the point of view of the last Defence Commandant. (It was first published in Russian in the *Vojennoistoriceski Zurnal* under the title 'The Fascist Clique's Agony'.) Weidling also said that he had liked working with me in the last difficult days, and that I had been a support and help to him during the most difficult period of his life.

It was the morning of 9 May and we had had our thin soup when a German- speaking Russian major rushed in, calling for Refior, Herrmann[17] and myself. I understood him to say: 'Transport to a prisoner of war camp with all your kit!' Then came my first body search. I had already heard how the others had had all watches, rings, nailclippers and all metallic objects taken from them, but this had not been the case with our group. They had kept their promises and left our personal packs undisturbed. My rucksack was now rummaged through.

We were loaded on to a truck with the generals and driven off under strong guard. Again we were unable to orientate ourselves as the truck was enclosed with a tarpaulin, and I lost my sense of direction, even though I was familiar with the Berlin area. We were unloaded on to an almost bare area that had once been Strausberg Airport, and we stood around in the fresh, sunny May weather. Off another truck climbed SS officers, such as Mohnke, Günsche,[18] and others.

The Russians, all in brand-new uniforms, were not hostile towards us. Their equipment, jeeps, trucks and aircraft, all appeared to be of American origin.

I stood next to Weidling. He repeated how good it had been working with me and how I had been a great help to him in this catastrophe, and then he said: 'Now we have to go through the worst part, the way into captivity, and hopefully we will remain together.'

And then with a glance at the scene before us, he said: 'These are the victors. They have the power! The light is coming from the east! What will they do? If they want to exploit the situation, they will need us [Germany], which could be an advantage!'

The first handling that we had experienced did indeed give the impression that they needed us. I say this now because I believe Weidling went to Moscow with this impression, although he was to change his mind in captivity.

The aircraft, a Douglas, was ready to leave, and we had to climb aboard. Altogether there were ten to twelve officers, a corporal, two Russian officers and two guards armed with sub-machine-guns. We sat on the side benches in the aircraft with the corporal next to me. At first, as we flew off, my attention was drawn to the ground below. How destroyed Berlin looked! It was the first time that I had seen it from the air, and the scene was shattering. Our battlefield at the Oder was only vaguely recognisable, as we were already too high.

I asked the anxious corporal sitting next to me: 'How do you come to be here? Are you a politician?'

He replied: 'No, I don't know what they want from me. I was called up into the *Volkssturm* and was captured north of Berlin but by the Polish Army. They put me into a grey uniform and handed me over to the Russians.'

This man was between fifty and sixty years old, and was a cigar merchant from Potsdam by the name of Trumann. The Poles had been attracted by his name and taken him for a relation of the US president!

After about a five-hour flight the machine prepared to land, and we saw below us a vast sea of buildings. It was Moscow.

THE BUTYRKA PRISON

We were conveyed in a sort of 'Black Maria' and by the time we reached our destination it was dark. We saw very little of Moscow, but I do remember the very wide streets.

After a short journey we stopped before a vast building complex, and a massive iron gate opened as if by a ghostly hand. The initial impression was almost friendly. We were led into a kind of reception hall, whose walls were whitewashed halfway up and whose floor was of colourful tiles. Behind a counter stood some people in uniform. On the wall were some large key racks, like those in a hotel, but the keys looked as if they came from the Middle Ages.

Our names were called out, but we could hardly understand what was being said, and there was no interpreter. We were then packed into a small room with benches along the walls. The strong door was closed behind us and locked from outside. The window was barred. This now looked like a prison. We sat there for hours, but we were alone and could talk to one another. The aircraft had been noisy, the sound of the engines too strong, and now we had no guards with us.

SS-Brigadier Mohnke said: 'I have already said that they will do us in!' And then he said to me: 'You with your negotiations! Why didn't you brief me?'

I had to remind him that there had no longer been any communication between the Reichs Chancellery and the Bendler Block, and that he had broken out with the 'Reichs Chancellery Group' at 2300 hours on 1 May, while I had only set off as parliamentary representative for the new negotiations on General Weidling's orders at 0100 hours on 2 May, two whole hours after his breakout.

Sometime or other we were given soup with a few blobs of fat and some fish eyes swimming in it looking sadly at us. But when one's stomach is empty, as mine was, one is obliged to go ahead and eat and not be choosy.

For at least a day we were held in this whitewashed cell before we were called by name and led out, Weidling and myself together again. 'With your packs!' they said. We were taken into a large room, well illuminated with lights. In the middle of this room was a large table with several Russians in uniform sitting around it, some wearing long white coats.

'Strip!'

I thought only my torso would be sufficient, but no: 'Completely!'

Then I saw the uniformed people shaking the contents of my rucksack out on the table and turning out the pockets of my jacket and trousers. I heard Weidling protesting, and he called out to me: 'Dufving, what is this? What do they want? This is outrageous!'

Then I saw that one of the searchers wanted to remove the photographs of my wife and children. This was too much! I wanted the photographs, which were in a folding frame, back. The man looked at me in a friendly way and offered me the frame!

After this strange administrative procedure, we were led back into a room, where the others were already sitting on the floor. The same thing that we had just been through had happened to them. We were then brought some mattresses that were as thin as floormats.

Later we were called out in small groups of two to four men. Refior, Herrmann, Witowsky and I were led down a long corridor and landed in a dark, unfriendly cell that was completely bare. But it was not long before iron bedsteads, mattresses, blankets, pillows, plates, mugs, wooden spoons and so on were brought in and we were gradually fully equipped. Then a fifth was packed into our cell; it was 'Mr Trumann'. Now things were really tight, for the maximum capacity for such a cell was only four men.

Colonel von Dufving returned to Germany after undergoing over ten years of imprisonment, much of it in solitary confinement. He joined the new Bundeswehr *in early 1957, being employed as a lecturer at the Staff College at Bad Ems and Hamburg for several years, and then at the Ministry of Defence in Cologne until his retirement in 1967, but continued working there for a while as a retired officer. Later on he did two six-month tours as an instructor with the Taiwanese Army. Colonel von Duvfing unfortunately died while this book was in preparation.*

NOTES

1. General Helmuth Weidling (1891–1955) had served as a subaltern in Zeppelins during the First World War, transferring to the artillery afterwards. By 1938 he held the rank of colonel and took part in the invasions of Poland, France and the Soviet Union. He was awarded the Knights' Cross as commander of the 86th Infantry Division in 1943 and became commander of the XXXXI Panzer Corps that autumn, being further awarded the oak leaves and then the swords to his Knights' Cross in 1944. In April 1945 he was appointed commander of the newly reconstituted LVI Panzer Corps as General of Artillery.
   In the withdrawal from the Seelow Heights following the Soviet breach of the German defences, LVI Panzer Corps was driven back on Berlin while seeking to rejoin the bulk of the parent 9th Army to the south. False orders spread by Seydlitz Troops for the elements of his corps to regroup west of Berlin led to both Hitler and the 9th Army commander accusing Weidling of desertion, so Weidling went to the Führerbunker in order to clear his name, which resulted in his being appointed Defence Commandant of Berlin.
   Weidling was to die in Soviet captivity in 1955.
2. Colonel Hans Refior was a friend and staff college colleague of von Dufving, and was appointed Chief of Staff to the Berlin Defence Area Headquarters when it was formed in early 1945. With General Weidling's appointment as Defence Area Commandant, von Dufving continued as his Chief of Staff for military matters, while Refior became his Chief of Staff for civilian affairs. After the war, Refior published his diary on his experiences in Berlin.
3. The Bendler Block, where General Weidling set up his command post, accommodated the headquarters of the Home or Reserve Army, from where Colonel

Claus Graf Schenk von Stauffenburg had launched his abortive assassination attempt against Hitler on 20 July 1944, and where he was subsequently executed. The signals bunker mentioned by von Dufving stood in the courtyard and was demolished after the war. The German Resistance Museum is now housed here.

4. General Hans Krebs was the last Chief of Staff of the Oberkommando-des-Heeres (OKH – Army GHQ) following the dismissal of General Heinz Guderian on 28 March 1945. Krebs had served as assistant military attaché in Moscow in 1939/40.
5. Major Siegfried Knappe was operations officer of LVI Panzer Corps. His book *Soldat – Reflections of a German Soldier 1936–1949* was published by Orion Books in 1992.
6. Martin Bormann was Hitler's secretary in the rank of Minister, and was also administrative head of the Nazi Party. He took part in the breakout from the Reichs Chancellery on the night of 1/2 May 1945 but committed suicide that same night.
7. SS-Brigadier Wilhelm Mohnke was in command of the troops guarding the Reichs Chancellery area within Defence Sector 'Zitadelle' (Citadel).
8. Defence Sector 'Zitadelle' was commanded by Lieutenant-Colonel Seifert, who was responsible for its peripheral defence, but not for the Reichs Chancellery area within it, which was SS-Brigadier Mohnke's responsibility.
9. General of the Army Vasili Dannovich Sokolovsky was the Deputy Commander of Marshal Zhukov's 1st Byelorussian Front.
10. Himmler's secret negotiations with Ambassador Count Folke Bernadotte of Sweden were revealed in a Reuters news broadcast in German from Stockholm on the evening of 28 April.
11. SS-Brigadier Dr Gustav Krukenberg had brought 350 volunteers from his former SS Panzergrenadier Division 'Charlemagne' to fight in Berlin and had then been given command of the 11th SS Panzergrenadier Division 'Nordland' on 25 April.
12. This was a catchphrase from their staff college days.
13. Von Dufving omits to mention the individual breakout option, which resulted in breakout attempts over the Charlotten Bridge in Spandau, the Weidendammer Bridge in Mitte and up Schönhauser Allee in Horst Wessel (Prenzlauer Berg).
14. Major Wolff was the Personnel Officer on the staff of the LVI Panzer Corps. Buksch was von Dufving's batman.
15. Berlin's many bridges carry the city's water, electricity and gas conduits, and, even when the bridge structures were demolished by explosives, these conduits tended to survive.
16. These were the two retired Generals Schmid-Dankward and Woytasch who had voluntarily offerred their services to General Weidling.
17. Luftwaffe-Colonel Harry Herrmann commanded the 9th Parachute Division.
18. SS-Major Otto Günsche was Hitler's *Waffen-SS* Adjutant.

Index

location references followed by 'm' refer to a map eg 42m
location references followed by 'n' refer to a note eg 232n

Action Barleycorn 58
Ahrensfeldef 157, 162
Albrechtstrasse 192
Albulaweg 188
Aldershot 138
Alexanderplatz 152, 163, 180
Alfons, VS-man 203–4
Alt Bleyen 74
Alt Landsberg 163
Alt Langsow 71
Alt Levin 28
Alt Mariendorf 191, 194
Alt Tucheband 41, 42m, 43, 72
Alte Oder stream 64, 72
Altenstadt 10
Alter Park 195, 196
Altner, Helmuth 232n
Amt Wollup 39
Ankogelweg 188
Annahof 64
Antwerp 138
Apolda 6
Attilaplatz 192
Aue, Lw-Gnr 50
Averdieck, Dr Fritz-Rudolf 71

Bad Dürkheim 13
Bad Ems Staff College 255
Bad Freienwalde 25
Bad Herrenalb 4
Baldersheimer Weg 188
Baltenplatz 171
Bärenfänger, Col/Maj Gen Erich 147, 154, 155, 171, 183n, 184n
Bartmann, SS-Serg Erwin W 131–8
Baruth 126, 130n, 190
Bavaria 151
Bayerischen Wald 88
Beelitz 136
Beerbaum 99
Belgium 138
Belzig 129, 136
Bendler Block 154, 234, 244, 248, 249, 255–6n
Bendlerstrasse 249
Bendlerstrasse Bridge 245–6
Berghausen 19
Berkenbrück 117
Berlin 24, 71, 99, 135
  Russians surrounding of 54, 69, 91, 92, 100, 139
  German defence of 154–83, 185–97
  escaping from 198–231
  surrender 233–55
  after World War II 138
  see also individual streets and places
Berliner Bridge 203, 204, 206, 232n
Bernadotte, Count Folke 256n
Bernau 54
Bernhardt, VS-Man 162
Berzarin, Col-Gen N E 184n
Besold, Dir 157
Biesdorf 148, 153, 154–8, 156m, 160, 161–2, 164, 183n
Biesdorf-Sud 165
Bietigheim 3
Bismarckstrasse 180
Blankenburg 24
Blankenfelde 187
Blanter, writer 236
Bobby, Lw-Gnr 25, 30, 36, 37, 40, 48
Böbmann, 2/Lt 141
Bohle, Gren Paul 210, 214, 217–8, 220–2, 224–7
Böker, Lw O/Cdt Herbert 88–92
Bolde machine factory 130
Bolle, Arno 147–8
Bommert, Lw-Lt 23
Borm, Ingeborg 212–3, 214, 216, 225
Bormann, Martin 235, 237, 238, 238, 241–2, 256n
Börner, Lw-Sgt 201
Börnicker Strasse 207
Brand, Major 139–43
Brandt, Lw-Gnr Kimme 52
Braun, Eva 235
Braun, Frau 228, 229
Braun, Horst 231
Breitunger Weg 189
Breker, Arno 48, 60
Brendl, Lw-Sgt 43, 44, 50, 52, 60
Brest-Litovsk 219
Bretthauer, Lw-Gnr 200
Briesen 133
British Army 53, 58, 92, 130, 138
  7th Armed Division 'The

Desert Rats' 232n
Northamptonshire Yeomanry 138
Britz 192
Bruness, Capt 103
Brunsbütteler Damm 225–6
Brunswick 138
Buckow Manor Farm 99
Buckower Chaussee 190
Buckower Damm 187
Buckow-West 187, 188, 190, 192
Bukow-Ost 192
Buksch, Gren 248, 256n
Bünde 88
Bundeswehr 195, 197, 255
Burgdorf, Gen Wilhelm 243–4
Burgwall 94, 95
Busse, Gen Theodore 96
Butyrka Prison, Moscow 233

Calbe-an-der-Milbe 129
Central Cattle Market 167–71, 169m
Channel Islands 106
Charlotten Bridge 205, 206, 222, 223–4, 256n
Charlottenburg 181, 222, 232n
Charlottenburg-Nord 147, 153
Chausseestrasse 188
Christl, Lw-Gnr 200
Chuikov, Col-Gen Vassilii 236, 237–9, 242
Cologne, Ministry of Defence 255

Dachau concentration camp 137
Daeschler, Maj 96
Dageförde, Maj 150
Dahlewitz 187
Danhauser, Lt–Gen 188
Dannstadt 13, 17
David, Lw-Sgt 51
Dehmsee lake 117
Denmark 1
Deven 101
Diedersdorf 187
Dihlmannstrasse 179
Dnepr Front 106
Döbberin 71
Döberitz 230, 232n
Döbrich, Cav Capt Erich 189, 190, 194, 188
Dolmatovsky, writer 236–7
Dolziger Strasse 171
Dombrowski, Jevgeny 145, 177, 179
Donath, Cpl 171
Donder, Sgt 94
Döpke, Lw-Gnr Heini 53
Dorfstrasse 187, 189
Dufving, Col Theodor von 233–56
Dukhanov, Lt-Gen 236

East Prussia 145, 229
Eberswalde 24
Ehrenburg, Ilya 91–2
Ehrhardt, Capt 191, 196
Eiche 162
Eichwerder 50
Elbe River 55, 92, 129, 136, 142, 178, 207, 243
Elbinger, Lw-2/Lt 10, 13, 16, 17, 19, 20
Eldenaer Strasse 167, 168
Engelhardt, Lw-Lt 198, 209, 211–29
Erstermann, Capt 141
Erzgebirge Mountains 130
Escher, VS-Coy Comd 177
Essen 229
Etzin farm 181
Eutin 58

Falkensee 1, 200, 202
Feddern, Lw-Gnr 35, 43, 46
Fehrbelliner Platz 196
Feldner, Lw-Gnr 210, 212, 214, 217, 222, 226
Fellman, Maj 101
Feuchtinger, Lt-Gen Edgar 139, 143n
Fignerweg 187
Finkenkrug 3, 200
Finow 99
Fischbeck 129
Fleck, 2/Lt 145, 149, 154, 164
Flohr, Maj 141–2, 143n
Flügel, Lw-Gnr 28–9, 38, 43, 47, 52
Forkenbeckplatz 171
Fösterei Bridge 75
Francke Park 192
Frankfurt-on-the-Oder 108, 112–3, 131
Frankfurter Allee 170, 171–3, 180
Frankfurter Chaussee 165, 167
Frede, Lw-Lt Martin 3, 6, 8, 19, 21
Freiburg 88
Frese, 2/Lt 141
Friedenstrasse 173, 175, 176
Friedersdorf 62–3
Friedrich, Lw-Gnr 18
Friedrichs, Maj 189
Friedrichsberger Strasse 176
Friedrichsfelde 149, 163, 164, 165–7, 166m, 180
Friedrichshain 173, 174
Fritsch, Lw-Sgt 207, 209
Fritsche, Hans 250
Fromme, Lt 97
Frömmert, Lw-Gnr 200
Funk, Maj 147, 154, 170
Fürstenbrunner Bridge 179, 180
Fürstenwalde 117, 133

Gahlke, Lw-Sgt Maj 202, 210, 214
Garbe, Lw-Sgt 201
Gardeschützenweg 87, 185
Gartenfeld 148, 179
Garthenstadt Gross Ziethen 187
Gatow Airfield 88
Gau 152, 183n
Gebhardt, VS Coy Comd 154, 171, 176–7, 182
Gensberger, O/Cdt Sgt 6, 7
Genshagen 187
Genthin 129, 136
German Army
Army Group 'Weichsel' 159
Armies
3rd Guards Tank

Index

Army 130n
9th 116m, 118, 128, 130n
12th 96, 127, 128, 130n, 233, 255n
69th 130n
Corps
IX SS-Panzer 109
XXXXI Panzer 255n
LVI Panzer 233, 235, 255n, 256n
Defence Sector 'Dora' 187, 195
Divisions
9th Parachute 256n
20th Panzer-grenadiers 71–9
21st Panzer 142
25th Panzer-grenadiers 62–70, 93–105
86th Infantry 255n
281st 101
606th 95, 105n
712th Infantry 114, 115
'Bärenfänger' 147, 154, 155, 159–60, 163, 171, 183n, 184n
Panzer 'Charlemagne' 256n
Panzer 'Kurmark' 108–17, 118
Panzer 'Müncheberg' 74, 79, 82
Regiments
Artillery 20 75
Artillery 25 101
Artillery 'Tannenberger' 140
Fahnenjunker-Grenadier 1241 'Wetzlar' 106–130
Fortress 57 147, 149
Fortress 60 'Berlin' 185–97, 186m, 191m
Infantry 106 106
Motorised Flak Regt 36 22–61
No 1 Tp 49, 50, 51, 52
No 2 Tp 49
No 4 Tp 43, 47, 49
No 5 Tp (later No 2) 22–61
Panzergrenadier 2 'Müncheberg' 82, 87n
Panzergrenadier 6 62–70
Panzerdrenadier 35 64, 101
Panzergrenadier 76 72, 74, 76
Panzergrenadier 90 71–9
Panzergrenadier 119 101
Panzergrenadier 125 140n
Panzergrenadier 'Kurmack' 118
Battalions
21st Armoured Reconnaissance 139–43
Panzer 8 72
Army Flak 292 93–105
'Lünenschloss' 185
'Skorning' 185–6, 190, 191m
Army Ammunition Technical School, Lichterfelde 185, 188, 189
Army Ammunition Technical School, Treptow 147–8, 152, 154
Battery 'Scharnhorst' 190
Hamburg Staff College 255
OKH (Army GHQ) 196, 256n
Reserve Field Hospital 122 190, 194
Wezlar Officer Cadet School 106
see also *Volkssturm*, *Waffen-SS*, *Wehrmacht*

German Resistance Museum 256n
Germaniastrasse 193
Germersheim 19
Gessner, SS–2/Lt 132
Gevezin 101
Geyer, Capt 104
Giese, 2/Lt 69
Gladsky, Lt Col 236
Glockenturm 210–1
Gnaden, Lw–Lt Col von 217, 221
Goebbels, Dr Paul Josepf 53, 91, 183n, 238, 239, 240, 241–2, 248, 250
Goebbels, Frau Magda 243
Goldap 67
Golm 117
Golzow 63, 64, 66, 68, 74–7
Gorgast 63, 64, 65m, 74–5
Göring, RM Hermann 54, 105n
Gosfort Camp, Edinburgh 138
Gottberg, von 140
Gottlieb-Dunkel-Strasse 193
Gottschewski, Lt 189, 190, 195
Götz, Capt 97
Grafenwöhr 151
Gransee 54
Grasdorf, Friedrich 22–61
Grömitz 57
Gross Neuendorf 62
Gross Sachsenheim 3
Gross-Ziethen 188
Grove 4
Gruber, Lw-Sgt 201
Gudenus, 2/Lt 99
Guderian, Gen Heinz 256
Günsche, SS-Maj Otto 252, 256n
Gustedt, Lt von 145, 149

Hackengrund 109
Hagenbach 4–5
Hahn, 2/Lt 149
Halbe 119–122, 120m, 124, 124–5m, 130n, 135, 140–1
Hammer 117–8
Hanover 22, 44, 49, 58
Hardenberg Line 82, 85

Harlander SS-NCO 122–3
Hartrampf, SS-Maj 118
Harz Mountains 233
Haselberg 97
Haselhorst 148, 150, 180
Hasenheide Garrison Cemetery 196
Havel 201, 203
Heckelberg 98
Heerstrasse 205, 207
Heidefriedhof 194
Heidelberg 20
Heilbronn 20
Heilig, Sgt 66
Heimann, Lw-O/Cdt 2–4, 6, 12
Heimstätten 77
Heinersdorf, Herr 250
Heinrichsdorf 26
Hellersdorf 160–1
Hellersdorfer Strasse 157
Hellersdorfer Vorwerk 155
Helmstedt 138
Henke, Lw-Gnr 202
Hermann Göring Factory 138
Herrmann, Lw-Col Harry 253, 254, 256n
Herzfeld, Lw-Gnr 202, 215
Hesse, Lw-Gnr 31, 51
Heydrich, Vs-Adjt 177, 180
Hildebrand, Fräulein 215
Himmler, Heinrich 239, 256n
Hindenburg Light 25, 60
Hitler, Adolf 139, 183n, 234, 251, 255n
  assassination attempt 56, 256n
  birthday 53, 91, 160
  death 235, 237–8, 241
Hitler Youth 128, 132, 196, 203, 249
Hof Göhren 104
Hoff, Heinten 90
Hoffman, 2/Lt 141, 210, 222, 226, 227–8
Hofmeister, Gren 66, 67, 68, 70
Hohenzieritz 100
Hohenzollern Canal 178–9
Hölschloch 6
Holstein 57
Hönow 161, 162, 163
Hönower Strasse 155
Hoppegarten 165
Horst-Wessel-House 180

Iron Cross First Class 6, 62, 90, 144, 171, 183
Iron Cross Second Class 104, 183

Jägerhof 101
Jean-Paul-Weg 187
Jenewein, Lt Alfons 62–6
Jerichow 136
Joachimsthal 54
Jonny, Lw-Gnr 23, 24, 25, 28, 36–41, 46, 48
Jühnsdorf 185
Juliusturm 200–6, 232n
Jungfernheide Volkspark 179
Junghans, SS-Lt Col 133–4
Just, Lw-Sgt 6–10, 17

Kaiser, Lw-Sgt Fritz 201, 203, 205, 206–7, 208–9
Kalliczec, 2/Lt 82
Karinhall 105n
Karlshorst 157, 162, 165
Karlsruhe 4, 88
Karstadt building 163, 183n
Käthner-Potthoff, VS-Sgt Maj 158, 161
Kaulsdorf 149, 154, 155–8, 156m, 160–2, 163m, 164m 183n, 170
Kern, Lw-2Lt 23–4, 26, 29, 31–5, 38–9, 42–7, 49, 51–2, 55, 57–8
Kersdorf 117
Kersten, Lt 101
Kerstenbruch 28
Kettinger Strasse 187
Ketzin 139, 140, 181
Kielhorn, 2/Lt 140
Kietz 74
Killian, Dr 78
Kippert, Lw-Gnr 35, 38
Kirch-Grubenhagen 102
Kleber, Capt 236
Kleinheisterkamp, SS-Gen Mathias 109
Kleinmeier, Lw-Gnr 26, 36, 38, 41, 46, 50
Klement, Dr Hans-Werber 93–105
Klinger factory 193
Kloppenburg, Lw-Gnr 28, 30, 33, 34, 44
Klust, SS-2/Lt 128
Knappe, Maj Siegfried 235, 244, 248, 249, 250, 256n
Knopf, Lt-Col 149
Koch, 2/Lt Hermann 62–70
Koch, VS Coy Comd 148
Kolberg, film 159, 183n
Köllner, Lw-Gnr 'Frieps' 28, 41, 49, 51, 53
König, Lw-O/Cdt Karl-Heinz 90
Königs Wusterhausen 139
Königslutter 137
Kontradewitz, Lw-Lt 6
Kortenhaus, Werner 139
Kovno 144
Kräger, Lt 150
Krause, Lw-SSgt 202, 218–9, 221, 226, 230
Krause, Maj 189, 196
Krebs, Gen Hans 234, 235–40, 242, 243–4, 249, 251 256n
Krell, Dr Otto 155
Kretzer, Lw-Gnr 200, 202, 215, 222, 226
Kreutzberg, Sgt Alfred 211–2, 213, 214–6, 217, 219, 221, 226
Kreutzberg, Harald 213
Kreuzmann, Lw-Gnr 48
Krüger, VS-QM 164, 180–1
Krukenberg, SS-Brig Dr Gustav 241, 256n
Krull, VS Bn Comd Erich 146, 154
Krupp-Druckenmüller Factory 193–4
Kruse, Lw-Gnr 35
Kruwe Farm 98
Kühling, Dr 98
Kuhlke, Lt 141
Kuhnke, SS-2/Lt 118
Kummersdorf 127, 135

Index

Kunersdorf 70, 94–5
Kursk 131
Küstrin 41, 44, 48, 60, 62–3, 71, 74, 79, 93–4, 105n, 112–3, 159
Kutzenhausen 5–6

Labes, Gren Günther 80–7
Labour Front (DAF) 148, 183n
Labour Service girls 210
Landau-Neustadt 13
Landes-Frauenklinik 194
Landesberger Platz 176
Landsberg/Warthe 144
Landshut 188, 189
Landwehr Canal 154
Lange, Ute 212–4, 215, 218–20, 222–3, 226–7
Langkeit, Col Wilhelm 109, 118
Lebed, Col 236
Lebus 108–11, 110m
Leinhard, 2/Lt 141
Lenaustrasse 187
Leonardo-de-Vinci Gymnasium 197n
Letschin 32–3, 34m, 39, 44
Ley, Dr Robert 183n
Lichtenberg 131–2, 167, 168
Lichtenrade 188, 189, 190, 191m
Lichtenrader Damm 187–8, 190
Lichterfelde 185, 187
Liebigstrasse 171
Limburg, Lw Sgt 10, 12, 14, 15–16, 17, 19
Linden 59
Lindenhof 109
Lindner, Maj Gen (O/Cdt) Rudi 106–30
Lindow 100
Lipke, Lw-Gnr 200, 210, 211, 212, 216, 222, 224, 227
Lösecke, Col Helmut von 71–9
Lötzke, Lydia 212, 213, 214, 219, 226, 228
Lötzke, Waltraut 212, 214, 218, 220, 223, 226, 227–9, 230–1
Löwenberg 100
Löwen-Böhmisch Brewery 173–7, 174m, 184n
Löwenstrasse 184n
Lower Silesia 139
Löwestrasse 173–5
Lübeck 58
Luck, Col Hans von 139, 140, 143n
Luckenwalde 141
Lüdersdorf 96
Luftwaffe 1–21, 22–61, 74, 77, 88–92, 94, 192, 202, 212
  1st Bty, 370th Flak Regt 198–232
  4th Bty, 1st Bn, 10th Flak Regt 6, 21
  5th Bty, 1st Bn, 10th Flak Regt 6
  9th Bty, 36 Mot Flak Regt 22–61
  Parachute Officers' School 166, 182
  War School, Berlin-Gatow 88
Luise, Queen 100
Lüneberg Heath 92
Lünenschloss, Maj 185, 189
Lyne, Maj-Gen Lewis 232n

Magdeburg 130
Mahlsdorf 154, 155–8, 156m, 160–1, 163, 183n
Mahr, VS Coy Comd dr 148, 149, 154, 162–3
Mally, Lw-Gnr Gert 6, 8, 11, 16, 17
Manschnow 41, 44, 72
Marburg 106
Marcks, Lt-Gen 139, 140, 141
Marienberg farm 94–5
Mariendorf 187, 189
Mariendorfer Allee 187
Mariendorfer Weg 194
Marienfelde 188, 189, 191
Marienfelder Chaussee 189
Mark Brandenburg 100
Markendorf 131
Markgrafpieske 134
Märkisch Buchholz 119
Marzahn 154, 157, 162
Marzahner Chaussee 165
Massow 124
Matthé, 2/Lt 96, 97
Mecklenburg 54, 102
Melzer, 2/Lt 141
Meyer, Lw-Gnr Jürgen 1, 6, 8
Mihan, Werner 1–21, 198–232
Mogel, VS-Man 166
Möglin 94
Mohnke, SS-Brig Wilhelm 235, 241–2, 252, 254, 256n
Molkow, Capt 188
Moscow 253
Mucho, Lw-Gnr 52
Müller, 2/Lt 102
Müller, Lw-Gnr Hermann 202, 210
Müller, VS Coy Comd 176
Müllrose 132
Müncheberg 80, 88–9, 117
Münster 142
Munsterlager 92
Murellenschlucht 209, 210
Mussehl Bridge 193–4
Muth, Lw-Sgt 3
Mutosov, Col 236

National Committee for a Free Germany 52, 54, 61, 91
Nauen 100
Nazi Party 146–8, 164, 177, 179, 183n, 184n, 187, 188, 196
Neu Bleyen 74
Neu Levin 28
Neu Manschnow 94
Neu Tucheband 65, 73
Neuberg-am-Rhein 4–5
Neubrandenburg 101
Neuenhagen 163
Neuentempel 117
Neuhaus an der Elbe 56
Neuhof 130n
Neukölln 183n, 193, 195, 196
Neuruppin 54, 99
Neustadt 49, 57, 212

Neustrelitz 54, 100
Niederkirchen 13
Nielandis, SS-Lt-Col 236, 240
Nienhagen 57
Niermann, Lw-Cpl 14, 15
Nietbalk, Vs-Man 164
Nonnendamm Allee 179
Normandy 139

Oder River 62, 73, 77, 93, 99, 111–2, 131, 185, 233, 251, 253
Oderbruch Valley 63, 71, 73, 88–9, 94, 107m
Oderstrasse 195, 196
Oerzan, family von 102
Ohlsen, Lw-Sgt 25, 26, 28, 30, 35–8, 43
Olympic Stadium 164, 180
Oppenheim 142
Oranienburg 54, 100
Orenstein & Koppel factory 226
Orly Airport 106
Oryvall, Capt 78
Oschatz Airfield 88
Ott, Dr 157
Ott, SS-Sgt 118

Paaren 230
Pallisadenstrasse 173, 175
Parchim 55
Peenhäusser 102
Petersdorf 133
Pettenkoferstrasse 167, 170
Pichelsdorf 209
Pillgram 131
Pinow 103
Pismühle 71
Podelzig 108
Police Bn 'Warnholz' 149, 161–2
Polish Army 253
Pongo, Lw-Gnr 23, 25, 28, 30, 35, 36–8, 40, 46, 48, 52
Potsdam 1, 6, 21, 139, 150, 151, 175, 181, 198, 231, 232
Potsdam Conference 232
Potsdamer Strasse Bridge 247
Pourroy, Dr Gustav-Adolf 144–84
Pozhersky, Dr 236
Prenzlau 100
Proell, Lt 101
Pronin, Gen 236
Protz, Lt 98
Pufendorfstrasse 176
Pursch, Frau 62

Rapstedter Weg 187
Red Air Force 89, 158, 201, 232n
Red Army 26–55, 62–3, 71, 73–4, 82–7, 89–92, 93–100, 104, 132–6, 139–43, 158–61, 165–81, 185, 190–6, 200, 203–5, 207–8, 210–1, 222, 232, 245–8
  1st Byelorussian Front 256n
  2nd Guards Tank Army 232n
  5th Shock Army 184n
  8th Guards Army 236
  4th Guards Rifle Corps 236
  35th Guards Rifle Division 236
  47th Army 50, 60
  69th Army 108–28
  102nd Guards Rifle Regt 236
  GPU 141, 143n
  Reserve Field Hospital, Pappelallee 181
Red Cross 245
Refior, Col Hans 234, 244, 247–54, 255n
Reichs Chancellery 154, 234, 235, 239, 241, 242, 243, 251, 156n
Reichs Sportsfield 210, 211
Reichsarbeitsdient (RAD) 18, 21, 22, 59, 106, 193
Reichsstrasse 1 69, 82
Reichsstrasse 96 185, 187–8, 189
Reitwein 62
Renner, Maj 140
Requardt, Lw-Gnr 51
Reuche 141
Reuters 256n
Rheinmetall-Borsig Factory 187, 190–1
Rheinpfalz 11
Rhine 19, 94
Rhineland-Palatinate 1
Richter, Sgt 97
Richter, VS-Coy Comd 177, 180
Richthofen, Manfred von 103, 105n
Richthofenstrasse 173–7, 174m
Rigaer Strasse 171
Rippen, Capt von 94, 95, 96–7
Rödiger, Lw-Sgt 198, 205–6, 214, 215, 221
Rohde, Lw-Sgt 215
Rohrdamm 150, 179
Rolf, VS-Coy Comd 177
Rolf, VS-CSM 177
Ronnenberg 58
Roop, Lw-Sgt 11–12, 14, 15–16
Roosevelt, Franklin D 91
Rosenbusch, SS-Lt Col 133
Rothen Manor Farm 102
Royal Air Force 71, 88, 158, 160, 232
Rudel, Lt-Col Hans-Ulrich 38, 60
Rudow 192
Ruhleben 152, 211
Ruhleben Barracks 150
Ruhlebener Strasse 205, 215, 220, 222
Rüskes, 2/Lt 141
Russia 106
Russian Liberation Army (POA) 61

Saatwinkler Damm 178–9
Sachsendorf 113–4
Sachsenhausen Concentration Camp 92
Sachte, Lw-Gnr 38
Samariter Strasse 170, 171–3, 172m

Index

Sanftenberg field hospital 142
Schäfer, Lt 150
Schäfergrund 109
Schaltwerke 157
Scharf, VS-Pmr 180–1
Schifferstadt 17–18
Schloss 101, 103
Schloss Bellevue 163, 183n
Schloss Biesdorf 155, 157
Schmalz, Lw-Gnr 17
Schmid-Dankward, Gen 256n
Schmidt, Lt 149, 164
Schneehage, VS Coy Comd 148, 154
Schoenebeck, Lt von 147, 154, 182
Scholze, Col 73
Scholze, Col Rudolf 185
Schöneberg 196
Schönefeld 127
Schönfliess 108, 114–7, 115m
Schönhauser Allee, 177, 181, 182, 256n
Schönwalde 200
Schorfheide 54, 100
Schrade, VS-Coy Comd 176
Schreckenbach, VS-Pl Comd 180
Schreier, 2/Lt 192
Schreyer, Dr 153
Schuckertplatz 179
Schuckmann, 2/Lt von 97
Schulenburg Bridge 208
Schulenburgring 236, 249
Schultz, Lw-Gnr 200
Schulz, Lt J 194
Schulzendorf 96
Schumacher, Lw-Gnr 43, 51
Schumann, Lw-Sgt 23
Schünke, VS Bn Comd 173
Schütz, Lw-Gnr 50
Schwärzler, 2/Lt 190
Schweikardt, Lw-Capt 166, 182
Schwerin 54, 70, 102, 103, 104
Schwetzingen 19
Schwiebertweg 148
Seelow 80, 81m, 89, 93–4, 113, 233, 251
Seelow Heights 63, 69, 73, 82, 159, 255n
Seelower Loose 82, 87n
Seifert, Lt-Col 235, 236, 241, 256n
Selchow 117
Selsower-See lake 117
Seydlitz Troops 117, 128, 133, 134, 136, 139, 141, 255n
Siebenbaum, Lw-Gnr Karl 24, 25, 29, 31, 35, 38, 44
Siemens 144–8
Siemens, Friedrich Karl 183n
Siemensstadt 147, 148, 150, 151, 157, 167, 177–80, 178m, 232n
Sinsheim 20
Skorning, Col Wolfgang 185–97
Skroda, VS-Man 165
Smolin, Col 236
Sobotta, Capt 170, 175
Sodemann, VS-Coy, Comd 177, 180
Sodt, Lw-Sgt 202, 210, 215, 222, 226
Sokolovski, Gen Vasili 239, 256n
Soldatensender 'Calais' 48, 49, 60
Sonneberg 229
Spandau 24, 198–232, 199m
Speyer 18–19
Spree River 88, 117, 179, 201
Spreeau 134
Spreenhagen 131, 134
Spreewald 116m
Sprung, 2/Lt 149, 163
Staaken 228, 230
Stach, Pte 141–2
Stauffenburg, Col Claus Graf Schenk von 256n
Steglitz, Capt 188
Steidle, Lw-Gnr 200, 215, 222, 226, 232
Steinbeck 97
Stendal 129
Stettin 100
Storkow 117, 133
Strausberg Airport 252
Streng, SS-Sgt Maj Ernst 118, 128
Strom Ditch 74
Stubenrauch Bridge 192
Südhafen 206, 209
Sweden 256n

Taiwanese Army 255
Tangermünde 129
Tannenhof 74
Tatge, Lw-Gnr 46
Tauernalee 188
Tegel 179
Teltow Canal 192–5
Teltow Redoubt 211, 220
Teltower Chaussee 205, 208
Teltower Strasse 215
Tempelhof 188, 195, 196, 236, 249
Tempelhof Airfield 195–7
Teschendorf 100
Thaer Strasse 171
Thoma, Maj 195
Thüringia 1–2, 26, 229
Tiefwerder Waterworks 200, 208, 212
Tiergarten 180
Tilsiter Strasse 173
Tirpitzufer 247
Tolkopyk, Col 236
Töpchiner Weg 188, 190
Torgau 139, 143n, 207
Trebbin 94
Treptow 147, 152, 154
Treutner, VS Coy Comd 148, 154, 169
Trockels, Lt 155, 175–6
Trumann, VS-Man 253, 255
Tschernitz, Lw-Cpl 200, 203, 205, 206

Übersreuther, Lw-Gnr 36
Ullstein printing works 192
Urbanitsch, Lw-Gnr 50, 53
US Air Force 71, 88, 158, 160
US Army 5, 7, 13, 16–17, 20, 53, 55–6, 92, 103–4, 136–8, 143n, 159, 178, 207–8
  102nd US Infantry Division 129
Utterodt, Lw-Cpl Paul 25, 53

Vaihingen 4
Vishnevsky, Vsevelod 236
Vistula River 73
Vlassov Troops 54, 61n
Volksartillerie 69
Volkssturm 18, 85, 106, 132, 142, 145–50, 159, 187, 188, 190, 192, 196, 203, 204, 249, 253
  VS Bn 'Schünke' 149
  VS Bn 'Wüstenhagen' 181
  VS Bn 3/115 'Siemensstadt' 146–84
  VS Bn 3/121 'Wagner' 161
  VS Bn 3/132 'Siemensstadt' 177–80
  VS Bty 'Blücher' 162–3, 164
  VS Bty 'Schill' 149
  VS Coy 2/311 188, 190
  VS Coy 3/311 194
  VS Coy 4/309 190
Völpke 130
Vorwerk Sachsendorf 113
Vossfeld Manor Farm 101

Waffen-SS 135-6
  SS Heavy Tank Bn 502 118
  SS Leibstandarte 'Adolf Hitler' 131, 187
  SS Panzergrenadier 'Norland' 179, 256n
  SS Regt 'Falke' 131
  SS Fusilier Bn 15th Latvian 236
Wahrer, Lt 96, 97
Waldhelm, Lw-Gnr 28, 35, 37
Waldorf School 59
Waldsportplatz 150
Warsow 104
Wartenberg 157
Warthegau 25, 60
Weber, bandmaster 23
Wehrkreis III (Berlin) 183n
Wehrmacht 49, 84, 92, 132, 138, 145–6, 148, 149–50, 155, 159–60, 164, 189, 197, 233
  Bn 'Trockels' 149, 155, 162
  Bn 'Krausse' 189, 191
Wehrmacht Report 97
Weidendammer Bridge 256n
Weidenweg 171, 173–4
Weidling, Gen Helmuth 165, 234–5, 243–5, 247–54, 255n
Weinholdt, VS Coy Comd Dr 148, 154, 158, 170
Weiss, Lt 42
Weissenburg 10–13, 21
Wenck, Gen Walter 175, 178, 181, 207–8, 220
Werbig 63, 71
Werner, 2/Lt 189, 194, 195, 196
West Wall 5
Wezlar 106
Wiesthaler, VS-Bn Comd 177, 179
Wilhelm-Borgmann Bridge 193
Wilhelmstadt 219, 232n
Wissembourg see Weissenburg
Witowsky 254
Wittbrietzen 127, 128
Wittenberg 142
Wittstock 54
Wolff, Maj 248, 249, 256n
Wörth 4
Woytasch, Gen 256n
Wriezen 26, 27m, 45m, 49, 50, 94
Wuhle Stream 155
Wuhl-Garten convalescent home 161
Wunder 126–7
Wurm, Lw-Sgt 14, 15
Würzburg 3, 20
Wüste Kunersdorf 111–3

Z-Cards' 146–8, 153
Zehdenick 54
Zehna Manor Farm 102
Zersch 130n
Zhukov, Marshal Georgi 239, 256n
Ziesar 129, 136
'Zitadelle' 235, 241, 242, 256n
Zobel, Capt Horst 79
Zoo Flak tower 154, 163, 195
Zossen 126, 190
Zunder, Helga 202-3, 207–8
Zunder, family 207–8
'Zur grünen Linde' 189
Zwanziger, 2/Lt 72
Zwicker, Capt 190, 192, 194